PLURALISM WITHOUT RELATIVISM

PLURALISM WITHOUT RELATIVISM

Religious Studies à la mode

JOSEPH C. McLELLAND

CLEMENTS ACADEMIC
Toronto

Copyright © 2008 Joseph C. McLelland

Published 2008 by
Clements Publishing
213-6021 Yonge Street
Toronto, Ontario
M2M 3W2 Canada
www.clementspublishing.com

ACKNOWLEDGMENTS
Some chapters have appeared in print:
1 *Toronto Journal of Theology* 5/1, 1989;
2 *Theological Education in Canada*, ed. by Graham Brown, 1998;
3 *ARC* (FRS, McGill) 23, 1995;
4 *Journal of Religious Pluralism* I/1, 1991.
Unpublished papers:
6, address to The Canadian Theological Society (1969);
7 to The Canadian Society for the Study of Religion (1995);
9 to an American Academy of Religion panel (1990).

Indexed by Jonathan McLelland

All rights reserved worldwide. No part of this publication may be reproduced, stored in a retrieval system, or transmitted, in any form or by any means, electronic, mechanical, photocopying, recording or otherwise, without the prior permission of the publisher or the Copyright Licensing Agency.

Library and Archives Canada Cataloguing in Publication Data

McLelland, Joseph C. (Joseph Cumming), 1925-
Pluralism without relativism : religious studies à la mode /
Joseph C. McLelland.

Includes bibliographical references.
ISBN 978-1-894667-89-0

1. Religious pluralism. 2. Christianity and other religions. I. Title.

BL85.M34 2008   261.2   C2008-901932-6

in memoriam
WILFRED CANTWELL SMITH
Colleague and Friend

The philosophers have only interpreted the world, in various ways; the point is to change it.
— Karl Marx, *Theses on Feuerbach, XI*

What the philosophers say about Reality is often as disappointing as a sign you see in a shop window, which reads: Pressing done here. If you brought your clothes to be pressed, you would be fooled; for only the sign is for sale.
— Kierkegaard, *Diapsalmata, Either/Or*

CONTENTS

Preface 9

Acknowledgments

1. *The Ambiguity of Philosophy of Religion* 13
   What Can We Prove? / Modernity: Beyond Argument
   Changing Streams in Mid-Horse / From Unity to Diversity
   Towards Definition

2. Which *Natural Theology?* 35
   Two Type of Natural Theology / Friends, Enemies, Hostages /
   Canada: a Case Study / C'est l'Hiver / Common Sense,
   Common Cause / Ideas and Idealism / Trends and Projects

3. *Via Postmoderna: Towards a Modal Theology* 53
   Pre-Amble / Minerva's Owls / Once More: "Via Moderna"
   Test Cases / "Possible Worlds" / Post-lude

4. *A Theory of Relativity for Religious Pluralism* 71
   Troeltsch's Dilemma / Escaping the Lemmas / Theory and
   Model / Paradigms of Christian Theology

5. *Science as Metaphor* 89
   Models and Metaphor / The Logic of Discovery / Theology
   and Relativity Physics / Paradigm Change is Not Enough
   Relativity without Relativism / Special Theory: Christian
   Theology / General Theory: Global Theology / Unified Theory:
   Modal Theology

6. *Dogma and Icon*   *111*
    Image and Icon / Seeing and Hearing / Perceptions of Spirit
    The Poetics of Space / The Dream and Truth of Picasso
    Remaking Reality / The Sur-real and the Super-natural

7. *Comparing the Incomparable*   *135*
    Category Mistakes / A Caveat from Karl Barth / What to
    Compare? / From GUT to TOE: problems with Universal
    Theory / Knowing about Knowing / Kierkegaard as
    Aristotelian / Conclusion

8. *Modes of Christology*   *157*
    Theology as Christology / Nicene Theology / "Modes
    of Being" / The "Extra Calvinisticum" / Christologies
    and the Christ

9. *Incarnation: Christology in Hinduism and Islam*   *177*
    THEOLOGY WITH OR WITHOUT CHRISTOLOGY:
    HINDUISM / Trinitarian Analogies / Incarnational
    Analogies / A Problem with History
    THE QUESTION OF BUDDHISM
    "CHRISTOLOGY OUTSIDE THEOLOGY:" ISLAM
    Jesus in the Qur'an / The Qur'an as the Christ
    "Appropriate to God"

10. *Speech and Silence*   *199*
    The Silence of St Thomas / Unio Mystica / Modus
    Loquendi Theologicus / The Silence of the Buddha
    Beyond Philosophy: Barth, Derrida / de Silentio
    Todo y Nada / Socrates' Raft

Index of Names   *223*
Index of Subjects   *228*

PREFACE

At last one reaches an age and stage when research projects tend to come together, reflecting the major concerns of one's past—Minerva's owl is calling. It's like the cartoon where an old professor, white of mane (looking much like one of my early mentors, Harry Wolfson), is seated at his desk surrounded by books and papers. He puts his hands to his head and exclaims: "By God, for a minute there it suddenly all made sense!"

The following are *essais* in the French sense: attempts at understanding. They are reflections on the state of the study of religion today, in this "postmodern" age. While diverse in nature, they share the common theme of options at a crossroads in the discipline of "religious studies" (*sciences religieuses*) in academia. They offer a "modal" theory of religion as contribution to the dialogue on religious pluralism.

The dedication to the late Wilfred Cantwell Smith indicates my debt to an outstanding Canadian scholar in this field. We were colleagues at McGill while he was composing his seminal book *The Meaning and End of Religion*. Sharing a common Reformed Church heritage, we discussed many issues, not least the significance of Karl Barth's thesis on "the abolition of religion." Since those days our paths crossed regularly, particularly at annual Learned Societies, while his writings

PREFACE

continued to bring profound insight to our discipline. He encouraged my efforts in these essays, and in a letter to me of 1995 agreed that "pluralism without relativism" summed up his own aim also: "Certainly it is an issue that has been a focus of engagement for me for several decades (and is central, might one not say, to my final book, *What is Scripture?*)." About the phrase itself, he suggested I put, "as Smith has been wont to say."

I have acknowledged the history of these essays above; those already published have been revised for this volume in the interests of a unified thesis. In part such revision has come through dialogue with the students in my annual graduate seminars. Where I would be content to read only the classics, they try to keep me up to date. My thanks for their part in the preparation of this book.

Gathering essays to form a single work means there are themes sometimes repetitious, with seams showing. There is also the risk of inconsistency, of trying to read all in light of a thematic unity not intended in the originals. For this I can but crave the reader's indulgence. In fact the issue of religious pluralism has travelled with me ever since my first teaching assignment in "History of Religions" some fifty years ago. So it was not difficult to identify the thread running through these essays, the earliest from 1969, the rest since 1989, as well as new material prepared for this volume.

The first two chapters deal with philosophy of religion as an appropriate way to engage the questions raised in the study of religion in general. This is because as a discipline it has prowled the borderlands of both theology and the scientific study of religion, and now faces a crisis of identity. I see two roles in our postmodern era: "philosophy of theology" and "philosophy of religions." These introductory chapters develop the thesis that the crisis arises from a distinct ambiguity in philosophy of religion, with two forms of natural theology at play.

The next two chapters consider postmodernism and pluralism, rehearsing the familiar problematics of three alternative theoretical solutions, and proposing a form of "modalism" as a possible way through, a resolution. In them a distinct thesis is advanced: that by according a form of "singularity" to the religions a reductive relativism may be avoided, insofar as a modalist theory allows for interdependence without denying absolute claims for disparate forms of religious encounter.

Then follow two chapters taking up the challenge of modalism, examining the nature of doctrine through analogues in the sciences and the arts as ways of understanding doctrines to reveal their revisionist potential.

The next three chapters turn more closely to "comparative studies," including case studies in a re-vision of trinitarianism and christology. Here are examples of the modality of dialogue in an age of explicit pluralism in which also a new encounter among world religions is taking place. The fact that this encounter has already produced variant forms of the crucial doctrines of God and revelation suggests the way ahead for the study of religion in its unique modality.

A final chapter considers the significance of language and silence in handling the complex and fragile data of religious experience: is transcendence so much so that only silence will honour its way of being? Or is the dialectic of thinking and speaking such that one may have "the last word" in a meaningful way?

Joseph C. McLelland
McGill University, Montreal
Spring of 2008

1

THE AMBIGUITY OF PHILOSOPHY OF RELIGION

Arguments for the Existence of Philosophers of Religion

The supreme paradox of all thought is the attempt to discover something that thought cannot think.
—Kierkegaard, *Philosophical Fragments*

The Western discipline of "philosophy of religion," forged definitively in the nineteenth century, faces a severe problem of self-definition these days. Its historical relation to theology has become complicated, even compromised, by the new disciplines of "religious studies" (*sciences religieuses*) and the new issue of pluralism. First we must ask: just what is the traditional image of philosophy of religion? A preliminary (and popular) answer is: *it seeks to prove the existence of God.*

Monty Python's Flying Circus was fond of takeoffs on Oxbridge philosophers, holding effete discussions on trivial points of language. One of their memorable sketches depicted a wrestling match between a bishop and an atheist to determine the question whether God exists. After a stirring match the result was declared: God exists, by two falls to a submission. That is what logicians like to call a "solid, knock-down argument." But those days are gone from theology and its sometime handmaiden, philosophy of religion. A severe chastening has fallen upon our discipline in recent decades, administered not least by that very Oxbridge style of doing philosophy, from logical positivism to linguistic analysis and beyond. This has proved therapeutic, cleansing us from sloppy habits of thinking, particularly of "God-talk." If the great thinkers of the past did not in fact claim to "prove" the existence of God, their arguments seemed to imply demonstrative plausibility, and their followers spilled much ink in refining the various ways to God in vogue ever since Plato. In his Gifford Lectures (1991) James Barr warned: "We may question whether all natural theology seeks to 'prove:' it may, on the contrary, merely *indicate*, merely register, what people *think* about God." Nor must it work always by sheer reason rather than social or cultural inheritance; moreover "it may be concerned not purely with the existence of God but much more with our picture of what God is like."[1] Despite this caveat, the popular if not academic view is that proving the existence of God is what philosophers of religion do most of their time.

WHAT CAN WE PROVE?

The vexed question of "arguing" for or against divine existence was never so crucial as extremists on both sides believed. Recall the classic models: Anselm's modal logic operating within his prayer life, or Aquinas's subtle treatment of cosmological and teleological "ways" opening on transcendence. (Not to mention his grand finale, dismissing his unfinished Summary and writing only a commentary on the Song of Songs: mysticism as the logical end of theology!). Indeed, Aquinas begins his great *Summa* by asking "whether sacred doctrine proceeds by argument." He distinguishes method in theology and in other sciences, concluding that while for the latter argument from authority is the weakest form of proof, in theological science it is legitimate to proceed

---

1. Barr, *Biblical Faith and Natural Theology* (Oxford: Clarendon Press, 1993), 2.

from articles of faith as *dogmata* to necessary corollaries.[2] This turn to scientific theology is significant, for it accepts the shift in understanding theology not as (with Augustine) rooted in personal experience but "an objective exposition and interpretation of the saving truth, as impersonally teachable as any other art or science."[3] A good example of the dilemma is that of Bernard Lonergan. His notorious "proof" in the early work *Insight* was considered merely a return to scholastic method, whereas later he acknowledged "the centrality of this dimension in fundamental theology." Lonergan"s "philosophy of God" provides a different map for fundamental theology and its companion "philosophy of Religious Studies." The latter involves analysis of the various ways in which religious phenomena are studied, surely a needed corrective to taking "religion" simply as one object of "philosophy." [4]

Such procedure provides a salutary lesson in theory of knowledge. Alisdair MacIntyre has called attention to the circularity of the arguments as a good thing (a "virtuous circle?"); the point is to move around the circle, not wish for a linear argument; indeed, "if religious beliefs are explanatory hypotheses, there can be no justification whatever for continuing to hold them."[5] Again, Wittgenstein remarked: "A proof of God's existence ought really to be something by means of which one could convince oneself that God exists. But I think what *believers* who have furnished such proofs have wanted to do is to give their 'belief' an intellectual analysis and foundation, although

---

2. *Summa Theol.* I.1, 7f; I.2, 2: "Whether it can be demonstrated that God exists?" See J. Pelikan, "Natural Theology and the Scholastic Method" in *The Growth of Medieval Theology (600–1300)* (Chicago: University of Chicago Press, 1978), 284ff.

3. E. Gilson, *History of Christian Philosophy in the Middle Ages* (NY: Random House, 1954) 64.

4. J. Kanaris, *Bernard Lonergan's Philosophy of Religion: from Philosophy of God to Philosophy of Religious Studies* (Albany: SUNY Press, 2002), 18; 118ff: "Lonergan's Philosophy of Religion."

5. A. MacIntyre, "The Logical Status of Religious Belief" in *Metaphysical Beliefs*, ed. Toulmin, Hepburn & MacIntyre (London: SCM, 1957), 196.

they themselves would never have come to believe as a result of such proofs."[6] Fergus Kerr has voiced similar concerns in his "Questions in the Philosophy of Theology," relegating the Proofs and their mentality to a side issue.[7]

The "arguments" do not call attention so much to the operative worldview, Platonic or Aristotelian, idealistic or empiricist, as to the deeper question of the roots and orientation of rationality itself. At the fountainhead of Western logic, Aristotle made two crucial distinctions. One was between formal and modal logic; the other was between two kinds of argumentation.[8] His *Topics* belongs within the *Organon*, the group of logical works dealing with the principles and method of proof. Socrates' "desire to syllogize" inspired Aristotle's conception of the logical syllogism. It yields the method of science when based on premises determined by the nature of things—Aristotle calls them "true and primary"—and provides "demonstration;" this form is handled in the *Posterior Analytics*. But when the principles under consideration are expressions of opinion only, the syllogism becomes dialectical or probable, and is the subject of the Topics:

> Our treatise proposes to find a line of inquiry whereby we shall be able to reason from opinions that are generally accepted about every problem propounded to us, and also shall ourselves, when standing up to an argument, avoid saying anything that will obstruct us. First, then, we must say what reasoning is, and what its varieties are, in order to grasp dialectical reasoning.[9]

---

6. L. Wittgenstein, in C. Barret, ed. *Lectures and Conversations on Aesthetics, Psychology and Religious Belief* (Oxford: Basil Blackwell, 1966), 85; cf. 59f on belief and evidence.

7. F. Kerr, *Theology After Wittgenstein* (London: SPCK, 1997) 168ff. See also S. Hauerwas's Gifford Lectures, *With the Grain of the Universe: The Churches' Witness and Natural Theology* (Brazos Press, 2001).

8. See J. Hintikka, *Aristotle on Modality and Determinism* (Amsterdam: North-Holland Publishing Co.—Acta Philosophica Fennica XXIX (1977) Issue 1) "Aristotle's Ways Out," 43ff.

9. Aristotle, *Top.* I.1, 100a18ff.

Aristotle mapped both kinds of reasoning. He begins his *Rhetoric*: "Rhetoric is the counterpart of Dialectic. Both alike are concerned with such things as come, more or less, within the general ken of all men and belong to no definite science."[10] He once remarked: "Not to know of what things one should demand demonstration, and of what one should not, argues lack of education."[11] In moral questions especially, "it is the mark of an educated man to look for precision in each class of things just so far as the nature of the subject admits; it is evidently equally foolish to accept probable reasoning from a mathematician and to demand from a rhetorician scientific proofs."[12]

This beginning of Western logic thus draws a crucial distinction, between the certain knowledge of scientific demonstration (*Quod erat demonstrandum*) and the probable conclusions of dialectical reasoning. Partly because the *Topics* was the only work of the Philosopher that he knew, Cicero promoted the New Academy view that we can only approximate truth; hence one needs a persuasive logic to convince others of probable truth.[13] Thomas Aquinas recognized the distinction: "holy teaching employs such authorities [e.g. philosophers] only in order to provide as it were extraneous arguments from probability."[14]

MODERNITY: BEYOND ARGUMENT

Immanuel Kant, of course, stands at the fountainhead of modernity not only in turning abstract ontotheology towards practice and ethics, but more fundamentally in seeing "natural religion [as] the substra-

---

10. *Rhet.* I.1, 1345a1.
11. *Meta.* IV.4, 1006a6ff.
12. *Nic. Eth.*I.3, 1094b24ff. See McLelland, *Peter Martyr's Loci Communes: a Literary History* (McGill Faculty of Religious Studies, 2007) 1ff.
13. Cicero, *Acad.* II.x.31; Q. Breen, "The Terms 'Loci Communes' and 'Loci' in Melanchthon" in *Christianity and Humanism* (Grand Rapids, MI: Eerdmans, 1968) 93–105. Breen cites the work of G. Grote, *Aristotle* (2 vols, London, 1872) on this point, especially I.2, "The Aristotelian Canon," 94n5.
14. Aquinas, *ST* Ia, 1,8, *ad sec.*

tum of all religion, and the firmest support of all moral principles."[15] He distinguishes "rational theology" from "empirical theology," based respectively on revelation and reason. This parallels the classic pair archetypal/ectypal (*theologia archetypa, ectypa*), corresponding to (a properly transcendental) knowledge of God by God, and the partial knowledge achieved by our concepts.[16] Kant's role in setting the stage of modernity unfortunately tends to reinforce some of the faults of classical theism. The thesis that we can establish God's existence but not nature ("that" God is, not "what" God is) places him within traditional negative theology, as D.M. Mackinnon argued.[17] Don Cupitt credits the deist John Toland with pointing out the fallacy of believing in "a being in Nature" without knowing what It was.[18] Still, Kant takes the lead, in the third *Critique*, in establishing the logical fallacy of "proving" divine existence: he may be credited with exploding the very idea of proofs for "God."[19] (His epistemology also implies or entails that "the transcendental unity of apperception" enables one to "create a God for himself.")[20] Since the category of being cannot apply to any Object lacking intuition, neither "God exists" nor "God does not exist" makes sense. We are faced rather with a limiting concept (*Grenzfall*). Alistair Mackinnon has argued that neither a determinate nor a heuristic use of "God exists" makes sense: the

---

15. I. Kant, *Lectures on Philosophical Theology*, trans. A.W. Wood and G.M. Clark (Ithaca: Cornell University Press, 1978), 26.

16. *Lectures*, 23.

17. See Don Cupitt, "Kant and the negative theology," in B. Hebblethwaite and S. Sutherland, eds., *The Philosophical Frontiers of Christian Theology: Essays presented to D.M. Mackinnon* (Cambridge: Cambridge University Press, 1982), 55ff.

18. Cupitt, *op.cit.*, 58; Toland, *Christianity not mysterious* (1696).

19. See Ned Wisnefske, *Our Natural Knowledge of God: A Prospect for Natural Theology after Kant and Barth* (NY: Peter Lang, 1990), 13ff: "The Annulment of Natural Theology."

20. Kant, *Religion within the Limits of Reason Alone* (New York: Harper & Row, 1960), 157.

THE AMBIGUITY OF PHILOSOPHY OF RELIGION

first is false and the second "has as its grammatical subject a term which is plainly not a concept in anything like the traditional sense."[21]

Kant's friendly critic J.G. Hamann produced an incisive rebuttal, unpublished in deference to their relationship. "The Metacritique of the Purism of Reason" charged that Kant had divided the empirical from the theoretical too deeply, missing completely the significance of language in the constructs of our understanding. "Not only does the whole ability to think rest on language . . . but language is also the central point of reason's misunderstanding of itself."[22] This anticipation of twentieth-century linguistic analysis has a radical edge. Hamann sees the Socratic dialogue as entailing a strange exigency to human speech: it remains disconnected, like a series of islands with no bridges. He wrote: "that living elegy of the philosopher perhaps made the sentences into a mass of little islands, which were not joined by any bridges or ferries." *The philosopher must learn to swim!* This "Magus of the North" influenced Kierkegaard, who also spoke of swimming "above seventy fathoms of water." Both carried the Lutheran emphasis on justification by faith alone to its logical extreme: when religion is freed from its legalistic modality, one is made open to sheer gift, what Pascal called "the motions of grace."

Paul Tillich applauded the arguments as "existential analyses" enlightening our human condition. Karl Barth saw that this philosophical focus on certain attributes, notably aseity, immutability and infinity, misses the point on which a concept of revelation must turn, namely that of "a *living* God . . . who lives in concrete decision."[23] A similar insight into the mistaken use of demonstrative proof leads

---

21. A.T. Mackinnon, "'Existence' in the 'Existence of God'" in *American Philosophical quarterly*, 9/4, 1972, 349–52.

22. J.G. Hamann, "Metacritique of the Purism of Reason" (1894) in R.G. Smith, *J.G. Hamann 1730–1788: a study in Christian Existence, with selections from his writings* (New York: Harper & Brothers, 1960) 216f.

23. Karl Barth, *Church Dogmatics* II.2, p 79, also II.1, 31.2 on "The Constancy and Omnipotence of God."

Wittgenstein to remark that "The difficulty is to realize the groundlessness of our believing." For "If the true is what is grounded, then the ground is not *true*, nor yet false."[24] Norman Malcolm defends such "Wittgensteinian fideism" by noting that since the "language game" of arguing one's position occurs within a system of thought, such justification must come to an end, since we cannot justify the very "framework principles" of the system itself.[25] This has sparked a considerable debate on "the groundlessness of believing." It relates to the sort of "evidentialism" associated with David Hume: "always proportion your belief to the evidence."[26] W.K. Clifford's famous essay on "The Ethics of Belief" took the high moral ground in defending the thesis: "it is wrong always, everywhere, and for any one, to believe anything upon insufficient evidence."[27] But this seemingly commonsense view falls before the obvious distinction between basic and dependent beliefs.

Some "Reformed epistemologists" have introduced a significant turn in debate on the Arguments. Alvin Plantinga develops the concept of "warrant" as the proper way to understand belief. He puts the case in two steps: the evidentialist claim does not apply to "basic beliefs," and religious beliefs should be counted among the latter. He thinks that evidentialism rests on "classical foundationalism," that is a belief is either itself properly basic, or else it depends on those that are. Plantinga appeals to Herman Bavinck, John Calvin and Karl Barth in the claim that knowledge of God is implanted in everyone (Calvin termed it *nisus*); Plantinga argues for

---

24. L. Wittgenstein, *On Certainty* (Oxford: Basil Blackwell, 1969), 166/24, 205/28.

25. N. Malcolm, "The Groundlessness of Belief" in L. Pojman, *Philosophy of Religion* (Belmont: CA: Wadsworth, 2nd ed. 1994), 463. See Wittgenstein's own understanding of well—established beliefs in *Lectures and Conversations on Aesthetics, Psychology and Religious Belief* (Oxford: Basil Blackwell, 1966), 53ff.

26. Hume, "An Enquiry Concerning Human Understanding," in *Philosophical Works* (London: Longmans, Green & Co., 1875), vol. IV, I.10.

27. W.K. Clifford, "The Ethics of Belief" in *The Ethics of Belief Debate*, G.D. McCarthy, ed. (Atlanta GA: Scholars' Press, 1986), 24.

the basicality of religious believing, for an "epistemic right" to believe without argument.[28] Nicholas Wolterstorff recounts "the migration of the theistic arguments: from natural theology to evidentialist apologetics," arguing that "the medieval project of natural theology was profoundly different from the Enlightenment project of evidentialist apologetics" (we shall pursue this theme of two natural theologies in the next chapter).[29] Indeed, classical Reformed teaching on natural law recognizes our problem of pluralism and handles it in a positive way.[30] Alvin Plantinga, like Charles Hartshorne, is also relevant to our thesis for analysing Anselm and for developing a modal ontological argument for divine existence.[31] Stephen Evans-analyses the debate and concludes

---

28. Also *sensus, notitia, naturali instinctu*: Calvin, *Inst.* I.3,1–3 cf II.8, 1 on the natural law, *inscriptam et quasi impressam superius dictum est*; A. Plantinga, "The Reformed Objection to Natural Theology" in Plantinga & Wolterstorff, eds., *Faith and Rationality* (Notre Dame, IN: University of Notre Dame Press, 1983) and *Warrant: The Current Debate* (New York: Oxford University Press, 1993).

29. Wolterstorff, "The Migration of the Theistic Arguments: From Natural Theology to Evidentialist Apologetics," in *Rationality, Religious Belief, and Moral Commitment*, edd. R. Audi & W.J. Wainwright (Ithaca: Cornell University Press, 1986), 38–81.

30. E.g. the leading second-generation Calvinist scholar Girolamo Zanchi's exhaustive treatment of law teaches that such knowledge "was inscribed upon the hearts of all people by God himself after the fall." D. Hieronymi Zanchii, *Operum theologicorum*, Tom. 4, *De primi hominis lapsus, de peccato, et de legi Deo* (1617), Cap. X, Thesis 8.

31. A. Plantinga, *The Ontological Argument, from St Anselm to contemporary philosophers* (Garden City, NY: Anchor Books, 1965); *Essays in the metaphysics of modality* (New York: Oxford University Press, 2003); cf. J.F. Sennett, *Modality, Probability, and Rationality: a critical examination of Alvin Plantinga's Philosophy* (New York: American University Studies, Series 5: Philosophy, 1992). Charles Hartshorne, *Anselm's discovery, a re-examination of the ontological proof of God's existence* (LaSalle, IL: Open Court, 1965); *The logic of perfection, and other essays in neoclassical metaphysics* (LaSalle, IL: Open Court, 1962). Cf. Plantinga's comment: "Kant's fashionable confusions about the ontological argument," *Faith and Rationality*, 64.

that a "responsible fideism" is the best way to show the reasonableness of belief.[32] Not many philosophers, even if partial to Anselm, test his thesis of *remoto Christo*: "Christ being set aside as if He had never been, [I] will prove by logically necessary steps that apart from Him salvation of man is impossible."[33]

Van Huyssteen argues that when foundationalism in both philosophy of science and theology is rejected in favour of nonfoundationalism ("one of the most important roots or resources of postmodernism,"), some form of *fideism* is in play. His project is twofold. First, the significance of contextuality must be recognized, "the epistemically crucial role of interpreted experience." Second, a "postfoundationalist notion of rationality in theological reflection" must look beyond local communities and cultures "towards a plausible form of interdisciplinary conversation."[34] Both aims are laudable and necessary, given the easy ride that "scientific" relativism has had in the humanities, and the awkward attempts of philosophers and theologians to establish grounds for universal propositions—including "groundless" reasons.[35]

CHANGING STREAMS IN MID—HORSE

The contemporary philosophic scene presents a baffling dilemma.[36] The great schools of philosophy—idealism, existentialism, empiricism—

---

32. C. Stephen Evans, *Faith Beyond Reason: a Kierkegaardian Approach* (Grand Rapids, MI: Eerdmans, 1998). See Ch. 2 for Malcolm and Ch. 3 for Plantinga.

33. Anselm, *Cur Deus Homo?*, Praefatio. He distinguishes the necessary from the fitting (*necessarium, conveniens*) in developing his argument *Aut Poena Aut Satisfactio*.

34. J. W. van Huyssteen, *Essays in Postfoundationalist Theology* (Grand Rapids, MI: Eerdmans, 1997), 3f.

35. Cf. John W. Cooper, "Reformed Apologetics and the Challenge of Post-Modern Relativism," *Calvin Theological Journal*, 28/1 (1993).

36. Cf. McLelland, "Arguments for the existence of philosophy of religion: A survey of recent writing," in *Studies in Religion/Sciences Religieuses* I/4 (1972)

seem less than eager to deal with the topic of religion except in restricted terms and tentative trials. More serious is the unease resulting from the profound shift in academia itself. This is evident on both flanks of the discipline called philosophy of religion, which is related historically to philosophy and to theology. On one hand is the movement of philosophy away from "philosophy of life" or questions of metaphysics and morality in the style of Kant and Hegel, to questions posed by the sciences, chiefly positivistic. (Most disciplines in academia, notably the social sciences, law and medicine, assume a positivist philosophy, usually without knowing it, and so, as Schleiermacher claimed, "fetter humans to the finite."). On the other hand, the new phenomenon of "medical ethics" suggests a return to the former orientation, establishing lines of contact and integration on campus, involving the curious irony of a return to Aristotle's *Nicomachean Ethics* for guidance in decision-making through phronēsis.[37] This shift would not be so bad if philosophers could shake the baleful effects of the "linguistic turn" and seek the meaning of language in its referential function. Thomas Aquinas saw the point, later enshrined in the Terminist debate: "The act of faith ends not in a statement but in reality."[38]

Again, theology no longer means simply "Christian theology", the historical determinant of Western culture and educational philosophy. In particular, its role as "queen of the sciences" (with philosophy as her handmaid) has long gone. The traditional hegemony of Christian thought has given way to two distinct ways of intellectual orientation. One is concerned with method. Although "methodology" usually is

---

361–69.

37. See Chas W. Allen, "The Primacy of *Phronēsis*: A Proposal for Avoiding Frustrating Tendencies in Our Conceptions of Rationality," in *The Journal of Religion* (University of Chicago, 1989) 35974: "All forms of thoughtful activity are at their best when *phronēsis* . . . plays the primary and most decisive role" (359) . . .

38. Actus autem credentis non terminatur ad enuntiabile, sed ad rem, *S.T.* 2a2ae 1, a. 2, ad 2.

misused to signify merely a particular method, in its proper sense it reflects "objectivity" and owes much to the modern development of phenomenology, to Husserl and Heidegger, and the search for appropriate ways of understanding the data designated "religious." A second way of orienting the study of religion is by recognizing the pluralism of the data. Christian theology is learning to come to terms with its context as one of many religions, without privilege about its teaching or ethics or spirituality. Perhaps the hottest debate as well as the most profound these days turns on this question of developing agreed models to discuss religious pluralism.[39]

Philosophers of religion (who exist not necessarily but contingently) are bemused and even baffled by such restructuring of traditional arts and disciplines. One significant tradition has taken us seriously insofar as we are apparently engaged in "fundamental theology." Roman Catholic theology recognizes this function as initiation into the theological enterprise, the concern for prolegomena that prepares for faith through applying natural reason and seeing how far it can go. This "functional specialization," to borrow Lonergan's term, is evident in Thomas Aquinas and other "scholastics" as they moved through fundamental to constructive to speculative theology. It is significant that evangelical Protestantism shares this approach, whether or not it accepts the nomenclature. It may call its enterprise simply (but provocatively) "Christian philosophy," or in a different vein "Reformed epistemology."[40]

The academic discipline called "religious studies" poses the question of the nature of religion in a new way. In distinguishing itself from "theology" it claims a neutral, objective basis for its theoretical work.

---

39. Among leading philosophers of religion who have moved into the "religious pluralism" debate are Ninian Smart (e.g. *Worldviews: Crosscultural Explorations* (New York: Scribners, 1983), John Hick (e.g. *Problems of Religious Pluralism* (New York: St Martin's Press, 1985) and John Cobb (e.g. *Beyond Dialogue* (Philadelphia: Fortress Press, 1982).

40. e.g. L. Lynch, *Christian Philosophy* (Toronto: Canadian Broadcasting Company, 19); A. Plantinga and N. Wolterstorff, as in fn 18 above.

THE AMBIGUITY OF PHILOSOPHY OF RELIGION

The roots of this distinction and the quarrel between the two lie in nineteenth century social science, particularly historiography. Ernst Troeltsch is a notable example of the dilemma, as we shall see.[41] Our contemporary situation falls under new rubrics, of which "postmodern" is the most striking and suggestive. We will examine this phenomenon below; here we note that a postmodern attitude to theory regards it as an ambiguous, even fruitless enterprise. On one hand, all data are "theory-laden," to use the familiar phrase of Norman Hanson.[42] That is, we no longer assume that we can begin with "facts" and work towards a theory to explain them. Rather, we recognize the more circular nature of our explanatory method, with its consequent tentativeness (or better, a ceaseless *dialectic* between theory and data). On the other hand, it seems that epistemology rather than ontology has priority in our theorizing, the apparent heritage of Enlightenment thinkers. Thus we are self-conscious concerning our method, raising "methodology" to a sort of meta-theory. Courses in methodology replace those once devoted to theory or the concept.[43] We focus on our knowing as object rather than the way by which (*quo*) we know something (*quod*). Thus we distort the actual union of subject and object in genuine knowledge.[44]

---

41. See next Chapter, "Troeltsch's Dilemma."

42. N.R. Hanson, *Patterns of Discovery* (Cambridge: Cambridge University Press, 1958), ch. 1.

43. In my days as graduate student in the University of Toronto, Etienne Gilson was offering a significant course entitled "Theory of the Concept." Bernard Lonergan thinks that when a "classicist notion of culture" prevails, theology is "a permanent achievement and then discourses on its nature;" when culture is "conceived empirically" theology becomes a process, "and then one writes on its method."—*Method in Theology* (NY: Herder & Herder, 1972), xi.

44. E.g. "When the intellect understands something other than itself, the thing understood is, so to speak, the father of the word conceived in the intellect, and the intellect itself rather resembles the mother, whose function is that conception takes place in her." J.F. Peiper, *The Concept in Thomism* (New York: Bookman Associates, 1952),157. Cf. the diagram in J. Maritain, *Distinguer pour unir: ou, Les degrés du savoir* (Paris: Desclée, 1963), 482.

FROM UNITY TO DIVERSITY

Current debates in academia suggest that philosophy of religion is in transition. It were easier to trace its rise in Spinoza and Kant and Hegel (for Hegel, there is a philosophy of everything) than to interpret the nature and direction of its career at the moment.[45] Italo Mancini bids us investigate religion "without ever trying totally to resolve it into a gnosis, spiritualism or metaphysic. This could be called the *Utopia* of religion."[46] (Utopia rather than Hegel's "Golgotha of Absolute Spirit!") But for the most part it is no longer a major subdiscipline within philosophy, judging by the proportion of its practitioners in those departments as distinct from religious studies or theology. Nor is it now related to theology itself so much as to history of religions or phenomenology. This shift in external relations reflects that of theology and religious studies themselves. On the one hand, theology is no longer an aggressive and consistent science, on the other the academic study of religion has come of age. The latter forces different options from earlier days, seeking coherence more than consistency, universal criteria aimed at the broad range of academic subjects rather than a rationale of the particular aimed at a community of faith.

This shift in problematics is further exemplified by the socalled problem of evil. Kant saw, *pace* Leibniz, that a philosophical theodicy is impossible. I would deny also a theological one. Both stumble on the attribution of "omnipotence" to deity, what Hartshorne labels a "theological mistake." An instance of this dead end is the strange game which philosophers continue to play, recently under J.L. Mackie's title "The Paradox of Omnipotence."[47] One is reminded of Kierkegaard's shrewd observation: "if God does not exist it would of course be impossible to

---

45. An excellent guide is provided by Alan P. F. Sell, *The Philosophy of Religion 1875-1980* (London: Croom Helm, 1988).
46. Italo Mancini, "Philosophy of Religion" in *Concilium* 136 (New York: Seabury, 1980), 65.
47. J. L. Mackie, *The Miracle of theism: arguments for and against the existence of God* (Oxford: Clarendon Press, 1982).

prove it; and if he does exist it would be folly to attempt it." Philosophy of religion must be able to follow this sort of modality of knowing if it wishes to do justice to its chosen field.[48]

There are monographs and even series devoted to the arguments still. Textbooks, on the other hand, show a broadening of the agenda, providing new context for traditional topics. To the familiar loci of Arguments and Theodicy most of us have likely added religious language and mystical experience, and some have developed courses in the religious dimension of science, of art, even of religions old and new. We team with world religions or social sciences to seek methods of enquiry appropriate to a wide spectrum of data. We mount panels to discuss our identity and our future in the context of Learned Societies that includes names like Religion or Theology. In short, we're clearly flexible, perhaps confused, and somewhat defensive.

The relations among philosophy, theology and philosophy of religion inform the current question of identity. It used to be common to say that philosophy "serves" theology. This meant that some form of classical philosophy—Platonism, or the *philosophia perennis*—provided theory of knowledge, even metaphysical categories, on which Christian thought could draw in developing its doctrinal system, particularly its doctrine of God. Today all three disciplines have altered so much that their relationship is quite other. Assuming that ours enjoys a relatively clear differentiation, we may distinguish a "philosophy of theology" on the one hand and a "philosophy of religions" on the other. The former locates us more credibly in relation to insiders' reflection on the data of "religion;" the latter reflects our interest in a more than Western tradition, our being seized by the problem of religious pluralism. Fergus Kerr has noted that philosophy of religion is "so identified with one set of problems (what used to be called natural theology or Christian

---

48. See Chas Hartshorne, *Omnipotence and Other Theological Mistakes* (Albany, NY: University of New York Press, 1984); S. Kierkegaard, *Philosophical Fragments* ((1844) Princeton University Press, 1936), p 31.

apologetics): we need practitioners of what Donald MacKinnon called 'the philosophy of theology.'"[49]

Another approach to discovering where we are or should be, rather than where we've been, is to distinguish leading streams or traditions that continue to inform our subject. For instance, the most influential, at least in Anglo-American institutions for some four decades after 1945, was analytic philosophy. Its narrow examination of religious language proved both therapeutic in critique and at times destructive in conclusion. Now analysis or critique is the central, perhaps decisive, role of philosophy of religion. One thinks of Ricoeur's depiction of Marx, Freud and Nietzsche as "masters of suspicion" who serve to cleanse religion of societal, infantile and immoral traits.[50] And of Walter Kaufmann or Kai Nielsen with their sharp objections to classical theism. Kaufmann's critique accuses the warring partners existentialism and analysis of shortchanging the crucial datum of experience: "Why must we either ignore anguish or treat it as man's central experience? Why must we spurn experience, either because it is too messy or because it is not messy enough?"[51] Iris Murdoch expressed similar sentiments about the false dichotomy in her book on Sartre: "The 'world' of *The Concept of Mind* is the world in which people play cricket, cook cakes, make simple decisions, remember their childhood and go to the circus; not the world in which they commit sins, fall in love, say prayers or join the Communist Party."[52] Such return to *experience* is salutary. Jerome Gellman, for example, posits the thesis that applying certain principles to "putative experience of God" should show that "it is strongly rational to accept that God really is experienced, and hence that God exists." The principles include connection to reality

---

49. Fergus Kerr, *Theology After Wittgenstein* (Oxford: Basil Blackwell, 1986), 171.

50. Ricoeur, *De l'interprétation: essai sur Freud* (Paris: Ed. du Seuil, 1961).

51. W. Kaufmann, *A Critique of Religion and Philosophy* (London: Faber & Faber, 1959), 27.

52. Iris Murdoch, *Sartre: romantic rationalist* (Cambridge: Bowes & Bowes, 1953), 42 .

and "strength in number greatness."[53] This approach is clearly superior to those that refuse to consider "faith" a viable datum in epistemology.

Besides critical-analytic there are synthetic forms of philosophy of religion. They serve to spark more inventive and explanatory hypotheses and analogies for constructive theses. If linguistic analysis played the former role, process thinking is a leading example of the latter. We should note, however, that some theologians can think philosophically in a way that incorporates the theo-therapy required to cleanse the idea of God from inappropriate anthropomorphisms. Thomas Aquinas is still outstanding in this regard, with his opening gambit (in the greater *Summa*) of apophatic method.[54]

TOWARDS DEFINITION

What *is* philosophy of religion? Not what it once was. Kant, Schleiermacher, Schelling and Hegel represent its early and heady days. Philosophy seemed well able to determine the limits of knowledge and hence the reach of dogma. Each in his own way illustrates the ambiguity, even dilemma, that haunts us. Kant began well in making God the necessary decision of human willing; but his end is significant: dabbling in the problem of radical evil he went too far; Goethe accused him of "slobbering on his professor's gown" by his appeal to religious (Pauline!) dogma in his book on religion within reasonable limits.[55] Schleiermacher was the careful methodologist, relating "philosophical theology" to Christianity through a point of departure logically "above" it, that is "in the general concept of a religious community or fellowship of faith".[56]

---

53. J.I. Gellman, *Experience of God and the Rationality of Theistic Belief* (Ithaca: Cornell University Press, 1997), 2: "The Argument," 45-56.

54. The analogical method is intended to show "how God is not" (*quomodo non sit*). The apophatic modality always outweighs the cataphatic in both Western classical theism and Eastern conciliar orthodoxy. See *S.T.* I.1,

55. Kant, *Religion within the Limits of Reason Alone* (Cambridge: Cambridge University Press, 1998).

56. F. Scheiermacher, *Christian Faith* (*Der Christliche Glaube*, 1821/22),

Thus he subsumed the phenomena of Christian faith under a universal religious consciousness. Hegel developed his various "philosophies"—of mind (*Geist*), of nature, rights, law, history, and especially religion—in the form of philosophical consciousness-raising. Philosophy of religion was an instance of *aufgehoben*, sublating dogma into concept. So he burdened theology with a "speculative Good Friday" which raised (reduced?) doctrine to Idea and made philosophy of religion the end of theology, and indeed of religion itself.[57] All four figures suggest the end of Enlightenment as a naive trust in instrumental reason, and the beginning of modernity as critical reasoning on data as phenomena.[58] Perhaps Schelling is more helpful yet in regard to our contemporary situation and debate. Tillich found him so, in developing categories appropriate for a history of religion free from the presupposition of a particular absolute: "For the philosophy of religion, the absoluteness of Christianity is a problem whose solution requires a concept of religion."[59] Schelling also warns of the modern split between the empirical sciences seeking causal laws and human sciences seeking hermeneutical rubrics.[60]

Today's context is marked by a fragmentation of the traditional academic pursuit of truth, resulting in confusion about intellectual roles. Individual philosophers of religion may play the gadfly, since the Socratic

---

Berlin: De Gruyter, 1980).

57. See McLelland, *Prometheus Rebound: the irony of atheism* (Waterloo: Wilfrid Laurier University Press, 1989), "7: The Speculative Death of God: Hegel, Feuerbach," 125-45.

58. Schleiermacher, *Brief Outline of the Study of Theology* (1811), §33.

59. P. Tillich, *Christianity and the Encounter of World Religions* (New York: Columbia University Press, 1963).

60. Tillich, *The Construction of the history of religion in Schelling's Positive Philosophy*, (1910 doctoral dissertation) trans. V. Nuovo (London: Associated University Presses, 1974), esp. Part III. Cf. *Mysticism and Guilt—Consciousness in Schelling's Philosophical Development*, 1912 dissertation for Licentiate in Theology, University of Halle, trans. V. Nuovo (London: Associated University Presses, 1974). I have treated the foundational figures in *Prometheus Rebound*. Cf. Jas Collins, *The Emergence of Philosophy of Religion* (New Haven: Yale University Press, 1967).

model is always useful in refuting conceptual naivety and pomposity. Others may continue traditional functions of supporting or complementing Christian theology, especially in seminary situations. Most of us, I suspect, are less confident about pursuing a discipline whose brief bright hour seems fading, as paradigm shifts occur about us. Philosophers of whatever kind are no longer the arbiters of academic good taste. It is some time since a "philosophy of life" disappeared from philosophy departments; what seems closest now to a public authority is philosophy of science, particularly in addressing medical ethics and related topics. In theology meanwhile, liberation and feminist approaches question the very integrity of our functional differentiations. Social sciences add their critique, reinforced, if complicated, by ethics offering itself as criterion for true conceptuality. The issues of who shall live and die, of nuclear power and ecological stewardship, dominate the minds of students and search committees and granting agencies. In this context we sound like rather prim Victorian aunts recalling the youngsters to more restrained and genteel habits of mind and heart. Ah, for the good old days!

If we are to develop a method appropriate to our data, it must reject the imagined polarity of "objectivity" and "subjectivity." The former relies on abstraction and so risks distortion; the latter relies on commitment and so risks coercion. Perhaps these parameters imply a kind of spectrum of rationality, between scepticism and credulity. The motion between would be governed by a kind of Uncertainty Principle. Instead of the position/velocity of physics, we attempt to understand origin (relation to world) and reference (relation to transcendence). Such a dynamism operates much like the traditional concept of analogy, which involved the dialectical play of *signum* and *res*. Between homonym and synonym (Aristotle) or univocity and equivocity (Aquinas) there is a subtler relationship between disparates, a "proper proportionality" which breaks formal logic in favour of new modalities of presence and absence. Both "opposites" are denied, anthropomorphism on the one hand and agnosticism on the other.

I see philosophy of religion as the pursuit of that *logos* appropriate to a higher *mythos*, not as its apologue or defender, but simply as its friendly critic. We stand in danger of equating scientific method with metaphysics; we should rather cultivate a spirit that knows its way around in the history and philosophy of the human pursuit of ultimates. To be a gadfly is relatively easy, and compatible with the Socratic view of philosophy as the practice of dying. We need a hardier breed, whose critique allows us to consider and compare the rich and varied forms of the celebration of *living*. This would constitute a proper "phenomenology", a subject objectified ("disciplined") by its own data so that it responds in appropriate categories. The data of religion, after all, do not include the datum "religion"—Wilfred C. Smith has argued this point most cogently. He argues that "The idea that believing is religiously important turns out to be a modern idea."[61] That is, the difference between "belief" and "faith" measures the distance between propositional truth and personal commitment. Philosophers ask, "What do you believe?" The "believer" answers, "I know Whom I trust." Herein lies the dilemma—its two horns—of *philosophy* of *religion*.

Here is a thesis: *the proper subject-matter of philosophy of religion is "natural theology."* That is, our discipline is able to handle only the outer court of theology's object/Subject; it borrows its categories from certain theological prolegomena. In doing so, it trades on questionable assumptions, primarily that "existence" applies to God, as the Arguments assume.[62] This initial category-mistake blunts the edge of its critical function, and narrows the scope of its impact. It makes our

---

61. See his exposition in *Belief and History* (Charlottesville: University Press of Virginia, 1977), Preface and 36ff, "The Modern History of 'Believing'."

62. A noteworthy example of this critique is that of Henri Duméry, *The Problem of God in philosophy of religion*, trans. C. Courtney (Evanston, IL: Northwestern University Press, 1964). Duméry's kind of antitheism posits God as Unity rather than Being "apperceived" through radical transcendence. See H.R. Burkle, *The Non-Existence of God: Antitheism from Hegel to Duméry* (New York: Herder & Herder, 1969), esp. 147ff, "The Reduction of God."

efforts preliminary and therapeutic, but less constructive or edifying. The following chapters intend to illustrate this thesis.

Now let us look at natural theology as a phenomenon, a case study to test the thesis that natural theology is the only possible subject-matter of philosophy of religion, and therefore makes room for an alternative philosophy of theology, allowing for the possibility of a positive theology. Then we will be able to turn explicitly to the issue of religious pluralism, the testing ground for a universal theory of religion and for our contemporary mood of positivism or relativism.

2

WHICH "NATURAL THEOLOGY?"

I certainly see—with astonishment—that such a science as Lord Gifford had in mind does exist, but I do not see how it is possible for it to exist.
— Karl Barth[1]

The natural theology of Western thought is Natural Theology—so we concluded in the first chapter. We stated that there appear to be two types of philosophy of religion, the traditional inheritor of nineteenth century European philosophy, and a more recent form of what Donald Mackinnon called "the philosophy of theology."[2] Reflecting on Wittgenstein's musings on the subject, Fergus Kerr called for "practitioners of *the philosophy of theology*."[3] T.F. Torrance claims to be exploring "the philosophy of theological science," cutting through "idealist and positivist assumptions alike" in epistemology, and so

---

1. *The Knowledge and the Service of God According to the Teaching of the Reformation*, Gifford Lectures 1937–38, trans. J.L.M. Haire and I. Henderson (London: Hodder & Stoughton, 1938), 5.
2. D.M. Mackinnon, *Explorations in Theology* 5 (London: SCM, 1979), 147.
3. F. Kerr, *Theology After Wittgenstein* (Oxford: Basil Blackwell, 1986), 171; see Ch. 8: "Questions in the philosophy of theology," 168ff.

achieving "the restoration of ontology in the proper sense."[4]

TWO TYPES OF NATURAL THEOLOGY

We must note the radical shift in natural theology from its medieval authors, whose arguments for divinity were partners to their faith. Anselm's Ontological Argument was a form of prayer, of "faith seeking understanding" (*fides quaerens intellectum*), while the "five ways" of Aquinas are a minor component in his magisterial sum of theology proper. Nicholas Wolterstorff has made this point well, describing the history as "the migration of the theistic arguments" from natural theology to "evidentialist apologetics."[5] The earlier form distinguished those truths of revelation accessible to natural reason, and proceeded to mount demonstrative arguments, "for apologetic and polemical purposes." Wolterstorff also discerns another "project of natural theology," namely thinking through articles of faith, an advance in belief through the "seeing" of reasoned discourse: "We *transmute* believing into seeing, faith into vision."[6] On the contrary, the experiment of modernity begins with a presumption of agnosticism or even atheism, attaching foundationalist conditions to theology, and so displacing faith with rational commitment.[7] This constitutes an "evidentialist" criterion for faith, a form of the fallacy of misplaced concreteness.

Another thesis has emerged in recent decades: that "natural theology" as an independent discipline should be displaced by a different sort of natural theology integrated with philosophy, or with the philosophy of

---

4. Torrance, *Reality and Scientific Theology* (Edinburgh: Scottish Academic Press, 1985), 131.
5. N. Wolterstorff, "Can Belief in God Be Rational If It has No Foundations?" in Plantinga and Wolterstorff, *Faith and Rationality* (Notre Dame: University of Notre Dame Press, 1983).
6. With John Locke in mind, Wolterstorff calls on Thomas Aquinas for the distinction within sacred science, e.g. *S.T.* IIaIIae, q. 2, art. 10.
7. E.g. Antony Flew, *The presumption of atheism, and other philosophical essays on God, freedom and immortality* (London: Elek for Pemberton, 1976).

theology. This is most apparent in the work of Karl Barth and Thomas Torrance. Barth's notorious ploy at the Gifford Lectures, devoted to natural theology, was to challenge the very idea of such a subject by expounding its opposite, namely confessional theology. His lectures are entitled "the knowledge of God and the service of God according to the teaching of the Reformation," offered as an "indirect" contribution to the clarification of the subject. "I do not see how it is possible for it to exist. I am convinced that so far as it has existed and still exists, it owes its existence to a radical error." Barth's point is that natural theology "is thrown into relief by the dark *background* of a totally different theology." The latter—a theology of revelation—is that by which the former lives, "in so far as it must affirm what the other denies and deny what the other affirms." Barth therefore offers that "other theology" with which natural theology co-exists as antithesis.[8] He pursued this theme elsewhere: "Natural theology (*theologia naturalis*) is included in and brought into clear light in the theology of revelation (*theologia revelata*); in the reality of divine grace is included the truth of the divine creation. In this sense it is true that 'Grace does not destroy nature but completes it.'"[9] For Barth, it is human autonomy that posits its own source of knowing God, and so he challenges his own Reformed Church tradition—notably in the *Confessio Gallicana*—which not only displaces revealed theology but compromises the Church's independence of the state (for Barth these two always hang together). Barth's concern is not rationality but autonomy. He seems to regard traditional natural theology as a form of that "works-righteousness" so strongly rejected by the Reformers. Thus he sees only one kind of natural theology, leading inexorably to "natural religion;" the alternative of a more modest "theology of nature," forming a natural (!) bridge to rev-

---

8. Karl Barth, *The Knowledge and the Service of God*, 5ff.
9. Barth, *Theology and Church* (London: SCM, 1962) 342. See *C.D.* I/2, 305 for Barth's analysis of Rom. 1 and Acts 17, the two crucial biblical passages for the topic. See Aquinas, *S.T.* I.1, 8 *ad sec.*

elation, is rejected apriori. [10] In fact, as James Barr, a more traditional sort of Gifford lecturer, points out cogently, Barth is mistaken about the Reformers themselves, ignoring their own form of natural theology.[11] But Barr is also mistaken about Barth, in the sense that what the dogmatician seeks to identify is the very object of dogma itself: "Wouldn't it be pitiful if theology wished to retreat to the notion that its object was not God but merely faith—as if it would not immediately fall into the same dilemma about how to deal with God as the object of faith or whether perhaps faith too was something without an object?"[12]

Thomas F. Torrance has sharpened Barth's thesis and developed it in a unique way.[13] His books in recent decades have made the case for a "theological science" in harmony with "natural science," and for both as rejecting an independent Natural Theology. He begins from Barth's view that natural theology springs from "a whole movement of man in which he seeks to justify himself over against the grace of God."[14] But

---

10. *C.D.* II/1, 127. The Gallic Confession of 1559 (echoed in the Belgic in 1561) declared two kinds of revelation, "in his works" and "in his Word" (art. 2). Wisnefske notes Barth's account of the "subjective bases of natural theology" in CD II/1 and the "objective bases" in CD IV/3 and 4—*Our Natural Knowledge*, 58f.

11. Barr, *Biblical Faith*, 9, 104ff.

12. Barth, *Fate and Idea in Theology*, (*Schicksal und Idee in der Theologie*), trans. Geo. Hunsinger, in *The Way of Theology in Karl Barth*, ed. H.M. Rumscheidt (Allison Park, PE: Pickwick Pubs., 1986), 35.

13. Barr treats Torrance only in footnotes, and refers only to one article, "The Problem of Natural Theology in the Thought of Karl Barth" in RS 6 (1970). By regarding Torrance as simply "Barthian" Barr misses his novel contribution, particularly in terms of the dialogue with the sciences; he rejects the very idea of "theological science," regarding theology strictly as a humanistic discipline (181f).

14. Torrance, "The Problem of Natural Theology in Karl Barth," in *Religious Studies* 6 (1970) 1212–35, recast as "Natural Theology in theThought of Karl barth," ch. 5 His thesis here is the contrast between "dualist" and "interactionist" theologies. See the excellent survey in A.E. McGrath, *Thomas F. Torrance: An Intellectual Biography* (Edinburgh: T. & T. Clark, 1999) Ch. 8: "The Place and Purpose of Natural Theology."

there is a legitimate theology of creation, of nature, that reaches a valid conclusion: as *creation*, everything is *contingent*, so that both chance and order obtain, reflecting both the Hebrew heritage of the personal will of a Creator and the Greek heritage of cosmic orderliness. This idea of *contingent order*—the basis of experimental method—becomes a major theme, as Torrance explores "the philosophy of theological science." He argues for "a proper natural theology" that is not "an *independent* conceptual system, *antecedent* to actual or empirical knowledge of God upon which it is then imposed, quite unscientifically, as a set of necessary epistemological presuppositions!"[15] Thus "belief in order" derives from "the structure of created being," and "constitutes an ultimate regulatory factor in all rational and scientific activity."[16]

A second theme for Torrance is the detrimental role of dualistic philosophy in Western thought, caused by the "closed mechanistic universe" of nineteenth-century science (followed by most academic disciplines these days!). While the dualism of the classical age tended to prevent the development of experimental method for centuries, the modern form is more sinister, limiting science to positivism and denying the breakthrough of relativity theory, thus maintaining an outdated "receptacle or container" theory of space. But with relativity theory and quantum physics a new cosmology is in order: the "relational" concept of space—time. It is significant that Einstein himself insisted on his own "intuition" in apprehending the contingent order of reality, and so dissociated himself "from all positivist accounts of the discovery of Special Relativity."[17]

---

15. Torrance, *Space, Time & Resurrection* (Grand Rapids: Eerdmans, 1976) 1. Cf. "Divine and Contingent Order," in A. R. Peacocke, ed. *The Sciences and Theology in the Twentieth Century* (Notre Dame, IN: University of Notre Dame Press, 1981), p. 81–97.

16. Torrance, "Transcendental Role of Wisdom in Science," in *Ground and Grammar of Theology* (Belfast: Christian Journals Ltd., 1980), 131f.

17. Iain Paul, *Knowledge of God: Calvin, Einstein and Polanyi* (Edinburgh: Scottish Academic Press, 1987), 87.

As analogue for the "radical reconstruction" he calls for, Torrance cites Einstein's view of the relation between geometry and physics. Even four-dimensional geometries entail "a profound correlation between abstract conceptual systems and physical processes," since the space-time continuum constitutes "a continuous, diversified but unitary field of dynamic structures." Torrance takes this as parallel to the intrinsic relation between natural and revealed theologies. Natural theology "cannot be undertaken apart from actual knowledge of the living God as a prior conceptual system on its own, or be developed as an independent philosophical examination of rational forms phenomenologically abstracted from their material content, all antecedent to positive theology."[18] Such insistence on the unity of the two disciplines sees the function of natural theology as a sort of "theological geometry" within positive God-talk. When pursued as an independent science antecedent to physics, Euclidean geometry was found to be "finally irrelevant to the actual structure of the universe of space and time." But when introduced into "the material content of physics," a four-dimensional geometry became a "natural science" as Einstein called it. Similarly, natural theology may function as "a complex of rational structures arising in our actual knowledge of God." Therefore natural theology "cannot be pursued in its traditional abstractive form, as a prior conceptual system on its own, but must be brought within the body of positive theology and be pursued in indissoluble unity with it." Natural theology may provide a "necessary condition" for actual knowledge of God, although not "a sufficient condition."[19]

---

18. Torrance, *Space, Time & Incarnation* (London: Oxford University Press, 1969), 69. *Summa Theol.* I.1, 7f; I.2, 2: "Whether it can be demonstrated that God exists?". See J. Pelikan, "Natural Theology and the Scholastic Method" in *The Growth of Medieval Theology (600–1300)* (Chicago: University of Chicago Press, 1978), 284ff.

19. Torrance, *Reality and Scientific Theology* (Philadelphia: Westminster Press, 1982), 39ff.

WHICH NATURAL THEOLOGY?

FRIENDS, ENEMIES, HOSTAGES

Philosophers and theologians are on a similar quest, but too often unsure or unwilling to admit that the objects of their desire are related: "Being" and "God." They have been in turn friends, enemies, and hostages to each other's demands. The very definition of the two fields is tendentious, inasmuch as they may be considered identical, absolutely different, or overlapping (rather like Aristotle's concept of analogical relations). Of course there has always been a philosophical theology, and as James Horne notes, a companion sceptical philosophy to dispute its arguments.[20] The former is usually propaedeutic—a Justin Martyr invoking philosophical customs in thought and dress, or Clement and Origen of Alexandria developing their Christian Platonism, the latter in stark contrast to Tertullian's rejection of Athens. Such a traditional agenda occupying theologians of an apologetic or irenic approach became specialized as an academic discipline in the nineteenth century. Protestant seminaries called it "Apologetics;" Roman Catholic "Fundamental Theology," in keeping with the Thomist tradition.

As for the nature and role of natural theology, its history is significant, originating in Roman times with Cicero and Varro, the latter attributing it to philosophers in distinction from poets and lawgivers. The word "theology" as referring explicitly to Christian doctrine comes much later, probably with Abelard. The Thomist distinction between natural knowledge and grace is the heart of classical theism, but this harmony was soon challenged by Occamists and the Enlightenment. Such scepticism, however, did not destroy faith but shifted it to fideism on the one hand and rationalistic theism on the other. Kant's critical limitation on reason "making way for faith" really meant faith in moral reasoning rather than in a personal God. After Kant and Hegel, natural theology became philosophy of religion. Modern philosophy of religion

---

20. James Horne, "Philosophical Theology as 'Science of Religion'" in Abraham H. Khan et al., "Symposium," *Toronto Journal of Theology*, 5:1 (1989), 37.

is decidedly post-Hegelian, although Michel Despland is correct to insist on its pre-Hegelian history.[21] Unfortunately, this approach to religion is now losing its confidence and even its self-esteem. Is this due to the lack of a strong theology to provide a reference point for philosophical thinking? After all, as Barth claimed, we need the horizon of such a theology to know where we are. What, then, is the current state of relations between philosophy and theology?[22] Let us consider the case of Canadian letters.

CANADA: A CASE STUDY

Traditional natural theology is clear from earlier philosophy and theology in Canada, with parallels and slight differences as regards the USA. Studies of our intellectual history—by Irving, Johnson, McKillop and others—bear this out.[23] A significant, and ironical, case is the definitive "essay on philosophy and culture in English Canada" by Armour and Trott which names our earliest "philosophers"—in fact they are all *theologians* of a Natural bent. The authors intend to cover "philosophy in its usually understood academic sense" and to uncover "the working concept of reason" in our history.[24] I maintain that they have begged the question of what both philosophy and reason meant in this history, distorting the role philosophers played in academia, and obscuring the proper domain

---

21. M. Despland, *The Education of Desire: Plato and the Philosophy of Religion* (Toronto: University of Toronto Press, 1985). Cf. James Collins, *The Emergence of Philosophy of Religion* (New Haven: Yale University Press, 1967).

22. See G. Ebeling, *Studium der Theologie: Eine Enzyklopädische Orientierung* (Tübingen: J.C.B. Mohr, 1975) and E. Farley, *Theologia: the Fragmentation and Unity of Theological Education* (Philadelphia: Fortress Press, 1983).

23. C.F. Klinck, ed. *Literary History of Canada* (University of Toronto Press, 1965): J. Irving and A.H. Johnson on philosophy 431-550, 576-597; J.S. Thomson on religion and theology 551–575; Conclusion by Northrop Frye. A.B. McKillop, *A Disciplined Intelligence* (Montreal: McGill-Queens University Press, 1979).

24. L. Armour and E. Trott, *The Faces of Reason: an essay on philosophy and culture in English Canada 1850-1950* (Waterloo: Wilfrid Laurier University Press, 1981), xxiiif.

of philosophy of religion.[25] A recent survey of "analytic philosophy of religion" likewise deals with philosophers of religion debating the same topic, but here with clearer understanding.[26]

In my own case, as an undergraduate I had learned of the harmony of philosophy and theology from Frank Waters at McMaster University, but soon experienced a different understanding. At the University of Toronto in the late 'forties, in order to study the two disciplines at once I required permission from both Walter Bryden, Principal of Knox College, and Fulton Anderson, Chairman of the University's Philosophy Department. Within my first day I had been warned by Bryden about the dangers of philosophy and by Anderson about the dangers of theology. I soon learned the politics at work, given the Barthian emphasis at Knox and the anti-theological stance of many philosophers.[27] Interestingly, neither suggested that I consider the famous Catholic philosophers at the Pontifical Institute, Etienne Gilson and Jacques Maritain, whom I discovered on my own. Such was the triple play of the subject in that era.

C'EST L'HIVER

Northrop Frye taught us to start with the question "Where is here?" Canada inherited the European tradition in which philosophy was

---

25. A similar critique of the tendency to dissociate philosophy from "theology" as early as possible is provided by Bruce Kuklick, *A History of Philosophy in America, 1720–2000* (Oxford University Press, 2001). In his *Churchmen and Philosophers: From Jonathan Edwards to John Dewey* (New Haven: Yale University Press, 1985) he showed the significance of Trinitarian Calvinism as the common language of both philosophers and theologians.

26. Mostafa Faghoury, ed. *Analytical Philosophy of Religion in Canada* (Ottawa: University of Ottawa Press, 1982). The essays consider Terence Penelhum, Kai Nielsen, Alastair McKinnon and Donald Evans.

27. Anderson had called Bryden an "irrational enthusiast" in a 1941 review of his book *The Christian's Knowledge of God*; see J.A. Vissers. *The Neo-Orthodox Theology of W. W. Bryden* (Princeton Theological Monograph Series 56, 2006), 217.

either handmaid of theology (French and Catholic) or friendly critic and support (British and Protestant); but another element needs to be noted, namely, that of local context. If I am correct that (to parse the thesis) "the natural theology of Canadians is natural theology," then one important influence on our thinking must be the peculiar geography of this place, what Frank R. Scott called "the country of the mind." Ours is a wintry land: we live, in Al Purdy's phrase, "north of summer;" in Gilles Vigneault's popular song, "Mon pays, ce n'est pas un pays, c'est l'hiver." This fact is significant for the origins of theological education in the valiant efforts of those ecclesiastical frontiersmen taming the wilderness to establish congregations, convert native peoples, and establish academies, e.g., Pictou Academy, Nova Scotia and Wesley College, Winnipeg. It may also help explain why even our notorious "two solitudes" (Hugh MacLennan) share a common spirituality, a sort of "wintry theology," what Ronald Sutherland dubbed "The Calvinist-Jansenist Pantomime."[28] The Jansenism of Québec and the Calvinism of the early settlers east and west reflected a similar theology of nature responding to our climate, and a theology of grace appropriate to those who struggle for that "survival" noted by Margaret Atwood as the defining characteristic of Canadian literature.[29] It seemed to both Catholic and Protestant in the pioneer generations that this life is a *purgatoire sur la terre*. I believe it has something to do also with the fact that Scottish "common sense" philosophy found a second home in France before migrating to North America. The *auld alliance* between Scotland and France (formed against their common enemy England) involved trade in ideas, so that the philosophie écossaise was the quasi-official philosophy of nineteenth-century France, and in turn influential in Quebec.[30] (This fascinating story seems strangely absent from the rhetoric of Québec nationalism these days).

---

28. Ronald Sutherland, *Second Image: Comparative Studies in Quebec/Canadian Literature* (Toronto: New Press, 1971), 61ff.

29. Margaret Atwood, *Survival: a thematic guide to Canadian literature* (Toronto: Anansi, 1972).

30. L. Marcil-Lacoste, Claude Buffier and Thomas Reid, *Two Common*

WHICH NATURAL THEOLOGY?

Traditionally, Catholic theology has handled the apologetic agenda with links to the *philosophia perennis* on the one hand, and to developments in existentialism and phenomenology on the other, for example, in Transcendental Thomism. Here, at least, relations were always cordial, provided one followed the privileged Thomist philosophy and avoided that "false philosophy" to which in his 1907 encyclicals Pope Pius X attributed much of the heresy of "modernism." Protestant theological education followed the nineteenth-century curriculum, with philosophy of religion serving as introduction and handmaid to systematic theology. It handled the prolegomena: religious experience, the nature of religious language, and the arguments for the existence of God and against it, most notably the problem of evil. It played a strong, even decisive, role in educating clergy and engaging sceptics during those earlier times of confidence in reason to arbitrate in metaphysical debates. If this role has largely passed before the storm of postcritical and postmodern thinking, we need to recall it briefly in order to situate our North American tradition. Two strong movements came with our first philosophers/theologians, namely, Scottish Common Sense and German Idealism.

COMMON SENSE, COMMON CAUSE

If at first Canadian theologians and philosophers seem identical it is because both were committed to natural theology. Philosophy's part in Apologetics was well established: to demonstrate Christian and church religion (*demonstratio religiosa christiana et ecclesiastica*). This suggests a more theological context for reason than Armour and Trott recognize in selecting the theory of knowledge ("the faces of reason") as the best way into this subject. Now epistemology may be our modern paradigm, but for our forebears *knowledge* reflected *being*, and both relate necessarily to a theistic worldview. One important influence on their approach was the "classical theism" that synthesized nature and

---

Sense Philosophers (Montreal: McGill-Queen's University Press, 1982).

grace, symbolized in the famous Thomist statement already noted: "Grace does not destroy nature but perfects it."[31] The Enlightenment shifted the balance to make room for autonomous reason, losing the dynamic of Thomas's moderate realism in the process. By the time Canada happened, the influence of German Idealism was not yet apparent; the Scottish Common Sense school was dominant (most famously through Princeton's James McCosh), complemented by the English deistic approach. Both streams stressed moderation, harmony, and a theology stronger on creation than redemption. The argument from design was still powerful, and nothing human was alien from God.

In 1850 James Beaven published *Elements of Natural Theology*. Formerly professor of divinity at King's College, Toronto, he joined the new University there as professor of metaphysics and ethics. Armour and Trott observe that the move "marks both Beaven's personal transition from professional theologian to professional philosopher and the transition of academic philosophy in English Canada from a fiefdom of religion to an independent concern."[32] This perception, of course, is a modern take on what Beaven and his generation thought of the relation between philosophy and theology. The academic establishment matched the ecclesiastical—it was difficult *not* to be Christian in either sphere. Beaven reflects the two currents of our "colonial philosophers," Scottish common sense and moral intuitionism, a combination of Hamilton and Butler.

The other players in the drama of academic philosophy in the period 1850–1890 include William Lyall (1811–1890), George Paxton Young (1818–1889), and John Clark Murray (1836–1917). Lyall's concern for experience and his emphasis on the affections reflect a continuing stream in Maritime Canada as well as New England. His moral philosophy is mediating (Kant as well as Augustine, for instance) and this too would prove to be distinctively Canadian. Murray was a disciple of

---

31. Aquinas, *ST* I.1, 8 *ad sec.: gratia non tollat naturam sed perficiat*.
32. Armour & Trott, *Faces of Reason*, 32.

William Hamilton, although he developed an "eclectic idealism" in his mature works on ethics.[33] Young is a more complex and controversial figure. As professor at Knox College from 1853, his chair included "logic, mental and moral philosophy" and "evidences of natural and revealed religion." This agenda denotes the role of philosophical apologetics in the seminary, the harmony of our two subjects. By 1864, according to his friend D.J. Macdonnell, Young had concluded that he could no longer accept the Westminster Confession of Faith, and resigned from his chair.[34] The striking saga of this remarkable scholar includes his return to Knox in 1870 to teach philosophy, with no duties pertaining to theology. One year later he became professor of mental and moral philosophy at University College, Toronto. Young rejected the "common sense" philosophy of his early years in Scotland, in part because of its connection with the harsh Presbyterian doctrine he abhorred. His critique of William Hamilton's epistemology and of theological determinism leads to a form of idealism, anticipating that of T.H. Green. Young's conscience and career express the agony of the age.

IDEAS AND IDEALISM

The dominant figure for the Canadian story is John Watson, teaching at Queen's from 1872, on his arrival from Glasgow, until retirement in 1922. He helped transmute the tradition of nineteenth-century mental and moral philosophy into the secularized and academic philosophy of the twentieth. McKillop has noted the stance of "the Anglo-Canadian moral imperative" from Thomas McCulloch through Grant, Morton, and Innis to Northrop Frye: Watson played a crucial role in its development and transmission.[35] Watson's thorough study of Augustine, Hegel,

---

33. John Clark Murray, *Outline of Sir William Hamilton's Philosophy* (1870), and *A Handbook of Christian Ethics* (1900).
34. See J.C. McLelland, "The MacDonnell Heresy Trial," *Canadian Journal of Theology*, 4:4 (1958), 273–284.
35. McKillop, *Contours*, 96–110.

Spinoza, and Leibniz established his defence of the Hegelian dialectic as the comprehending unity overcoming all contradictions in thought and life.[36] He called his mature position "Constructive Idealism" and offered it as being "in essential harmony with that which was embodied in the life and teaching of the Founder of Christianity," and also as "the conception of a divine principle which manifests itself in every part of the universe, but predominantly in man."[37] Moreover, the combination of idealist metaphysics and social ethics provides the key to much Canadian philosophy and theology, providing a social and political conscience informing public life. Our original thesis, that earlier Canadian philosophy was really natural theology, still holds, however. Watson's own words in his inaugural lecture—the year is 1872; he is 25 years old—form a sort of motto: "In thus revealing necessary truth, Philosophy at the same time reveals Him who is Truth itself."[38]

From the 1920s, new departures in philosophy and theology proved revolutionary. The Victorian consensus, what has been termed the "evangelical creed" guiding morals and ideas, was breaking down.[39] Philosophy of science grew in significance, inspiring Oxbridge logical and linguistic analysis, in contrast to the existentialism of the Continent. In Canada, philosophy departments lost interest in metaphysical issues, charging theology with "non-sensical" propositions. Neither philosophy nor theology regarded the other with much interest. Wittgensteinian fideism appears to have impressed philosophers more than theologians.

The modern giants Karl Barth and Paul Tillich seemed destined to polarize the relationship of our two subjects as either kerygmatic or

---

36. John Watson, *The Philosophical Basis of Religion* (Glasgow: James Maclehose, 1907), 430–431.

37. John Watson, *Christianity and Idealism* (1897), and *The Interpretation of Religious Experience* (1912). See Armour and Trott, 216ff.

38. Klinck, *Literary History*, 439.

39. M. Gauvreau, *The Evangelical Century: College and Creed in English Canada from the Great Revival to the Great Depression* (Montreal: McGill-Queen's University Press, 1991).

apologetic, either polemical. or congenial. I have argued elsewhere that Barth's position is much more open than usually assumed, a matter of emphasis on the dialectical imbalance typical of Barth's method, rather than a rejection of philosophy in Tertullian's manner.[40] What Barth made clear, ironically in his Gifford Lectures and polemically in his *Nein!* against Brunner, was the difference between a theology *of* nature and a theology *from* nature. The former acknowledges creation, its traces of creative Spirit, and draws suggestive arguments therefrom; the latter mounts persuasive arguments from natural reason, and so forms Natural Theology. Brunner's *theologia naturalis* "refracts" its divine origin, whereas Barth's "revelation-positivism" (*Offenbarungspositivismus*), as Bonhoeffer termed it, rejects it as "philosophical fantasy," while allowing a pragmatic use of things natural.[41] In Canada the debate centred in Toronto's Trinitarian Society and Knox College, where Walter Bryden taught philosophy of religion in "Barthian" fashion (his students summed it up as "no grace in Greece"). Barth's own redress of the balance in "The Humanity of God" was still to come; meanwhile the liberal/neo-orthodox dichotomy was strongly felt and expressed.

TRENDS AND PROJECTS

Certain recent trends have invested the interdisciplinary matrix of our subject with new life and hope. First, we should note the famous "linguistic turn" associated with the name of Heidegger and with the explosion of hermeneutics. Heidegger's meditation on being led to his critique of mere thinking about essence, so that the critical turning-point (*Kehre*) reveals the very limits of ontology by recognizing a

---

40. J.C. McLelland, "Philosophy and Theology—A Family Affair (Karl and Heinrich Barth)" in H-M. Rumscheidt (ed.), *Footnotes to a Theology: the Karl Barth Colloquium of 1972* (Toronto: CCSR: *Studies in Religion Supplements*, 1974), 30–52.

41. Karl Barth, "No!" in Karl Barth, *Natural Theology* (with Brunner's "Natural Theology"), Peter Fraenkel, ed. (London: Geoffrey Bles, 1946), 51, 81.

"withdrawal" within being and so the overcoming of metaphysics.[42] The idea of a postmodern critique of modernity involves rejection of the ontotheology of classical theism. Whether the attack of Nietzsche, Heidegger, Barth, and other critics of Enlightenment rationalism seems cogent to either philosophers or theologians these days, something is afoot that warrants our attention. We may reject the jargon and the often studied frivolity of Derrida, Lyotard, or Taylor, but we cannot evade their challenge to our traditional confidence as wordsmiths. Philosophy itself now requires apologetics too. If neither discipline can look into the mind and find a "mirror" of reality,[43] then we need each other as never before to discover how to think without mirrors.

A second way in which philosophy and theology are related these days stems from the debate on *selfhood*, the critique of the atomic individual posited by the Enlightenment project on behalf of an authoritative virtue or sovereign good.[44] In part this trades on the distinction within reasoning yielding what Aristotle termed *phronēsis*, and in part it explores the way that autonomy backfires, the old story of freedom's bondage. I have explored the latter dilemma through the myth of Prometheus, the engagement between Zeus *tyrannicus* and Prometheus *heroicus* that runs between tragedy and comedy, as Aeschylus saw.[45] I

---

42. Heidegger: "Language is the home of being, it is in it that man establishes his abode. The thinker and the poet are the guardians of this habitation." (*Letter on Humanism*, 1946). See Jean Grodin, *Le Tournant dans la pensée de Martin Heidegger* (Paris: presses universitaires de France, 1987).

43. Richard Rorty, *Philosophy and the Mirror of Nature* (Princeton: Princeton University Press, 1979).

44. e.g. Jeffrey Stout, *The Flight from Authority: Religion, Morality and the Quest for Autonomy* (Notre Dame: University of Notre Dame Press, 1981); Alisdair Macintyre, *Whose Justice? Which Rationality?* (Notre Dame: University of Notre Dame Press, 1988); Iris Murdoch, *The Sovereignty of Good* (London: Routledge & Keegan Paul, 1970); Charles Taylor, *Sources of the Self* (Cambridge, MA: Harvard University Press, 1989).

45. McLelland, *Prometheus Rebound: the irony of atheism* (Waterloo, ON: Wilfred Laurier University Press, 1989). See also Daniel C. Dennett, *Consciousness Explained* (London: Penguin Press, 1991), esp. 13: "The Reality of Selves," 412–30.

do not know the complete answer but I am pretty sure the question is somewhere about, and that it will take all our efforts—philosophers, theologians, religionists—to find it. And it will not be discovered by repeating old saws about (absolute) omnipotence on the one hand or (autonomous) reason on the other.

Finally, philosophy of religion, the obvious connection between philosophy and theology, is shifting ground. It has moved away from its historic partner, systematic theology, to a more positive relation with world religions. This is largely in response to the challenge of religious pluralism. Wilfrid Cantwell Smith's call for a world theology is relevant, as is the universalizing of John Hick and Ninian Smart. What we might call "philosophy of religions" attempts to approach the data of world religions without yielding intellectual rigour. This involves thorny questions of historicism and relativism, aiming at a way through their dilemma to a properly universal context for belief and unbelief. This is the direction I call "modal" to signify the step from typical categories analyzing ordinary human experience to those responsive to possibilities on a cosmic scale, as I will argue. It seeks the logic of possible states of affairs compatible with relativity theory and quantum physics. Thus we may attempt a theory of what is *universally* possible to provide context for our *global* problem of religious pluralism; or we may discover that such a universal theory is impossible.

By choosing a historical approach to our topic I have neglected a more thematic one. I trust, however, that along the way I have suggested not only some ways our two subjects have been related, but also possibilities in contemporary academia. Philosophers of religion may continue to haunt the traditional no-man's-land looking for grounds for believing or traces of irony. Or they may take courage at the memory of how well philosophy has served theology in our history, intentionally in earlier days, more occasionally since. Such philosophical commentary, advice and critique are more necessary than ever, if academic theology is to move beyond current demands which are often mere passing fads. The pressure is great—who can be against professionalization, technique, contextualization? We all wish to be relevant in our good works. What is more demanding yet, however, is the need for theologians to be justified by a faith forever seeking understanding.

3

VIA POSTMODERNA: TOWARD MODAL THEOLOGY

'Reality' cannot be conceived ... To conceive reality is to reduce it to possibility ... 'reality' in logic is only a 'reality' which is thought, i.e. possibility.
— Kierkegaard[1]

PRE-AMBLE

Words are strange things. The "linguistic turn" that led us into today's proliferation of what Richard Rorty calls "posties"—poststructuralism, postliberalism, postmodernism, postfoundationalism ... even Derrida's "postcards"—has proved confusing, if not discouraging of serious scholarship. The term "postmodern" has had a brief and heady career, beginning in literature and architecture. In the latter it denotes a break with the dominant International Style and a response to pluralism with its relativism and eclecticism. In this context it had been said that "we live in a post-modern era, the information age where plural cultures compete and there is simply

---

1. *Journals: a Selection*, ed. A. Dru (Oxford: Oxford University Press, 1938), (1850), 373.

no dominant cultural style."[2] Here the "coded language" of relativism is formed in concrete and glass.[3] From architecture the mode has spread to the social sciences, thence to philosophy and theology. In the last it seemed at first a label invented by the American Academy of Religion, where an elite group read papers to one another annually in a kind of self-fulfilling prophecy. But the very range of disciplines exploring its meaning suggests a certain convergence, a growing critique of what we have assumed—particularly we liberal humanists—to be the enlightened understanding of understanding. (And now there seems to be a new shibboleth: "cultural theory" is what the Humanities do. This still perpetuates the thesis that the particular is preferred to the general, the local to the universal).

Neonatal care is required, to monitor symptoms and provide prognosis. Although definition works better with hindsight at the end of a journey, we must start somewhere. Social scientists typify "modernity" by categories such as rationalization (Max Weber), autonomy, individualism, nationalism. Its breakdown or demise is described as alienation, *anomie*, "life lived in fragments" (Baudelaire-in 1846!), "the broken centre" (Nathan Scott, following Yeats); in short, "the Death of God." Philosophers favour the explanatory concept of an "Enlightenment project" (Jeffrey Stout, Alisdair MacIntyre) now doomed, so that we need to go beyond the kind of consciousness associated with the Cartesian ego, or Husserl's "solitary mental life." If "modernity" depicts a complex historical phenomenon, the above list of characteristics suggests something of its mood, what has been called "a Time, a Mentality, and a Malaise."[4] In

---

2. Chas. Jencks, *The Language of Post-Modern Architecture* (New York: Rizzoli, 1991) 2; *What is Post-Modern?* (New York: St Martin's, 1987). He coined the word "adhocism" to make a case for "improvisation."

3. See Terence Hawkes, *Structuralism and Semiotics* (Berkeley: University of California Press, 1977). I learned much about modern architecture from my former students, both practising artists, Celia Rabinovitch and Philippe Angers.

4. Thomas. C. Oden, *After Modernity . . . What?* (Grand Rapids, MI: Zondervan, 1990), 45ff; his charts on 48–50 and 73 are helpful.

short, the hypothesis of "modernity" as a distinctive period now expiring is the necessary presupposition for any definition of postmodernity. This obvious fact has weight, unless we find that the concept of modernity itself is questionable, throwing the periodisation of Western history in doubt. The irony is that even such terms as modern and postmodern imply the "grand récit" rejected by such postmodernists as Lyotard. We may observe that Lyotard himself wished to assign an absolute status to *justice*, in face of the dilemma articulated by Alisdair MacIntyre and others.[5] For, does not a complete relativism spell the death not only of grand narratives, but also of common humanity and its virtues? The demand for a global reign of nonviolence—promised by the Enlightenment's "civilising process" but crushed beneath wars and Holocaust and terrorism—entails some form of reconciliation or peaceful coexistence among religions as well as societies.[6]

Now "post-modern" in itself is an oxymoron—how can you progress "beyond" the "new"? There is some recognition that "modern" denotes the "measure" (*modus*) of the present (*modo*).[7] Lyotard makes the shrewd observation: "A work can become modern only if it is first postmodern. Postmodernism thus understood is not modernism at its end but in its nascent state, and this state is constant."[8] The formal idea of going beyond modernity may be construed as a return to a former

---

5. See Ch. 7 below, and M. Volf, *Exclusion and Embracer: a Theological Exploration of Identity, Otherness, and Reconciliation* (Nashville: Abingdon Press, 1996), "Many Names, Many Justices," 202ff.

6. See Volf, *Exclusion and Embrace*, "cosmic Terror," 286ff; Küng & Kuschel, *A Global Ethic: The Declaration of the Parliament of the World's Religions* (New York: Continuum, 1995).

7. J-F. Lyotard, *The Postmodern Condition*, English trans. Bennington and Massumi (University of Minnesota, 1984); Cf., A.M. Olson, "Postmodernity and Faith" in *Journal of the American Academy of Religion* LVIII/1 (Spring 1990).

8. Lyotard, "Answering the Question: What is Postmodernism?" in Hassan and Hassan, eds *Innovation/Renovation: New Perspectives on the Humanities* (Madison: University of Wisconsin, 1983), 338ff.

age, with various degrees of "conservatism" (young-, old-, and neo-).[9] Or it may be more pointed, rejecting the philosophical *subject* found in Cartesian solipsism.[10] In sum: "Meaning is local, community is tribal, society is pluralistic, and economics is the pragmatics of the marketplace. This is the age of the sign."[11]

This sits well with Heidegger's programmatic *Destruktion* of the history of ontology, aimed at retrieval of the proper question of what "Being" signifies.[12] Metaphysics dissolves reality, it entails the formation of "ontotheology" which posits divinity as the logical End of the hierarchy of beings. If ontology has lost Being, so to speak, then theology has lost "God." Ontology needs to be rescued—everybody says so, not only Heidegger but Barth and Tillich and Ayer and Derrida—from this category mistake. Regressive analysis is required, sometimes called "deconstruction." Here is another bothersome term. Better to speak of two kinds of postmodernism, "deconstructive-eliminative" and "constructive-revisionary."[13] For the lighthearted, there is also Jeffrey Stout's article-review of Davidson, Putnam and Rorty (a kind of "Princeton Lampoon"?) entitled "Lexicon of Postmodern philosophy."[14]

To sum up: "modern" signifies the historical period (in the West) from 17th to 20th centuries, born largely of the scientific revolution and Enlightenment, and characterized by trust in and exaltation of indi-

---

9. J. Habermas, *The Philosophical Discourse of Modernity*, English trans. by F. Lawrence (Cambridge: MIT Press, 1987).

10. F. Kerr, *Theology After Wittgenstein* (Oxford: Basil Blackwell, 1986).

11. Graham Ward, "Postmodern Theology," in *The Modern Theologians*, ed. D.F. Ford (Oxford: Basil Blackwell, 1997).

12. *Being and Time* § 6 (19). Robert P. Scharlemann argues that Karl Barth follows a similar agenda in a "destructive" reading of classical theism: "The Being of God When God Is Not Being God," *Deconstruction and Theology*, ed. T. Altizer (New York: Crossroads, 1982), 79ff.

13. D.R. Griffin, W.A. Beardslee, J. Holland, *Varieties of Postmodern Thelogy* (New York: SUNY, 1989), 1ff.

14. J. Stout, "Lexicon of Postmodern Philosophy," *Religious Studies Review* 13/1 (January 1987), 18-22.

vidual reason. "Post-modern" signifies the transition period of the 20th century, born largely of post-war disillusionment, recognizing the limits of scientific method as well as the new reality of globalization.

MINERVA'S OWLS

Masters of suspicion have long warned that the Enlightenment project contains the seeds of its own destruction. Their question is: *what is the reason for trusting reason?* That is, what evidence do believers in evidentialism have for demanding grounds for knowing something to be true? These "masters of suspicion" as Paul Ricoeur calls them, naming Marx, Freud and Nietzsche, may also include Hegel, Kierkegaard, Dostoyevsky, Barth, Heidegger. The most notorious is Nietzsche, the most tendentious Kant himself. Kant's "What is Enlightenment?" supplied the very motto of Enlightenment: "Dare to know!" (*Sapere aude!*). But was he not also facing Enlightenment's "impotence . . . its helplessness in the face of the questions it raised" as Kolakowski charges?[15] Did he not recoil before that final *aporia* noted in the First Critique: the "unconditioned necessity" which yawns like "an abyss on the verge of which human reason trembles in dismay"?[16]

It seems that Hegel is now enjoying the attention previously paid to Kant. The older Hegel of Kierkegaardian attack is yielding to the younger (*Phänomenologie der Geist*, 1807), the idealist to the existentialist—"there are several Hegels".[17] The question is whether Hegel's contribution to our aporetic dilemma leads to reunion or merely further estrangement. Is his "Spirit alienated from itself" (*Der sich-entfremdete*

---

15. L. Kolakowski, *The Alienation of Reason: a History of Positivist Thought* (New York: Anchor, 1969), 41.

16. I. Kant, *Critique of Pure Reason* (1781) "Transcendental Dialectic" II.3.5; Cf., McLelland, *Prometheus Rebound: the irony of atheism* (Waterloo, ON: Wilfrid Laurier University Press, 1989), 97ff.

17. M. Merleau-Ponty, "Hegel's Existentialism" in *Sense and Non-Sense*, trans. by Dreyfus and Dreyfus (Evanston, IL: Northwestern University Press, 1964), 63ff.

Geist) the temporary cost of creation ("production" for Marx) or a sign of permanent fault? Alan Olson argues that Habermas and those French philosophers influenced by Kojève's interpretation of Hegel are right to begin with Hegel's critique of Kant's philosophy of the understanding (*Verstehenphilosophie*). That is, Hegel is truly *post*-Kantian. Our still neo-Kantian age (especially its theologians) needs to hear this attack on transcendental reflection, with its argument for the existence of faith. Hegel's proposal involved a dynamism, "the *processual* element in a concept of faith as consciousness."[18] His dialectical logic posits the *identity* of identity and difference, and so reinstates analogy (or "metaphor" to use today's more fashionable term) at the heart of theological epistemology.

This positive interpretation is disputed by Mark C. Taylor, who follows Heidegger's reading of Hegel as having fulfilled (sublated!) the Cartesian turn to the subject.[19] Is this Hegel trumping Des-cartes: (pardon the pun), a sort of "It is thought, therefore Something is?"—*Cogitat, ergo* (*Spiritus*) *est?*. Thereafter, Heidegger's destructive analysis rolls over both players, replacing identity with Das Zwischen, the between, the difference that unveils (*Es gibt*) identity only in its differentiation. If Hegel sublates Descartes, elevating subjectivity to Absolute Subjectivity, then these postmodern critics need to subvert this subjectivity, through declaring the *difference* between identity and difference. Hence Derrida's neologism "différance" to trace the constant cleavage, "to save the tear" in order to celebrate the absence of presence.[20]

So the new saints of postmodernism—Derrida, Foucault, Lacan, Lyotard (and Taylor to break the francophone monopoly)—begin from the ironic insight into philosophy and theology caught in a rationality that spells its own doom. (Hegel warned us that the owl of Minerva takes flight only at nightfall: her wisdom begins at reason's end). Their

---

18. A.M. Olson, "Postmodernity and Faith" in *Journal of the American Academy of Religion* LVIII/1 (Spring 1990), 49.

19. M. Taylor, *Altarity* (University of Chicago, 1987), 3ff, 35ff.

20. Jacques Derrida, *Writing and Difference,* trans. Alan Bass (Chicago: University of Chicago Press, 1978).

noisy attacks produce a cacophony of "logics of disintegration."²¹ There is no longer universal reason, history as metanarrative (Lyotard's "grands récits"), individual identity. There is instead the peculiar nexus of language, texts as woven "texture," signifiers, a pastiche made by bricoleurs. "All is text." Taylor writes of "mazing grace, and erring scripture."²² Is this how a new age gets itself born, with whimpers rather than bang? What's so radically *new* here?

ONCE MORE: "VIA MODERNA"

In the later fourteenth century another Modernity was born. The *via moderna* challenged the dominant culture where harmony reigned in matters civil and ecclesiastical. It offered a new paradigm of faith/reason, rejecting the "realist" tradition (thus rendering it *via antiqua*) in favour of a linguistic turn ("nominalist") that questioned whether words terminate on things universal at all (thus *via moderna, terministae, nominales*). Occam was replacing Scotus: the terminism and nominalism would culminate in John Gerson (fifteenth century), enemy of Modistae and Scotistae in behalf of the *vita contemplativa* as the chosen way after the destruction of natural and rational theology.²³ Aquinas had been clear that "The act of the believer ends not in a statement but in reality."²⁴ But for William of Occam both Thomism, and even more its apparent rival Scotism, needed paring to the bone; his sceptical-critical philosophy resembles modern logical positivism. The self (as *synteresis rationis*) was no longer regarded as posited by God

---

21. P. Dews, *Logics of Disintegration: Post-structural Thought and the Claims of Critical Theory* (New York: Verso, 1987).

22. Mark C. Taylor, *Erring: a Postmodern A/theology* (U. of Chicago Press 1984), 99. Cf., M. Volf, "Adieu to Grand Narratives," *Expulsion and Embrace*, 105ff.

23. See Jill Raitt, ed. *Christian Spirituality: High Middle Ages and Reformation* (NY: Crossroads, 1988), 116ff.

24. —*non terminatur ad enuntiabile, sed ad rem*: Aquinas, *S.T.* IIa2ae 1, a.2, ad 2.

and invested with eternal truths; ontological connection was replaced by voluntary acceptance.[25] Voluntarism, and insofar anti-intellectualism, was shared with late medieval Augustinianism (the *schola Augustiniana moderna*)—Gregory of Rimini and John Major for example, influential in Renaissance and Reform. The stress lay particularly on the logic of merit (*ratio meriti*) of both Christ and ourselves. If our age has a "will to power," theirs had a will to salvation.[26]

Perhaps history is an unceasing dialectic or *querelle* of ancient and modern, in which each term is relative to the other, so that each Present Age, as Kierkegaard saw, has its own style which is also its doom. I have chosen the term *via postmoderna* to signify this connection with late medieval *via moderna*. Both share a critique based on language; for us, the failure of rationalist ideology to effect human selfhood and to secure moral reasoning. Here we stand, once again barren through the infertility of the rationalism/fideism polarization, the titanic clash of the disjunctive syllogism: All or Nothing.[27] Kant was able to make an end run around his antinomies, even if finally tackled by radical evil, just short of the goal. In our case some other play seems necessary, even some change in the groundrules themselves. Not a paradigm shift but more profound, like adding a dimension to plane geometry, or to a chessboard, so that the rules are changed to greater complexity and freedom.[28] My suggested name for this project is *modal*.

"Modal" intends to denote a shift in the way (*modus*) reality is reflected in and by human minds. It agrees tentatively with the labels "modernity" and "postmodernity" as working definitions of a historical dialectic. But it seeks to go beyond both modern and postmodern rationalities.

---

25. See D. Lage, *Martin Luther's Christology and Ethics* (Edwin Mellen, 1990), 12ff.

26. See H. A. Oberman, *Masters of the Reformation: the emergence of a new intellectual climate in Europe* (Cambridge: Cambridge University Press, 1981), 5ff.

27. See J. C. McLelland, *Prometheus Rebound*, 244ff.

28. Cf. Isaac Asimov, *Adding a Dimension* (New York: Lancer Books, 1964).

It "stands at the threshold between semantics and pragmatics."[29] It is a recommendation from what might be called "philosophy of theology" as to how theology (Christian and other) should proceed in view of the postmodern critique. If postmodernism is analytic and de(con)structive, modal will be synthetic and constructive. After therapy, wholeness.

TEST CASES

The obvious Christian concepts at issue concern Trinity and Incarnation. I will argue in the next Chapter that we need a "theory of relativity" for religious pluralism, one that will re-focus the global problematic in reference to the universal. This means hypothetical instantiation—extra-terrestrial—of forms of incarnation. An analogy from physics would be: christology developed in an "inertial field" of world history, and needs to be not globalized but universalized. An analogy from art would be: christology developed in impressionistic style and needs to become not expressionistic but cubist, even surreal. This were not to revive ancient forms of modalism, the monarchianism of Sabellius for instance. Patristic modalism debated intratrinitarian relationships and the concept of the personal (*prosōpon*); its idea of "modes of being" moved within a particular paradigm. But other forms of Logos christology insisted on a mode of divine being that maintains universality *at the same time as* the mode of human being: *kenosis* does not affect substantially the eternal being of Logos, *and therefore* leaves open the possibility of other forms of divine presence, whether quasi-incarnational or extra-incarnational. Examples of such modal thinking include Origen's teaching on accommodation and subordination, the twin concepts of *en-*and *an-hypostasia* of II Constantinople

---

29. Maurice Boutin, "Conceiving the Invisible: Joseph C. McLelland's Modal Approach to Theological and Religious Pluralism," in *The Three Loves: Philosophy, Theology and World Religions*, ed. Culley & Klempa (Atlanta: Scholars' Press, 1994), 5.

(553-4 CE) and the Lutheran-Reformed debate (16th century) dubbed *extraCalvinisticum*, the Calvinistic "extra" signifying the enduring universality which limits the globally incarnate Word. I will suggest that such re-conceptualizing will force a more adequate christology upon Christians, with corresponding reevaluation of divine accommodation in all earthly religions. If we acknowledge the validity of Kant's criterion of "universalizability" in the logic of obligation, must we not search for similar criteria in the logic of revelation and reconciliation?

The form "If p then q" at its simplest demands that theology—Christian most particularly—attend to the universal implications of its doctrinal system. We know enough about our universe now to have done with vestiges of the Ptolemaic-Aristotelian cosmology. I do not suggest a new astrotheology as the postmodern form of cosmological argument (like seventeenth-century insectotheology), nor do I wish to replace ontotheology by epistemotheology. Rather, I mean such development of doctrine as will satisfy the possibilities of our new exploration of space, our new appreciation of the immensity of the universe, our new knowledge of possibilities beyond the solar system. "If E.T. then . . . " is the form of theo-logic demanded. This suits the sort of modality required by astrophysics, to name but one discipline. Modal logic rejects the disjunctive syllogism (in the form *modus ponendo tollens*): "Either p or q; q; therefore not-p." This faces us with a "horned syllogism" offering escape either in between, or taking the dilemma by the horns and admitting the disjunction while denying the implication.[30]

Classical theism assumed that what was good enough for Christians was so for all other humans on earth. Modern theism assumes that while the case of "non-Christians" is more problematic, the implications of trinitarian/christological doctrine remain "universal." Postmodern theism, however, must answer new questions no longer merely academic:

---

30. The theo-logic that "solved" the dilemma of divine and human willing was the Scholastic distinction between two kinds of necessity, *nec. consequentiae* and *nec. consequentis*. See McLelland, *Philosophical Works*, Peter Martyr Library, vol. 4 (Kirksville MO: Truman State University Press, 1996), 192f, 280.

since (probably) there are conscious lifeforms on other planets revolving around the million suns in other galaxies, what does revelation (necessarily) and salvation (possibly) mean for them? After all, the "anthropic principle" notes that the earliest conditions of the universe made the evolution of life inevitable. Yet the principle applies not to our planet alone, either uniquely or singularly, but to all planetary systems in the universe.[31]

Such questions have been raised in principle ever since the Church Fathers (or the Pauline literature's cosmic Christ); now they have a bite, an exigency as test of universalizability. The dogmas of modernity about human experience and reason need to be deconstructed in order to allow more modern questions to be formulated, answers to be sought. The human "flesh" of the Christian Incarnation, for instance, is not a generic/universal category, but may serve as global metaphor for all lifeforms in the universe. We must attempt the larger and harder vision in order to come down to earth with appropriate statements. What works in such cosmic context provides *a fortiori* argument for its validity on earth—from the greater possibility to the lesser actuality. Such cosmic relevance imposes more limited, modest claims for our doctrines on the one hand, while on the other it provides a truly universal dimension in which they participate.

Such hypothetical universality should be fruitful in our interfaith dilemma of absolutism/relativism. Is the distinction between *incommensurability* and *incompatibility* relevant to interreligious dialogue? For example, Christianity's presupposition is original sin, and Buddhism's "original suffering" as it were; such diverse beginnings surely mean that attempts to discuss apparently similar doctrines of "salvation" are bound to pass each other like ships in the night. Raimundo Panikkar considers that dialogue aiming at a unitive theory

---

31. E.g. L. von Bertalanffy, *General System Theory* (New York: Geo Braziller, 1968), "The Relativity of Categories," 222ff; John A. Ross, *This Backlit Universe: Mysteries of Systems* (Chilliwack, BC: Shore Lines publishing, 1993), "System is a Mutual Affair,"407ff.

of religion, or "universal theology", is a mistake of Western metaphysics.[32] Thus our problem becomes not incompatibility but differing modes of measuring the human condition. The modal shift under discussion acknowledges the brackets around our finite ways of knowing and being, but offers a transposition to broader categories of classification.

Theology, I suggest, needs to develop its own modal thinking. Classical theism made modest use of modal categories in its explication of divine and human potency/impotency, with some echoes in the contemporary "Paradox of Omnipotence" debate.[33] Occam wrestled with the precious problem of God's foreknowledge of future contingencies, which God knows "evidently and with certainty."[34] Before him, William of Sherwood (?1200-66) explored signs according to the fourfold terminology *significatio, suppositio, copulatio, appellatio*. Such terminal talk entails "supposing that", particularly that copulative terms produce novel naming (Mark Taylor does this well).[35] My intention in "modal theology" is somewhat akin to this earlier terminism. I wish to push our frame of reference for the implications of human God-talk to the properly "universal." Unless the verification/falsification of our statements about Transcendence is truly *universal* rather than merely *global* we are not yet in a mode corresponding to the universe as we know it scientifically. And if theological implication is contradicted by scientific it suffers by the norm of possibility—that is, it is incompatible with certain possible states of affairs. Aristotle first noted that the principles which hold good for "everything that is" belong to the science of being qua being.[36] The

---

32. R. Panikkar, "The Invisible Harmony: A Universal Theory of Religion or a Cosmic Confidence in Reality?" in L. Swidler, ed. *Toward a Universal Theology of Religion* (NY: Orbis, 1987) 118–53.

33. McLelland, *Prometheus Rebound*, 54ff, 281ff.

34. Wm. Ockham, "God's Causality and Foreknowledge" in *Ockham: Philosophical Writings* (Edited by P. Boehner; Edinburgh: Thomas Nelson, 1957), 127ff.

35. Mark C. Taylor, *Erring: a Postmodern A/theology* (University of Chicago Press, 1984).

36. Aristotle, *Meta.*, 1003b, 15ff.

gloss by Leibnitz was well taken, that universals must be invariant for all possible worlds. Such connection between logic and ontology, remarked by Ernest Nagel for one, is the burden of my story.

"POSSIBLE WORLDS"

The idea of possible worlds is familiar to philosophers and logicians exploring problems in semantics and metaphysics.[37] Nicholas Rescher notes the "prime explanatory function which possible worlds perform (and certainly the function which was responsible for their current popularity as a formal logical device) is that of interpreting modal discourse."[38] Alvin Plantinga is one philosopher of religion who has experimented with such modalities, using the category "transworld" in behalf of his free will defence of theodicy.[39] Karl Barth is another who explored the properly universal modality of those *rationes* which participate in Truth and therefore are both distinct and true—as Anselm grasped in postulating a *ratio Dei* beyond noetic and ontic contrasts.[40] A further analogue comes from metamathematics, namely Gödel's Incompleteness Theorem: the price of completeness in axiomatics is inconsistency. This in turn resembles Heisenberg's principle of Indeterminacy, accounting for the inability to know both velocity and position of subatomic data. Do theological systems likewise have an open texture, like an infinite series of expanding sets, or an incompleteness in knowing their data?[41]

---

37. E.g. D. Lewis, *On the Plurality of Worlds* (Oxford: Blackwell, 1986), etc.; M.J. Loux, *The Possible and the Actual: readings in the metaphysics of modality* (Ithaca: Cornell University Press, 1979), esp. R.C. Stalnaker, "Possible Worlds," 225ff.

38. N. Rescher & R. Brandon, *The Logic of Inconsistency* (Oxford: Basil Blackwell, 1980), 14: "Modal Logic on Non-Standard Possible Worlds," 68–72.

39. A. Plantinga, *The Nature of Necessity* (Oxford: Clarendon Press, 1974).

40. K. Barth, *Anselm: Fides Quaerens Intellctum* ([1931] London: 1960).

41. See John R. Carnes, "Metamathematics and Dogmatic Theology" in

PLURALISM WITHOUT RELATIVISM

Modal theology will cast its doctrine in terms accountable to universal implications. It will acknowledge Bertrand Russell's point that the problem of universals has paid too much attention to substantives and adjectives and too little to verbs and prepositions, thus concentrating on the logic of *qualities* to the neglect of the logic of *relations*.[42] Maurice Boutin's analysis sees this as the result of failing to note Kant's own division in his Table of Categories: "reality" is a quality (linked to quantity), but "existence" is a modality (linked to relation).[43] Now the "possible worlds" theory issues a challenge to every particular or exclusive claim in dogma. One who saw this clearly was C. S. Lewis, himself a writer of science fiction. He warned that we know too little about possible extraterrestrial rational beings to speculate "on what theological corollaries or difficulties their discovery would raise." Yet he recognized the need for extending theories of redemption, and speculated on various alternatives if such beings proved to be rational and perhaps also sinful. His own scifi trilogy represents a remarkable experiment in such speculative theology: the human named Ransom (sic) travels to other planets and discovers there a reality of evil like a quantum leap beyond Earth's.[44]

Aristotle turned to modal logic to solve the crucial dilemma: can we find reasons to oppose the apparent determinism of all things? His solution turned on the category of motion, *kinêsis*.[45] Here was a way through strict causality to allow free choice (similar to Democritus' solution by the famous "swerve" of atoms, providing Karl Marx with both

---

Scottish Journal of Theology 29.6 (1976), 501-16.

42. B. Russell, *The Problems of Philosophy* (Oxford University Press, 1967) 52ff.

43. M. Boutin, "Conceiving the Invisible" in *The Three Loves*, 1–18.

44. C. S. Lewis, "The Seeing Eye," in *Christian Reflections by C. S. Lewis*, ed. W. Hooper (London: Geoffrey Bles Publishers, 1967), 172ff. His trilogy is: *Out of the Silent Planet, Perelandra* and *That Hideous Strength*.

45. Aristotle, *Phys.* III.1,200b12ff, *Meta.* 1013a7–11, 1019a15ff. See J. Hintikka, *Aristotle on Modality and Determinism* (Amsterdam: Acta Philosophica Fennica 29.1, 1977), "The Concept of Kinesis as a Way Out," 59ff.

thesis topic and philosophical agenda).[46] The Aristotelian solution to the problem of future contingents draws helpful distinctions: *dynamis-kinēsis-energeia*. They yield different kinds of potentiality or possibility, opening logic to the richness of a reality not encompassed by formal logic alone. *Possibility encompasses necessity*: this is what seized Kierkegaard in his search for logical categories able to handle his concept of "the leap" decisive for what he calls "my category," the unique individual self (*Den Enkelte*). He found in Trendelenberg's logical works the modal categories he needed.[47] The motion between differing lifestyles of the *Stages* is thus accessible, and also the "thought-experiment" of the *Fragments* and its *Postscript*. Kierkegaard's answer to Lessing's question ("Can eternal happiness be based on historical accident?") is thus formalized in dynamic categories appropriate to the Subject. Faith is not so much the conclusion of a reasoned argument as the resolution of a lived dilemma.[48]

Our thesis acknowledges W.C. Smith's challenge to develop a theology of world religions, accepting his warning against first reifying "religion" and then attributing to it "truth-claims." Calling the latter an "unhappy neologism," Smith notes that what is before us is not the correspondence of propositions with reality but rather what "becomes true" in a person's integrity and faithfulness. The Muslim "claim," for instance, consists in "bearing witness," like the early Christian "proclaiming."[49] If John Hick is the Galileo of religious studies, insisting

---

46. See McLelland, *Prometheus Rebound*, 147–49.

47. S. Kierkegaard, *Concluding Unscientific Postscript* (Princeton: Princeton University Press, 1944) 100, 267n; *The Point of View for My Work as an Author* (NY: Harper & Row, 1962); A. Come, *Trendelenberg's Influence on Kierkegaard's Modal Categories* (Montreal: Inter Editions, 1991).

48. See L.J. Pojman, "Subjectivity and Epistemology," in *Logic of Subjectivity: Kierkegaard's philosophy of religion* (University of Alabama Press, 1984) 54ff.

49. See his "Response" in Hick, ed., *Truth and Dialogue in World Religions: Conflicting Truth Claims* London: Sheldon Press, 1974) and "Theology and the World's Religious History," in Swidler, TUTR, 51ff.

e pure si muove of world religions around a global centre, Wilfred Smith is our Heisenberg, warning of the indeterminacy that attends all human comprehension. In physics, the more we learn about motion, the less we can know about position; in religion, the more we know about position, the less we can know about relation.

POST-LUDE

Finally, we need to look beyond the jargon of both modern and post-modern advocates, beyond the vicious circle of adding epicycles in order to qualify otherwise incompatible dogmas. Antony Flew's old charge of "death by a thousand qualifications" still applies unless we are willing to explore new dimensions of possibility.[50] If the modal project of probable conditions in possible worlds seems too "sci-fi" or fantastic, its intention is to open a window to ideas whose time is coming, forced by the pace of space exploration and the challenge of relativism. Relativity is not relativism, but unless we measure the difference we have only absolutism to fall back on.

Post-modernism, moreover, is afflicted with dandyism; as such it should heed the warnings of Kierkegaard on the superficiality of "immediacy" and of Camus on the "dandies' rebellion."[51] Nevertheless, it is trying to articulate the breakup of an age that proved overly proud of its mastery of word, thought, world. Ultramodernity is falling, and with it the foundationalism/evidentialism that drove both theism and antitheism lo these many years. When foundationalism is rejected one must make do with some sort of "intersubjective communication"[52]

---

50. A. Flew, "Theology and Falsification" in *New Essays in Philosophical Theology*, A. Flew & A. Macintyre, eds. (London: SCM, 1955), 97: "A fine brash hypothesis may thus be killed by inches, the death by a thousand qualifications."

51. See G. Malantschuk, *Kierkegaard's Thought* (Princeton University Press, 1971) 135, 209ff, etc.; Albert Camus, *The Rebel* (London: Hamish Hamilton, 1954).

52. J. Habermas, *The Philosophical Discourse of Modernity* (Edited by F.

or a form of "solidarity" that can survive the reign of "contingency" and the critique of "irony".[53] But this assumes only one form of postmodernism, the "deconstructive-eliminative" noted above. It is the "constructive-revisionary" that informs modal thinking and impels exploration of alternative forms of universal validity. I wish to move into the post-Newtonian, non-Euclidean, geodesic era of possibilities now within imaginative grasp. I wish to appropriate this new thinking for philosophy and theology, for a renewal of youth. It doesn't take a Hebrew prophet to tell us that old men dream dreams; that's all we have left, to turn our heritage into your project, and to welcome new generations to the only game in the universe.

Cubist poet Pierre Reverdy wrote: "Nothing is worth saying in poetry save the unsayable, which is why one counts greatly upon what goes on between the lines."[54] And in philosophy, theology and so on perhaps it is counting on those spaces "between" to which mystics, visionaries and even professors have pointed with varying degrees of confidence or desperation. That would be a modality of communication worthy of Koheleth himself.

Lawrence; Cambridge: MIT Press, 1987).

53. R. Rorty, *Contingency, irony, and solidarity* (Cambridge University Press, 1989).

54. *Le livre de mon bord: notes 1930–1936* (Paris: Mercure de France, 1970).

4

A THEORY OF RELATIVITY FOR RELIGIOUS PLURALISM

Things fall apart; the centre cannot hold;
Mere anarchy is loosed upon the world
—W.B. Yeats[1]

A spectre is haunting the study of religion: the spectre of *relativism*. The subject of religious pluralism has emerged as a crucial debate in religious studies. Its object of study has become pluralized, while theology's borderlands are shifting from biblical and historical to comparative studies. And something new is happening among Humanists: calls for "a theology of world religions" are heard in the land; "in the next phase of world thought, the basis for theology must now be the history of religion."[2]

The term "pluralism" denotes a complex phenomenon. Western "perennial philosophy" assumed a unity and order behind the manifold of impressions—the One behind the many, or the Creator behind creation. The Enlightenment displaced an authoritative Other by the

---

1. "The Second Coming." Cf., Nathan A. Scott, Jr., *The Broken Centre* (New Haven: Yale University Press, 1966).

2. W.C. Smith, *Towards a world theology: faith and the comparative history of religions* (Philadelphia: Westminster Press, 1981). 55

individual subject's essence: I think, doubt, choose and so create my world. The quest for autonomy and maturity seems to imply a solipsism of both knowledge and ethics: *pluralism entails relativism.* Sometimes foundationalism is rejected in favour of nonfoundationalism, in denial of firm foundations for belief-systems, arguing "instead that all of our beliefs together form part of a groundless web of interrelated beliefs."[3] Indeed, an interesting analysis of pluralism into six types—normative, soteriological, epistemological, alethic and deontic—is given by Muhammad Legenhausen in his critique of John Hick. [4]

Meanwhile, a new form of pluralism has surfaced in Western consciousness. "Religious pluralism" refers to the relatively sudden ending of the Christian establishment in society and religion. As early as 1959 Wilfred Cantwell Smith noted the phenomenon, recalling his own experience as teacher in Lahore in the years leading up to the partition of India in 1947. The dreadful consequences of the clash of rival faiths constitute a warning that our search for peace must deal at root with religious pluralism. Smith scored "the distorted ideal itself—the basic doctrine that we are saved, outsiders are damned," and concluded that "the Christian community is at the moment theologically unequipped for living in the 20th century, with its pluralist mankind."[5] Current debate on this phenomenon begins from traditional contraries of absolutism and relativism, and advances to the current rival theories of exclusivism, inclusivism and pluralism.[6] The first continues the traditional self-understanding of classical theism (Arnold Toynbee called it a "plague");

---

3. J. Wentzel van Huyssteen, *Essays in Postfoundationalist Theology* (Grand Rapids, MI: Erdmans, 1997), 3.

4. M. Legenhausen, *Islam and Religious Pluralism* (London: Centre for International and Cultural Studies, 1999), 1.4., "John Hick's Religious Pluralism."

5. Smith, "The Christian & the Religions of Asia," address to the Couchiching Conference, Geneva Park, Ontario 1959, unpublished.

6. Typology first coined by Alan Race in 1938 (*Christians and Religious Pluralism*) according to Gavin D'Costa: "The Impossibility of a Pluralist View of Religions," *RS* 32 (1996) 223.

the second recognizes some validity for every religion, while assigning normative value to the Christian revelation; pluralism (which critics call simply relativism) seeks theoretical parity of all religions. This chapter attempts to move away from such categorization by offering a theory of relativity as catalyst in the debate.

TROELTSCH'S DILEMMA

Ernst Troeltsch (1865–1923) provides a magisterial statement of our problem. He came to view the new historical consciousness as a radical questioning of the Christian claim to absoluteness. Contrasting historical method with "dogmatic," he noted the difficulty in establishing normative values by historical enquiry. This resembles Lessing's critique of the "spider's thread" of history by which Christian faith is suspended, although the problematic of Lessing and Kierkegaard concerned not so much contingency and necessity as the tension between historical judgment and doctrinal claims.[7] Troeltsch acknowledged our agenda and its dilemma: how to supersede supranaturalistic dogmatism without reducing historical religions to abstract patterns or types. This "Heraclitus of historiography," as James Luther Adams called him, advanced the thesis that "The historical and relative are identical." That is, he saw the absolute developing out of the relative, hence the need to examine "evolutionary apologetic" as the problematic of *Historismus*.[8] In his intellectual journey he advanced from "The Absoluteness of Christianity" (his 1901 book) to its non-absoluteness (his final lecture of 1923). But the latter position involved a significant thesis, not unlike our "modal" proposal: that Christianity is absolute for Christian, as other religions are for their adherents. This "relative

---

7. Cf., G.E. Michalson, *Lessing's "Ugly Ditch:" A Study of Theology and History* (University Park: Pennsylvania State University Press, 1985).

8. *The Absoluteness of Christianity and the History of Religions* (Richmond: John Knox 1971, Intro. by J .L. Adams) 51ff. For his four principles of historiography, see his "Historical and Dogmatic Method in Theology," in *Religion in History* (Philadelphia: Fortress Press, 1991), 11–32.

absoluteness" resembles also the theory of John Hick, whose comments on Troeltsch include notice of the baneful effects of religious absolutism in world history.[9]

Now every study of human behaviour, particularly the rites and values of groups, requires a methodological, even a cultural relativism. But Troeltsch seems to demand a more consequential relativism, both epistemological and ethical, which surrenders canons of truth and value in face of diversity. Relativism is taken as reductionism; it remains sceptical about the truth-claims of its subject. Here is the threatening form of the new spectre.[10]

A noteworthy critique of this way of stating the question was advanced by H. Richard Niebuhr's *Christ and Culture*. His thesis was that Christianity itself moves within these data as polarities: "The relation of these two authorities constitutes its problem."[11] His answer to Troeltsch was that despite differing descriptions or roles of Jesus based on the variety of Christian experience, "it is the same Christ who exercises these various offices."[12] Niebuhr's typology is helpful—Christ against or for culture, with three other relationships that attempt to hold the two together: Christ fulfilling culture, or transcending it, or else its converter. While attending strictly to the Christian polarity with culture, this thesis reminds us that every religion occurs in a similar polarity, so that the question of relativism is not simply one between religions abstracted

---

9. John Hick, "The Non-absoluteness of Christianity," in *Disputed Questions in Theology and the Philosophy of Religion* (New Haven: Yale University Press, 1993), 77ff. See also Glyn Richards, *Towards a Theology of Religions* (London: Routledge, 1989), 25ff: "The Response of Relativism: Troeltsch, Toynbee."

10. See S. Oakley, *Christ Without Absolutes: a Study of the Christology of Ernst Troeltsch* (Oxford: Clarendon Press, 1988), "The Nature of Troeltsch's Relativism," 5ff; cf. Koestler and Smythies, eds., *Beyond Reductionism: new perspectives in the life sciences* (Boston: Beacon Press, 1968); R. Bernstein, *Beyond Objectivism Relativism* (Philadelphia: University of Pennsylvania Press, 1983).

11. H.R. Niebuhr, *Christ and Culture* (London: Faber & Faber, 1952), 26.

12. Niebuhr, *Christ and Culture*, 28.

from their social milieu, what W.C. Smith termed their "cumulative tradition." A related question is whether or not "historical criticism is a single, and fairly simply identifiable, entity."[13] Gordon Kaufman argues that the issue of historicity sees every religion "as one perspective, one worldview."[14]

ESCAPING THE LEMMAS

The question of the relationship among religions is not new, nor is relativism, a theory Plato ascribed to Theaetetus. Apart from implicit teaching on universal salvation in Church Fathers, one of the first to devote a work to the question of the salvation of "heathen" was "The Calling of All People" by Prosper of Aquitaine, best known as defender of Augustinianism in the Semi-Pelagian controversy.[15] He distinguishes humanity *ante legem, sub legem* and *sub gratia*. Such threefold periodisation is familiar enough, but the idea that the corollary of grace is universal salvation was far from a popular idea before the Renaissance.

We noted that theories of the relationship among world religions are generally called exclusivism, inclusivism and pluralism. There remains a deadlock between traditional exclusive or imperial theology and modern historicism or relativism. Since the new science of religion was taken (by Max Müller for instance) to deny the absolute truth—claim of Christianity, its disciples did indeed tend to posit a relativist explanatory thesis as they tried to assimilate the wealth of data from myths and

---

13. John McIntyre, "Historical Criticism in a 'History-Centred Value-System'" in *Language, Theology and The Bible: Essays in Honour of James Barr*, ed. S. E. Balentine & J.Barton (Oxford: Clarendon Press, 1994), 370. The idea is from Barr's *Old and New in Interpretation* (1966).

14. Gordon Kaufman, "Religious Diversity, Historical Consciousness, and Christian Theology," in *The Myth of Christian Uniqueness*, ed. John Hick and Paul Knitter (Maryknoll, NY: Orbis, 1987), 9.

15. *De vocatione omnium gentium* was formerly attributed to Leo the Great; PL 51, 647ff.

symbols—Frazer's *The Golden Bough* is notorious for its eclectic charm. As the sciences in general moved into preoccupation with methodology in search of criteria for truth, the dogmatism of exclusivist models in every field was displaced by relativism.

Among those who acknowledged the point of Troeltsch's critique was Paul Tillich. In his closing years he pondered the need for a new approach to the history of religions, one which would honour his category of "ultimate concern" and its related "religious substance."[16] His approach resembles that of inclusivism, promoted as a way of rescuing the Christian claim of absolute role for Jesus as the Christ—notably Karl Rahner's idea of outsiders as "anonymous Christians." Hans Küng's valiant attempt to critique the claim for the universal finality of Christ seems also to stop short of the Rubicon.[17] Indeed, Rahner's first thesis is "that Christianity understands itself as the absolute religion . . . The proposition is self-evident and basic for Christianity's understanding of itself. There is no need to prove it or to develop its meaning."[18] Although well intentioned, such attempts seem simply a more sophisticated form of inclusivism; they do not stand the test of the data of religious studies which show divergence and conflict.

We should add that the way of *dialogue* is taken by some as a fourth relational model rather than simply a way of proceeding. That is, it operates with assumptions of acceptance and of inclusive logic that prove more fruitful than other approaches. For some it extends the

---

16. *The Future of Religions* (New York: Harper and Row, 1966); "Absolutes in Human Knowledge and the Idea of Truth" in *My Search for Absolutes* (New York: Simon & Schuster, 1967), 64–83.

17. As Paul Knitter charges in "Hans Küng's Theological Rubicon," in Swidler, *Toward a Universal Theology of Religion* (Maryknoll, NY: Orbis Books, 1987), 227f.

18. K. Rahner, "Anonymous and Explicit Faith," in *Theological Investigations* (Baltimore: Helicon Press, 1961); on the conflict, see (e.g.) D. T. Suzuki, *Mysticism: Christian and Buddhist* (London: Allen and Unwin, 1957). A good summary of the literature is offered by the review essays in the CSSR *Religious Studies Review* 15.3 (July, 1989) 197–207.

modern phenomenon of "ecumenism" to its original meaning, "the whole inhabited world." The differences among cultures and religions are accepted as a normal topic for dialogue among equal partners. Thus the dialogical method is itself a way of mirroring reality (H.G. Gadamer) or of establishing a place where truth may show itself (David Lochhead, John Cobb).[19] Thomas Merton expected change on both sides through dialogue, as does John Dunne's "passing over" and C.S. Song's "transposition." Such views are in accord with our proposal of a modal theory of the religions, accepting the differentia as decisive rather than occasional.

One noteworthy contribution to the debate on religious pluralism is the distinction between "faith" and "belief." That some such distinction is in order has long been observed, to honour the categories produced by the religions themselves as they sought to understand the relation between inner drive and outward manifestation. An early attempt was that of the Pseudo-Dionysius, who noted the upward movement from biblical phenomena through cataphatic critique to the highest stage where unity with the Subject overcomes all negations.[20] Frithjof Schuon termed the two chief moments "esoteric" and "exoteric," and posited a higher "transcendent unity of religions." His thesis was that the exoteric believer rests content with the outward, in which form and content tend to be one, a kind of absolute mode. The esoteric, however, proceeds beyond, to a mode-less Highest Universal, and therefore moves towards abstractness for the exoteric but concreteness for the esoteric.[21] This resembles Wilfred Cantwell Smith's famous distinc-

---

19. H.G. Gadamer, *Truth and Method*, (New York: Seabury, 1975), G. Barden and J. Cumming, trans.; D. Lochhead, *The Dialogical Imperative* (Maryknoll, NY: Orbis Books, 1988); John B. Cobb, *Beyond Dialogue* (Philadelphia: Fortress Press, 1982).

20. C.E. Rolt, ed., *Dionysius the Areopagite on The Mystical Theology and The Divine Names* (London: Macmillan Co., 1920).

21. Frithjof Schuon, *The Transcendent Unity of Religions* (Wheaton, IL: Theosophical Publishing House, 1984), with Introduction by Huston Smith.

tion between "faith" and "cumulative tradition," mirrored in his subsequent exploration of the difference between faith and belief.[22] Bernard Lonergan has also contrasted the distinctive forms of our beliefs with a more universal faith.[23]

Two leading figures in the debate on religious pluralism may illustrate the deadlock. John Hick pays tribute to Wilfred Cantwell Smith's pioneer efforts to change "the way in which many of us perceive the religious life of mankind."[24] Hick sees this change as entailing a kind of Copernican revolution, according to which the old model of exclusivist religions is replaced by a new "universe of faiths" in which all religions move in planetary orbit around "God." This means a God-centred rather than a Christianity-centred universe.[25] In subsequent writings, notably in "the myth of God incarnate" debate, Hick proffers a theory that religions should be judged on their role as "salvific communities," that is, whether they provide routes along which "people are enabled to advance in the transition from self-centredness to Reality-centredness." This raises not only the familiar problem of conflicting truth-claims, but the even sharper question of "grading religions."[26] Such a pragmatic or functional criterion, involving "maps" of the transition from one mode of being to another, relies on value-judgments about the soteriological worth of any

---

22. W.C. Smith, *The Meaning and End of Religion* (New York: Macmillan, 1962); *Faith and Belief* (Princeton, New Jersey: Princeton University Press, 1979).

23. B. Lonergan, "Faith and Beliefs," paper presented to the American Academy of Religion, Newton, MA, 23 October 1969. See Kanaris, *Bernard Lonergan's Philosophy of Religion* (Albany, NY: SUNY, 2002), 12ff, etc.

24. John Hick, ed., *Problems of Religious Pluralism* (NY: St Martin's Press, 1985).

25. Hick, *God and the Universe of Faiths* (London: Macmillan Press, 1973, 1988), esp. Ch. 9, "The Copernican Revolution in Theology," and 11, "Christ and Incarnation."

26. "On Grading Religions," in *Problems of Religious Pluralism*, 67–87; *An Interpretation of Religion: Human Responses to the Transcendent* (New Haven: Yale University Press, 1988), Ch. 6; Hick, ed., *The Myth of God Incarnate* (London: SCM Press, 1977).

given religion, and so seems to replace a simple relativism with a complex kind of inclusivism. The theory turns on the question of "whether they promote or hinder the great religious aim of salvation/liberation," a question that begs others: is salvation the universal quest? And if so, what standard do we use to evaluate "salvation/liberation?"[27] Hick himself is well aware of the questions raised by his bold theorizing. By glossing "The Ultimate" as "The Real" he admits: "The paradigm of the real *an sich* and its varied manifestations to human consciousness has to justify itself by its power to illuminate the history of religions." He states that our "overlapping mental images of God are all produced by the impact of divine Reality" which then are subjected to an exclusivist self-understanding as their limiting factor.[28] Thus relative human responses to the Real represent valid modes of faith, "different 'lenses' through which the divine Reality is differently perceived," a theory Alister McGrath dubs "complementary pluralism."[29]

Paul Griffiths, on the other hand, holds that every religion is unique in its teachings and history. He notes that the other world religions share the Christian belief in the absolute nature of their own faith. Doctrines form "community rules" reflecting spiritual experience, and are instruments of both catechesis and evangelism. Thus the crucial question of salvific efficacy depends logically on the particular set of doctrines. The Christian christological claim to "universalism and exclusivism" resists the concept of "timeless truth" and posits a historical event as decisive. Griffiths offers his thesis as preferable to "the kind of superficial, pragmatic reasons suggested by Hick and others."[30]

---

27. "On Grading Religions," 86. Hick's point is that while "pluralism" is a hypothesis deriving from religious studies, exclusivism and inclusivism reflect dogmatic stances.

28. See Hick, "The Real and its Personae and Impersonae," in *Disputed Questions*, 164ff.

29. A.E. McGrath, *The Christian Theology Reader* (Oxford: Blackwell, 1995) 335, quoting Hick's *Second Christianity* (London: SCM Press, 1983) 82–87.

30. Paul Griffiths, in *Christian Uniqueness Reconsidered: The Myth of*

In the same volume opposing the Hick-Knitter symposium, John Cobb laments its narrow definition of pluralism, assuming a common "essence" of religion. He posits a broader view that sees the religions as "ways of being in the world," diverse traditions (Smith's category) that resist every essentialist definition. This in turn implies "a pluralism of norms," a more difficult problem. He asks, "Are we forced to choose between an essentialist view of religion, on the one hand, and conceptual relativism, on the other?" In answer, Cobb appeals to actual dialogue as a heuristic way through.[31] Even Kenneth Surin, friendly critic of the "Myth of Christian Uniqueness" conference, considers the quest for this kind of pluralism to be "the dream of a common language" (quoting Adrienne Rich) and the result of Western rationalization. He recalls Max Weber's view of modernity as "the rationalization whereby each realm of discourse . . . proceeds by its own 'inner logic'" to effect an autonomous product.[32] We will return to this question in Chapter 7.

The latter position sits well with the thesis we are advocating, that there are modes of being and believing, distinct—particularly in epistemology—yet not separate in ontological terms. One thinks of Whitehead's later philosophy of organism in which he proposes that in its becoming, a unity ("concrescence of prehensions") forms a distinct nexus or society.[33] The differentia among religions will inevitably spell contrast and conflict; but if they are related dialectically then dialogue represents the way towards mutual understanding and acceptance, towards *Shalom*. Still another voice should be heard just here, that of Mark Heim. His writings on our topic resemble modal theory, for his thesis is that

---

a Pluralistic Theology of Religions, ed. Gavin D'Costa (Maryknoll, NY: Orbis Books, 1990).

31. John B. Cobb, "Beyond 'Pluralism'" in *Christian Uniqueness Reconsidered*, 81–95.

32. Cited by Tom Driver in *The Myth of Christian Uniqueness: Toward a Pluralistic Theology of Religions*, ed. Hick & Knitter (NY: Orbis Books, 1977) 204ff.

33. A.N. Whitehead, *Modes of Thought* (Cambridge; Cambridge University Press, 1938).

"distinct religions and practices lead to equally real but substantively different final human conditions." The focus on "multiple religious ends" means that there can be several "salvations, different paths to different ends that they value supremely."[34] Thus several ends may be attainable, each not only viable but proper according to the goal of a particular religion. Heim draws on philosopher Nicholas Rescher's theory of "operational pluralism," according to which there is no objective stance, free from the religious dimension, that would allow us to judge all religions objectively.

Wilfred Cantwell Smith himself was perhaps more radical than either Hick or Griffiths. His close study of the subject of transcendence, for instance, led him to conclude that genuine transcending means "also its transcendence over language, and even over propositions, their [philosophers'] beloved location for it." Thus he regards linguistic analysis as necessarily falling short of its goal of understanding, since *comprehension* of *the Transcendent* is a contradiction in terms.[35] Smith made this important point in a 1978 lecture: "It is a monumental fallacy that propositions can be true or false. Propositions are always historical and mundane. What is true or false is what they mean to historical persons." Rather, through propositions we may "participate in truth."[36] The new theory that "all is text" implies that "all is hermeneutics" and throws the problem back upon theories of the subject's role in interpreting data.

---

34. Mark Heim, *Salvations: Truth and Difference in Religion* (New York: Orbis, 1996); the thesis of this seminal book is developed in "Many True Religions, And Each One An Only Way," *Ars Disputandi* Vol 3 (2003).

35. W.C. Smith, "Religious Pluralism in its Relation to Theology and Philosophy-and of these two to each other," in Culley & Klempa, eds., *The Three Loves: Philosophy, Theology and World Religions* (Atlanta, GA: Scholars' Press, 1994) 183, a lecture given at my Festschrift.

36. Smith, "History in Relation to Both Science and Religion," paper presented to the Conference on "Emerging Religious Consciousness," Carleton University, Ottawa, 1978 (*SJRS* 1981.2), 10.

Among the ways to escape from a dilemma, we are suggesting that "escaping between the horns" is the best method, rather than "taking by the horns" or rebutting. This entails denying the original disjunctive premise, in this case the claim that one cannot posit singular claims for faith while avoiding relativism. It is the nature of theory itself that has caused scholars to construct the dilemma, so that a new theory is in order that will honour the singularity of religious faith without either assigning an absolute claim to a particular religion or placing all on the grid of relativism.

THEORY AND MODEL

Terms such as theory, model and paradigm function somewhat ambiguously in both scientific and religious studies. Ian Barbour provides a taxonomy illustrating four chief ways of understanding in the two areas: naive realism, positivism, instrumentalism and critical realism.[37] Naive realism views theory as realistic (either true or false) and model as literalistic; positivism and instrumentalism tend to reduce theory to descriptive summary and model to useful fiction; critical realism sees theory as abstract symbol system and model as limited and imaginative. Human reasoning appears to follow a dialectical method, oscillating between data and theory. Since all data are "theory-laden" (R. Hanson) the process is not reducible to a naive "scientific method" of pure induction, what Michael Polanyi scored as the "cult of total objectivity." Polanyi's thesis is that the "personal coefficient" is a constant in human knowledge, and so "bridges . . . the disjunction between subjectivity and objectivity."[38] In between empirical observation and developed theory falls *model*. As theory seeks to correlate observations it uses imaginative models postulated by analogy with familiar data or constructs. Thomas Kuhn has

---

37. Ian G. Barbour, *Myths, Models and Paradigms* (London: SCM, 1974), pp. 34ff; cf *Issues in Science and Religion* (Englewood Cliffs, N.J.: Prentice Hall, 1966), pp. 162f.

38. M. Polanyi, *Personal Knowledge: Towards a Post-Critical Philosophy* (NY: Harper, 1958) 17.

popularized the term "paradigm" for imaginative models that carry the weight of theory and analogy.[39] His thesis concerning "paradigm shifts" as revolutionary changes affecting our fundamental apprehension of reality has been borrowed by theologians in their quest for models to accommodate the patterns of religious pluralism

Clearly the doctrine of the Incarnation of the Word seems to entail some form of exclusivism, claiming universal relevance for the Christ's theanthropic nature and atoning work. So far the two opposing camps mount conflicting theories, with incompatible models of the universe of faiths. In this debate the familiar distinction among graces, "prevenient/accompanying" or "general/special" appears to serve a strictly inclusivist agenda, as with Karl Rahner. On the other hand, Hick's thesis requires a sharp distinction between incarnation and myth. Granted that *Logos incarnatus* is not to be taken literally, is the correct alternative a "mythical" meaning? Hick suggests that the properly *religious* sense of this key doctrine is that Christians are led by their experience to worship their Mediator. "Jesus is the concrete image of God through whom our worship is focused, and the idea of the Incarnation is an effective mythic expression of the appropriate attitude to him." Now if it is "appropriate" then the myth is "true," but by turning it into a hypothesis, Hick claims, we falsify its character and also "generate implications that would make impossible any viable theology of religions."[40] His move to embrace a form of pluralism is not intended as a reduction to lowest common denominator, or mere acceptance without criteria. Developing his earlier epistemology of faith as "experiencing-as," he identifies the essence of religion as transformation from ego-centred to reality-centred being.[41]

---

39. T. Kuhn, *The Structure of Scientific Revolutions* (Chicago: Chicago University Press, 2nd ed. 1970).

40. Hick, *Universe of Faiths*, Ch. 12, "Incarnation and Mythology," 165ff.

41. John H. Hick, *An Interpretation of Religion* (New Haven, Conn.: Yale University Press, 1989); Hick, ed., *The Myth of God Incarnate* (London: SCM, 1977); cf. G. D'Costa, *John Hick's Theology of Religions: A Critical Evaluation*

PARADIGMS OF CHRISTIAN THEOLOGY

We have noted the ambiguity in the use of *modus* in both modernity and postmodernity. We might add also those modalities of genre or type familiar through Northrop Frye's *Anatomy of Criticism* and theory of myths. I also have in mind what is in play when "modal" is used in logic and in science. Modal logic is the logic of *if*—"If p then q." It explores the possibilities in conditional statements. Ancient forms developed by Philo of Megara and by Aristotle were suspect in earlier Christendom, but later studied by the scholastics, then neglected until the 1930s. Since C.I. Lewis and others, modern logicians have developed systems of implication to account for *alethic* (what is true) modalities of possibility and necessity, *deontic* modalities of obligation, and *epistemic* modalities of what is considered true.[42] Indeed, modal logic has become the dominant field in logical studies, its "most active and influential part."[43]

A good example of modal thinking is the modern distinction between typical and modal science. Classical physics cherished the Aristotelian classification of types, since typicality was the foundation of method. With relativity and quantum theory, however, a radical shift was required, inasmuch as "universality" advanced from limited fields to properly cosmic dimensions. Typical science involves special laws for certain classes of subject; modal science involves general laws for more abstract subjects—e.g. the move from Special to General Theory of Relativity, and thence to Unified Field Theory. Universal explanation requires a kinematic mode (itself indirect) for "describing" states of affairs.[44] The

---

(NY: University Press of America, 1987) and C. Gillis, *A Question of Final Belief: John Hick's Pluralistic Theory of Salvation* (Basingstoke: Macmillan, 1989).

42. See N. Rescher, *The Coherence Theory of Truth* (OX: Clarendon, 1993) V: "Criteria of Alethic Eligibility and Epistemic Decision Theory," 98–140; David Lewis, *On the Plurality of Worlds* (Oxford: Basil Blackwell, 1986) etc, and the excellent overview in A.N. Prior *et. al.*, "History of Logic," *Enc. of Phil.*, ed. Paul Edwards (NY: Macmillan 1967) IV, 513–71.

43. N. Rescher, *Studies in Modality* (OX: Basil Blackwell, 1974) ix.

44. M.D. Stafleu, *Time and again: a systematic analysis of the foundations*

difference between Euclidean and non-Euclidean geometries implies the change required in modes of apprehending, even of reasoning itself. This is more than Kuhn's famous "paradigm shift" since it connotes a change in the very way of understanding phenomena. The inductive method belongs to the "youth" of science, as Einstein remarked, whereas mature science relies more and more on hypothetico-deductive models: "the train of thought leading from the axioms to the empirical facts or verifiable consequences gets steadily longer and more subtle."[45] The trap of evidentialism set by Hume ("A wise man, therefore, proportions his belief to the evidence") is not the whole story, even for Hume himself.[46]

Christian classical theism tended toward a theoretical model dominated by the disjunctive syllogism, an All-or-Nothing opposition, in which "the Absolute in history" is a contradiction in terms, reflecting Kierkegaard's "infinite qualitative distinction between time and eternity."[47] The crucial issue is posed by christology, bearing the weight of revelation and salvation: how this doctrine developed in Scripture and Councils, whether it was itself pluralist (Logos, Sophia, etc), whether Buddhology presents a parallel movement, and so on.[48] The hard question is what a World Council of Churches study termed "the

---

of physics (Toronto: Wedge, 1980) 220ff.

45. Einstein, "Space, Ether and the Field in Physics" in *Relativity, the Special and General Theory* (NY: Henry Holt, 1920).

46. See David Hume, "An Enquiry Concerning Human Understanding," in *Philosophical Works* (London: Longmans, Green & Co., 1875) vol. IV, I.10, "Of Miracles." Just afterwards, Hume deals with evidence "derived from witnesses and human testimony" which "is regarded either as a proof or a probability" according to the experience. From "experiments and observation" we reach a conclusion on "the degree of evidence, proportioned to the superiority" of one side or the other.

47. Cf. McLelland, *Prometheus Rebound*, esp. 251, 281ff. See Kierkegaard's "Interlude" on the concept of becoming, *Philosophical Fragments*, 59ff.

48. E.g. C.F.D. Moule, *The Origins of Christology* (Cambridge: Cambridge University Press, 1977).

finality of Christ in the age of universal history." Close by is the philosophical discussion of pluralism and monism as metaphysical theories (e.g. Spinoza's substantival monism or Russell's logical atomism) as these provide context for theories of absolutism and relativism. In epistemology this implies the debate about foundationalism, contrasted with both fideism and positivism.

Ian Barbour notes that "the data of religion are experiences and events which are interpreted by imaginative models."[49] As with science, in religion too there is no uninterpreted experience. What we seek in both disciplines is a common rationality: "In fact rationality in science relates to the reasonableness or a more basic kind of rationality that informs all goal-directed human action."[50] Historically, the terms "experience" and "experiment" (both from the Latin *experior*) were thought by Christian Fathers to support the data of religion, the creedal dogmata. While not subject to strict demonstrative proof, the latter were nonetheless taken as reliable since they came from authoritative hearsay and were tested by experience. The two obvious forms of religious experience are the numinous and the mystical. Whether these are different in degree or kind remains unclear; masters of novices traditionally encouraged everyone to ascend the ascetic ladder whose goal is mystical union.[51] The harder question is why there are two types of mystical union, theistic (self with Self: "I taste salt") and monistic (losing one's self in the One: "I am salt"). The Christian idea of mediation holds that we come to know God in a way that John Baillie called "mediate but direct."[52] That

---

49. Ian Barbour, *Myths, Models and Paradigms* (NY: Harper & Row, 1974) 119.

50. J. W. van Huyssteen, *Essays in Postfoundationalist Theology* (Grand Rapids, MI: Eerdmans, 1997) 164.

51. Richard of St.Victor, for instance, offers his *Benjamin Minor* ("The Twelve Patriarchs") as preparatory meditation, with little hint that anyone is excluded from this vocation if they have the leisure.

52. John Baillie, *Our Knowledge of God* (London: Oxford University Press, 1959). Baillie returned to his theme in his final Gifford Lectures, *The Sense of the Presence of God* (London: Oxford University Press, 1962).

A THEORY OF RELATIVITY FOR RELIGIOUS PLURALISM

is, mediated knowledge (e.g. knowing another self through bodily acts) is not thereby indirect, or something less than "immediacy" implies. Similarly, for Barbour, "Our knowledge of God is like knowledge of another self in being neither an immediate datum nor an inference."[53] Such an epistemological role for the Mediator, however, does not satisfy the harder question of uniqueness. It would seem necessary to accept Cobb's idea of "ways of being in the world" which resist an essentialist theory. Again, George Lindbeck's thesis that the traditional model of religion as "experiential-expressive" should be replaced by one of a "cultural-linguistic" nature, avoids the necessity of universalizability.[54] Is it true that "all paths lead to the top" of Mount Fuji? Is the Kantian *noumenon* behind *phenomena* relevant to our problem? If not, the quest for "Religion as such" is futile.

Should Incarnation play the decisive role—for or against claims to uniqueness—in our debate? If so it functions as absolute standard, like the velocity of light in relativity physics. (One must acknowledge the bite of M.M. Thomas's warning that pluralism means "risking Christ for Christ's sake.")[55] But to proceed thence to larger questions of relations among systems such as non-incarnational religions is to beg the question of criteria for applying one system to another, of appropriate field laws. Raimundo Panikkar recognizes the point, identifying a new stage in interreligious relations, so that overlapping or dual allegiance contradicts traditional expectations.[56] Such a model being sought by Hick or Panikkar shifts the focus from what is believed to how (fides

---

53. *Myths, Models and Paradigms*, 125.
54. George A. Lindbeck, *The Nature of Doctrine: Religion and Theology in a Postliberal Age* (Phila: Westminster Press, 1984).
55. M. M. Thomas, *Risking Christ for Christ's Sake* (Geneva: WCC Publications, 1987), esp. Ch. 1, "The Challenge of Pluralism."
56. R. Panikkar, *The Trinity and the Religious Experience of Man* (New York: Darton, Longman and Todd, 1973); *The Unknown Christ of Hinduism* (Maryknoll, N.Y.: Orbis Books, 1981). The latter is in part a response to M.M. Thomas, *The Acknowledged Christ of the Indian Renaissance* (London: SCM, 1969).

quae, qua creditur), admitting a plurality of salvific communities, and so advances from special to general theory that can relate variant fields. But it is not yet clear what a "unified field theory" for all religions would be like. A preparatory step will be to reexamine analogies with science; this is the burden of our next chapter. Then we will examine other aspects of paradigm shift, with analogies from art and other dimensions of a philosophy of the religions. .[57]

---

57. W. B. Yeats. See Nathan A. Scott, Jr., *The Broken Centre* (New Haven: Yale University Press, 1966).

5

SCIENCE AS METAPHOR

Thesis: the development of relativity theory from Special to General to Unified Field offers a strong analogy to the development of doctrine from exclusivist to inclusivist to pluralist.

This and the following chapter explore the question whether theological data have helpful analogies in other disciplines, in order to clarify how far modal theory can revise traditional expressions of belief in light of the dialogue imposed by religious pluralism. First we turn to the sciences. We have seen how some scholars view the two disciplines, appealing to such categories as paradigm shift to enlighten the way religious concepts function. There is also an important sense in which both begin with a kind of faith: the scientist's belief in an orderly universe is analogous to religious trust. Einstein made this clear: "I assert that the cosmic religious experience is the strongest and the noblest driving force behind scientific research . . . The basis of all scientific work is the conviction that the world is an ordered and comprehensive entity, which is a religious sentiment."[1] This relates to the "intuition" Einstein credits with a formative influence on his

---

1. A. Einstein, *Cosmic Religion, with other opinions and aphorisms* (New York: Covici-Friede, 1931), 52, 98. See also A.T. McKinnon, *Falsification and Belief* (The Hague: Mouton, 1970) on the "faith" with which science begins.

development of the Relativity theories.[2] Here we will examine the nature of models and of scientific discovery for clues in our quest.

MODELS AND METAPHYSICS

A *model* may be defined as "an imaginative construct developed as a theoretical guide for techniques of research and action." It is obvious that models will function differently in various disciplines; what is decisive, however, is to recognize that in all disciplines there seems to be a dualism to model-building, resulting in alternative ways of theorizing. These alternatives have been expounded at length by Max Black and Ian Ramsey.[3] Black calls the two types "scale" and "analogue" models, while Ramsey prefers the terms "picturing" and "disclosure" models. The first kind, scale or picturing, is a working or descriptive model, an ostensible replica of reality—Lord Kelvin's model of the ether is a notorious example. Analogue or disclosure models, on the other hand, claim to be only proximate constructs which guide the seeker to insight through their isomorphic similarity to the "object" in question. Their heuristic role makes them decisive in experiment or exploration.

The natural sciences, to a marked extent, show a passage from a mechanistic worldview dominated by scale models to a growing sense of the elusiveness of reality and a consequent reliance on analogue models. Probably the most striking example of this passage is the short history of atomic physics, in which an original model of the atom, Bohr's miniature solar system, taken as scale replica, proved unable to function under certain conditions and had to be complemented by a quite different model, of energy quanta. The latter forced physicists to re-think their concept of models, resulting in an acceptance of both as analogue models, related by what Bohr calls "a principle of complementarity."

---

2. See Iain Paul, *Knowledge of God: Calvin, Einstein, and Polanyi* (Edinburgh: Scottish Academic Press, 1987), 86ff.
3. Max Black, *Models and Metaphors* (Ithaca: Cornell University Press, 1962); I.T. Ramsey, *Models and Mystery* (Oxford University Press, 1964).

Obviously this is a complicated story, with several factors at work. For instance, is Bohr's "principle" itself an analogue model, as he seems to think when he uses it to enlighten other areas of tension such as science and religion?[4]

Ian Ramsey noted this shift in natural science and rightly accused social science of anachronism, inasmuch as it takes its models, mostly mechanistic and mathematical, to be scale rather than analogue. Certainly the decision to seek quantification within the human studies was a fruitful and liberating one; but was it not a stage rather than the goal? Ramsey states: "Let not psychology repeat the errors of a Kelvin; let not psychology sponsor picturing models and then repeat the pseudo-puzzles and the tall stories which characterized physics in an earlier day. The 'mathematical' models cannot reach the person who will never—logically never—be transparent to any or all models, still less covered completely by picturing models." Hence let psychologists identify with physicists in working with disclosure models, not pictorial models. If so, "their models too are fulfilled in insight, that is, acknowledging that experimental psychology deals with persons like ourselves."[5]

This warning echoes the wise fears of Wilhelm Dilthey, who rejected the name of science for what he called the "human studies" (although *Geisteswissenschaften* may do, if we take it properly).[6] Fred Ferré has explored this issue, trying to "map the logic" of models in science

---

4. Niels Bohr, *Atomic Theory and the Description of Nature* (Cambridge: Cambridge University Press, 1934); Cf., C.A. Coulson, *Science and Christian Belief* (London: Oxford University Press, 1955). The point could be visualized as two separate diagrams for particle (A) and wave (B) theories; then uniting them in a complementary dialectic (A <—> B); finally a new theory posited over against them: (A—B) <—> (?). See also W.H. Austin, *Waves, Particles, and Paradoxes* (Houston, TX: Rice University Studies 53/1, Spring 1967), 1ff.

5. Ramsey, *Models and Mystery*, 28f.

6. See H.A. Hodges, *The Philosophy of Wilhelm Dilthey* (London: Routledge & Kegan Paul, 1952), 84ff for his differentiation among the disciplines.

and theology.[7] Ferré sees conceptual models as giving concreteness or form to theories. They serve purposes of interpretation, integration and heuristic stimulation. For theory tends towards what Ernest Nagel called "abstract calculus", a symbolic context that remains highly indeterminable. To such a context a model brings catalytic power, to probe and to suggest and to define. Thus model and theory enjoy a relation that is "mutually supportive," assisting and qualifying each other: "sometimes powerful models may lead to important modification of theories, just as theoretical requirements may sometimes result in the limitation or abandonment of models."[8] In "metaphysical" models, according to Ferré, where the criterion of all-inclusiveness obtains, it is the *scope* of the model's application that is in focus. Here the model functions as paradigm, an archetypal form of life opening on a horizon or vision of reality. The "fit" between theory and model is decisive, and the very criteria invoked to judge appropriateness are part of the horizon in view. Thus a metaphysical model functions heuristically and judgmentally, making demands of commitment or self-involvement.

The word "metaphysical" should not be allowed to mislead us. In fact it is from those models which are most "scientific" that there derives the recognition of the subject's involvement, and even more: the involvement of "science" itself in "meta-physics". Philosophers of science (the new "meta-physicists?") have been showing the way, not without considerable opposition. Probably the opposition itself proves their point: that models are so decisive for one's total view of things that a shift in models is a traumatic experience which summons hordes of antibodies to the site of the wound. Scientists as diverse as Karl Popper, Michael Polanyi and Thomas Kuhn have developed this thesis at length.[9] Let us concentrate on Kuhn's

---

7. F. Ferré, *Basic Modern Philosophy of Religion* (Scribners, 1967), Chapter 13: "Cognitive Possibilities of Theistic Language"; cf., "Mapping the Logic of Models in Science and Theology," *The Christian Scholar* XLVI.1 (Spring 1963).

8. F. Ferré, *Basic Modern Philosophy of Religion*, 377.

9. Karl Popper, *The Logic of Scientific Discovery*, 1959; M. Polanyi, *Personal Knowledge*, 1958; Thomas Kuhn, *The Structure of Scientific Revolutions*, 1962.

SCIENCE AS METAPHOR

concept of paradigms for a moment. He defines them as "universally recognized scientific achievements that for a time provide model problems and solutions to a community of practitioners."[10] This is an obvious extension from grammar, where paradigm functions as an example of which replications are expected. The scientific paradigm is a problem-solving model arising from actual practice and driving on into exploration. But—and this is Kuhn's point—"normal science" will discover new conditions under which the paradigm produces "anomalies" which precipitate "crisis." "All crises begin with the blurring of a paradigm and the consequent loosening of the rules for normal research . . . And all crises close with the emergence of a new candidate for paradigm and with the subsequent battle over its acceptance."[11] During the crisis, "extraordinary science" carries the burden of work, as in every "pre-paradigm" or speculative era.

One theologian in active dialogue with philosophy of science in this area is T. F. Torrance. He has published a trilogy that constitutes a solid engagement in behalf of theology as a special science: *Theological Science*, *Space, Time and Incarnation*, and *God and Rationality*. Torrance agrees that we do not have to do with "theoretical transcripts of reality" but with "models of a different kind." The latter could best be termed "analogue"(following Mary Hesse), a kinetic model that is to be "operationally defined" (in Einstein's sense), and must never be allowed to become fixed or rigid, for that would suppress its intended function in discovery.[12] Torrance begins with a call to "emerge from the cultural split" resulting from the common view that "science" works with a deterministic worldview, reducing "religion" to a subjective/existential domain. This charge of a "disastrous dualism" features in most of his writing in this area. He declares the old determinism as passé, and calls for "a profounder and more unitary grasp of the intelligible con-

---

10. Kuhn, *Structure*, x.
11. Kuhn, *Structure*, 84.
12. Torrance, *Theological Science* (O.U.P. 1969), xv, 240.

nections in the contingent order of the universe."[13] Indeed, he considers modernity an aberration in that it moved away from the unitary universe of classical thought—John Philoponus is an outstanding example—to posit dualism of mind and matter, of phenomena and noumena. Hence the postmodern (like Polanyi"s "postcritical") return to unitary vision recovers the proper perspective for scientific advance.

THE LOGIC OF DISCOVERY

The key to model-building is this "function in discovery," the heuristic intention. The analogue operates in a paradeigmatic rather than iconic way: it opens up reality for exploration, rather than closing it for reflection. Thus there is an "indeterminate scope" or revelatory potentiality, for analogue models. For Polanyi this becomes linked with his thesis of *tacit knowledge*: "we can know more than we can tell."[14] In this sense our language—and in particular our philosophy of language—will reflect our understanding of models and their relation to reality. A simplistic acceptance of scale models, for instance, will tend to attract a theory of language which reduces its revelatory role and tacit dimension accordingly: the debate between B.F. Skinner and Noam Chomsky is pertinent. But an acknowledgment of analogue models will suggest a more open view of language, a recognition that the analogical relation of models to reality may require a brokenness of speech or a tentativeness of theory as its running mate. This was true of the "Goettingen circle" of physicists and theologians who saw in Karl Barth's work a parallel methodology to that of modern physics. [15]

---

13. Torrance, "Emerging from the Cultural Split," in *The Ground and Grammar of Theology* (Belfast: Christian Journals Ltd, 1980), 19f. A similar critique of dualism is mounted by Gerard Siegwalt in *Dogmatique pour la Catholicité Evangélique (Système mystagogique de la foi Chrétienne*, vol. 2 (Paris: Labor et Fides, 1987).

14. *Personal Knowledge*, Part Two: "The Tacit Component;" *The Tacit Dimension* (Garden City, NY: Doubleday, 1966), 4ff on "tacit knowing."

15. e.g. Günter Höwe, "Parallelen zwischen der Theologie Karl Barths und

SCIENCE AS METAPHOR

When arguing for theology as a special science, Torrance makes much of the "analogic" of the Chalcedonian Definition as the paradeigmatic model for Christian theology: "a compound existence-statement derived by tracing certain basic existence-statements back to their biblical sources and through them to an empirical relation, in worship and faith, to Christ Himself".[16] uch a view suggests at least two things of significance for theological method. First, the parallel with natural science holds here too:

Method	Scientific Example: *Relativity Theory.*	Theological Example: *Doctrine of Trinity*
a) Particular Case:	Special Theory	Historical Jesus
b) General Implications:	General Theory	God the Father
c) Field Consequences:	Unitary Field	Holy Spirit

That is, given the general theory of analogue models and their logic, the method of articulation involves a direction and procedure that seem identical in the two disciplines. Barth's Anselmic method thus transports us into the centre of the epistemological concern of modern science.[17] Barth's point was that there is only one "way" or method for human reason to proceed, whether in natural or in human sciences, namely to understand our experiential data, asking "how is the actual possible?"—Anselm's *fides quaerens intellectum*.[18] Barth's analysis of Anselm shows the latter's alethic trinity, as it were: the rational experi-

---

der heutigen Physik," in *Antwort* (Barth Festschrift, 1956).

16. Torrance, *Theological Science* (London: Oxford University Press, 1969) "The Logic of Existence-Statements," 226–46 and "The Logic of Coherence-statements," 246–63.

17. See Karl Barth, *Anselm: Fides Quaerens Intellectum*, 1931, especially 1.4 on the threefold *fidei ratio*. Torrance argues that Anselm reflects the "forcing" from the side of Supreme Truth (*Ground and Grammar*, 99).

18. The subtitle of Barth's book on Anselm. See also van Huyssteen, *Postfoundationalism*, 6: "Systematic Theology and Philosophy of Science: the need for Methodological and Theoretical Clarity in Theology," 105ff.

ence of faith, its conformity with its object, and ultimately the ratio of Truth as such.

Second, this motion from particular to general is not the old "inductive method" of popular scientific historiography. Natural science itself must accept the postmodern critique of any pretension to being the sole way to truth, dismissing all else as "excluded knowledge," as Huston Smith charges against Bertrand Russell.[19] It is rather a method that proceeds dimensionally, so to speak, moving through paradigms that work well in a horizon of determinate dimension but which must break down and make way for a more complex paradigm as new dimensions come into view. Such a shift occurred with the Copernican revolution, but the best example is that of the shift from Newtonian to Einsteinian concepts of space and time. Einstein does not destroy Newton but perfects him (as Aquinas would say). In one sense, the advent of quantum mechanics and relativity theory proves and establishes the Newtonian worldview, but only by a strict delimitation of its scope, while not surrendering the goal of Newton's method, "strict causality."[20] (That is, we live our ordinary daily life within the bracketed Newtonian space and time, while outside it is Einstein's space-time continuum that operates in micro- and macro-reality). Similarly, an analogy from geometry is well known: the shift from plane to solid geometry begins to work with added dimensions and therefore discovers a change in rules; for example, there are no straight lines in a gravitational field. Karl Heim was fond of this analogy, using it in his theoretical construct of polarized spaces held within the space of divine omnipresence, the dimension of dimensions.[21] This idea of a

---

19. See Huston Smith, *Beyond the Postmodern Mind* (New York: Crossroads, 1982), esp. "Checkpoints," 162ff. But in considering Hume's view of induction, Russell also insists on the need for "novelty in fundamental hypotheses," the role of imagination in inductive reasoning—*Our Knowledge of the External World* (New York: New American Library, 1960), "Our Notion of Cause," 163–88.

20. E.g. A. Einstein, *Relativity, The Special and General Theory* (London: Henry Holt & Co., 1920).

21. E.g. *Christian Faith and Natural Science* (London: SCM Press, 1953).

dimensional breakthrough which allows for multipresence or coinherence is also familiar in fiction—Edwin Abbott's *Flatland: a romance of many dimensions*, as well as the "Christian fantasy" of Charles Williams and C. S. Lewis. One could adduce similar models from mathematical cases—Georg Cantor's transfinite numbers and endless endlessnesses or Gödel's theorem concerning insoluble problems and consequent infinity of system-building—and of course the fantastic drawings of Escher.[22] And so on.

In *Space, Time and Incarnation* T. F. Torrance argues for a "differential" language apposite to the unique multi-dimensional field established by the theological horizon. "The interaction of God with us in the space and time of this world sets up, as it were, a coordinate system between two horizontal dimensions, space and time, and one vertical dimension, relation to God through His Spirit. This constitutes the theological field of connections . . . He generates within these connections His own distinctive and continuous 'space-time track', and forms a moving and creative centre for the confluence of world-lines within the plenum of space-time."[23] Remembering—as Torrance himself does—that this is analogical thinking and not some new theosophy, we may well reflect on the possibilities of such borrowing and cross-fertilization in both method and model. And since it is simply such possibility which this first section wished to open up, its business is done.

THEOLOGY AND RELATIVITY PHYSICS

Theoretical studies of religion parallel those of modern science, particularly relativity physics. This is not to say that the two are identical in method or aim, but only that they show striking similarities, and in the last analysis claim to interpret the same "world." Some theoretical reso-

---

22. See Stanley Jaki, "Gödel's Shadow," in *God and the Cosmologists* (Washington: Regnery Gateway, 1989), 84ff.

23. Torrance, *Space, Time and Incarnation* (London: Oxford University Press, 1969), 72.

lution of differences and tensions is required if we are to avoid a schizoid intellectual standoff. To begin, we should recall that antique physics (from Ionians to Nominalism) gave way to classical physics (Copernicus and Galileo, dominated by Newtonian mechanics) and thence to modern physics (Planck, Einstein, Bohr) with its relativity theory and quantum mechanics. Classical physics had sought proper universality through abstraction, but theology can learn more from modern irreducible modal descriptions. The familiar complementarities of matter/force and particle/wave signify heuristic models most relevant to the role of dogmata.[24] That is, we claim that the analogy of paradigm shift is poor in heuristic power; a richer one is offered by the process of physics itself toward field theory, toward a single concept to explain all the fundamental forces of nature. This will entail a "logic of inhomogeneous classes" to replace traditional logic of homogeneity, since "The kind of connection found in field theory can be so elastic and flexible that it requires on our part a new logic to cope with it."[25]

Thomas Kuhn claimed that a scientific paradigm tends to outlive its capacity to explain new data. Anomalies and qualifications increase and reach a critical mass; for instance, "The state of Ptolemaic astronomy was a scandal before Copernicus' announcement." A traumatic shift becomes inevitable as the data force on us a simpler, more elegant paradigm. John Hick used Kuhn's example to meet the challenge of world religions. Just as the Ptolemaic cosmological model had become overly complex by adding ellipses and devices to meet new data, so classical theism had added too many qualifications to its trinitarian doctrine to survive the test of interpreting the "universe of faiths." A radical shift is being provoked by new data and a new consciousness of what "religion" means

---

24. Cf. Stafleu, *Time and Again,* esp. 220ff.
25. Torrance, *God and Rationality* (London: Oxford University Press, 1971), 15. Torrance cites Elasser's work on quantum logic ("an irreducible logical complexity") in *Atom and Organism* (Princeton: Princeton University Press, 1966).

to others, outsiders to one's own spiritual community. Such a Copernican revolution will produce a "new map of the universe of faiths."[26]

The way in which analogue models function to explain new data and to correlate apparently contradictory fields bears a striking resemblance to the theo-logic of analogy articulated by Thomas Aquinas. His relationship of "proper proportionality" established the mean between univocity and equivocity, anthropomorphism and agnosticism, literalism and fictionalism. Analogy (or isomorphism) remains crucial in our search for a theoretical model that will correlate vastly different data. Moreover, Christian theology has its own principle of complementarity which allows it to live with apparent paradox (e.g. "both divine and human;" chance and providence; *simul iustus et peccator*). Ricoeur's "rule of metaphor" is a modern theory of analogical predication, tracing the incongruity between human language and its transcendent Object/Subject. Nor is the search over for the sufficient principle of interpretation, the paradigm or archetypal analogue.

Thus the theological analogatum is like the scientific explanandum, and its analogans like the explanans. The crucial point in analogical reasoning is how to begin. *Classical physics* began with absolute space and time; *classical theism* began with an absolute historical singularity. Then something decisive happened to qualify both paradigms. Newtonian mechanics was bracketed or limited by quantum theory; classical theism is being limited by the need for more embracing coordinates of explanation. *Can the Incarnate Word continue to provide the test case for truth-claims in all religions?* If so, the contradictory claim of the religions of India, for example, which regard history in a different way, remains incompatible. It is significant that some theologians are interpreting Vatican II documents as encouraging a dialogue in which Christian faith is no longer the normative premise.[27] But the

---

26. John H. Hick, *God and the Universe of Faiths* (London: Macmillan, 1973), esp. 9 and 10; cf. *Problems of Religious Pluralism* (New York: St. Martin's Press, 1985).

27. E.g. Hans Küng, "Christians and World Religions: A Dialogue with

recent Declaration *Dominus Iesus* seems content to revert to exclusivist categories.[28]

Partly in response to christology, Christian anthropology stressed the concept of *sin* as decisive. Thus it misses the Eastern insight, as in C.S. Song's gnome "I suffer, therefore I am" (*Patior, ergo sum*), echoing the first Noble Truth of the Buddha concerning *dukkha*.[29] By beginning with history, incarnation, salvation from sin as its *analogans analogata*, Western theology is powerless to engage Eastern thought in a coordinate structure of meaning. There remains between East and West not only an essential incommensurability in anthropology, soteriology and theology, but incompatibility as well. There are complementary paradigms *within* both West (e.g. Logos/Messiah/Spirit in christology) and East (e.g. the Absolute as *advaita, visistadvaita* and *dvaita*); but the two hemispheres do not seem patient of higher sublation under more general coordinates (e.g. as if *salus* and *mukti* were complementary).

PARADIGM CHANGE IS NOT ENOUGH

"Copernican revolution:" this is itself a metaphor. It signifies any radical shift in perspective or horizon, like that from the Ptolemaic-Aristotelian to the Copernican cosmology. Consider the shift from a worldview in which Christianity is the centre of the universe of faiths to one in which a different sort of centre becomes the orienting norm. As heliocentrism was to geocentrism, so pluralism is to exclusivism—so runs the analogy. But if we take the cosmological analogy properly, it pushes us beyond solar system to galaxies, to the uttermost limits, just

---

Islam," pp. 192ff in L. Swidler, ed., *Toward a Universal Theology of Religion* (Maryknoll, NY: Orbis Books, 1987) hereunder TUTR.

28. *Dominus Iesus: on the Unicity and Salvific Universality of Jesus Christ and the Church* (Vatican City: Congregation for the Doctrine of the Faith, 2004).

29. C.S. Song, *Theology from the womb of Asia* (Maryknoll, NY: Orbis, 1986)—see "Suffering Community," 135ff.

as Newton recognized that the law of gravity must account for moving planets as well as falling apples.

What is being termed "paradigm shift" in theology cannot serve the need for a universal theory of religion. This thesis may be tested by the report of the recent symposium on "Paradigm Change in Theology," edited by Hans Küng and David Tracy.[30] Küng sets the stage: "Thus in *physics*: macromodels for scientific global solutions (like the Copernican, the Newtonian, the Einsteinian model) . . . Similarly in *theology*: macromodels for global solutions (the Alexandrian, the Augustinian, the Thomist model)." But this is faulty reasoning: the scientific and the theological macromodels do not correspond. What the Alexandrians or Augustine or Thomas proposed was not (like Copernicus or Newton or Einstein) a model which displaced or relativized the former, but merely a shift in emphasis or exemplars *within* the governing paradigm of classical Christian theism.[31] The examples are not properly incommensurable, necessitating a principle of complementarity to relate them positively. Therefore they are not properly "macromodels." They do not force a shift in conceptuality comparable to the scientific shift from substance/matter to process/form. Langdon Gilkey has raised the question whether there might be more fundamental changes, "what I shall call 'continental shifts' or 'epochal shifts'."[32] His examples are the rise of modern science and of modern culture since the Enlightenment. Here again one wonders whether such historical phenomena imply such profound anomalies as to provoke a fundamental shift, a truly contradictory position demanding new theory.

---

30. H. Küng and D. Tracy, eds., *Paradigm Change in Theology: A Symposium for the Future* (New York: Crossroad, 1989).

31. Even those archetypal theologians of East and West, Origen and Augustine. do not conflict in a way that denies their acceptance of the paradigm of classical theism—cf. McLelland, *God the Anonymous: a study in Alexandrian philosophical theology* (Cambridge, MA: Philadelphia Patristic Foundation, 1976).

32. Langdon Gilkey, "The Paradigm Shift in Theology," Küng & Tracy, *Paradigm Change*, 368ff.

Such a basic mistake in analogy hinders the debate on religious pluralism from advancing beyond the polarity of inclusivism/relativism. Küng's "two constants" are human experience with its contingency and change, and "the Judeo-Christian tradition which is ultimately based on the Christian message, the Gospel of Jesus Christ." But when the latter is privileged as a constant or absolute, we impose historical uniqueness as criterion for judging every other truth-claim. Thus only those who acknowledge ultimate revelation/salvation in Jesus as the Christ would have normative "religious experience." The point becomes clear when we compare Küng's constants with "Planck's constant" in quantum physics; the former is limited to one planetary history, the latter is intended "for all times and for all civilizations, even those which are extraterrestrial and nonhuman."[33] The theological "paradigm shift" under discussion is still from one deductivist system to another. This means that we have not experienced a Copernican revolution. We still resemble Newton, whose absolute space and time provide analogues: we have not yet developed a theory of relativity to provide coordinates across different systems with contrary paradigms. Much less are we working on unified field laws to embrace every (religious) system in the universe.

Raimundo Panikkar has grasped the problem well in using the category of "universalizability." He fears that the thrust toward (religious) unified field theory reflects Western intellectualism, reducing all data to those that are conscious and comprehensible. Genuine pluralism "has to do with final, unbridgeable human attitudes . . . mutually exclusive and respectively contradictory ultimate systems." If worldviews prove incompatible, we must acknowledge "the *relativity* of truth, once it is distinguished from relativism."[34] Panikkar sees the ambiguity of the term

---

33. Max Planck, quoted by Carl Raschke, *Theological Thinking: An inquiry* (Atlanta, GA: Scholars Press, 1986), 41.

34. "The Invisible Harmony: A Universal Theory of Religion or a Cosmic Confidence in Reality?" in Swidler, 118ff. Cf. M. Dhavamony, "Indian Perspectives in the New Paradigm of Theology," *Toward a Universal Theology* in Küng & Tracy, 424ff.

"universal"—its reference to terrestrial humanity suggests a (Kantian) theoretical object for Western intellectual imperialism. But what if it were to refer to higher lifeforms elsewhere in the universe? Would these also be objects for the epistemological and soteriological theories of classical theism? Questions of criteria for relatedness depend on the paradigm of universalizability governing standards and relations.

RELATIVITY WITHOUT RELATIVISM

Two major paradigm shifts in Western science inform analogies with religious studies: from Ptolemy to Copernicus and from Newton to Einstein. The effect of the first was a displacement in cosmology, but the second presents a more complex case. Relativity theory limits Newtonian absolutes, but they continue to function within its parentheses as *typical* science is maintained for defined data (e.g. the sun "rises" daily), even if these same data are sublated under *modal* laws—that is, a dual transposition that both conserves and displaces: Hegel's *aufhebung*, Derrida's *la relève*. Modern physics shifted from typical to modal description, the rigid bodies of particular motion becoming the kinematical subjects (wave packets) of quantum physics. Certainty becomes probability and final explanation becomes tentative description, unable to provide complete explanation for typical structures.

The names of Einstein and Hawking suggest our agenda: progress toward unified theory at the highest level, entailing necessarily abstract modalities. If the study of religion is at a post-Copernican stage, we need models analogous to the relativity theories of Einstein. He moved from special theory of relativity (STR) to general (GTR) and thence to the unfinished quest for unified field theory (UFT) or "Grand Unification Theory." An important preliminary point is that *relativity theory does not claim that everything is relative, nor does it imply ethical relativism*. (The crucial search is for the *invariant* phenomenon; in philosophical terms, the universal particular may be correlated in the *singular*, similar to the "singularity" posited by contemporary physicists.) The most fruitful analogues for our purpose include the process

PLURALISM WITHOUT RELATIVISM

from special to more general theory, from empirical to mathematical data, and from Euclidean to non-Euclidean geometries. T. F. Torrance has explored what he terms "the integration of form" in natural and theological science, remarking on the shift from rigid absolutes in science to "a more profoundly objective but dynamic relatedness inherent in the structure of the universe, invariant for any and every observer."[35] The new non-Euclidean four-dimensional continuum shifts human knowing of reality to a process of relational transformation. It bids us seek the theological form of critical realism in our theory building.

We submit that this threefold process in scientific theory offers a more fruitful paradigm for the shifts required by the challenge of religious pluralism. The analogy would operate as follows. STR relates two systems (e.g. electrodynamics and optics) by establishing coordinates for both, but relying on an empirical law (e.g. velocity of light). This resembles exclusivist theory in theology. GTR relates coordinate systems, of mathematical rather than physical import, moving toward more general laws. This resembles inclusivist and some pluralist theory, attempts to construct global theocentric models. UFT seeks one set of field laws governing all parallel coordinate systems in the universe (electromagnetic, gravitational, strong and weak nuclear fields, and a possible fifth). This resembles a modal theory raising global theology to universal scope. The new question becomes: what are the *laws of transformation* between Systems seen in the modality of universal phenomena?

If religions are like the "fields" of STR, incarnational revelation/salvation can function as absolute standard, governing a comparison of theories of incarnation—unique or unrepeatable? and of salvation—from sin or from suffering? But *special* theories relate only two systems of belief, e.g. Christianity and Islam (and Judaism, the third Abrahamic religion). Thus we would be discussing differing ways of understanding monotheism, or the idea of revelation through Word of God. GTR

---

35. T. F. Torrance, *Transformation and Convergence in the Frame of Knowledge* (Grand Rapids, MI: Eerdmans, 1984), 68ff.

introduces other types of system, seeking more general laws governing the faith and ethics of human being. But what if two theories rest on different and unrelated theoretical foundations, as with relativity and quantum theories—Buddhism and Christianity for instance? This was Einstein's dilemma (akin to Troeltsch's?) as he searched for "the grand aim of all science, which is to cover the greatest possible number of empirical facts by logical deduction from the smallest number of hypotheses or axioms." This aim is served as "predominantly inductive methods appropriate to the youth of science are giving place to tentative deduction." The process of simplification follows a principle of the "natural laws" of coordinate Systems, extending itself toward the unitary field.[36] A genuine UFT must include every kind of religious belief and behaviour, ancient to modern, fringe to mainstream, cosmic as well as terrestrial.

SPECIAL THEORY: CHRISTIAN THEOLOGY

Traditional models of Christianity in relation to other religions are limited to special theory. They operate with coordinates and paradigms developed within a Christian continuum which functions like an enclosed inertial system. The inclusivist attempt to embrace all religions on such a basis is not therefore an advance to general theory, much less the final step of unified theory. The analogy (A:B::C:D) for understanding the relation between Christianity (A) and extra-Christian religions (B) seems as follows: exclusivism postulates truth (C) and error (D); inclusivism sees full or explicit (C) compared with partial or implicit truth (D); pluralism relates one partial truth (C) to another (D). At this stage the crucial question is: what are the "protocol sentences"

---

36. "Space, Ether and the Field in Physics" in *Relativity, the Special and General Theory* (New York: Henry Holt, 1920); cf. P. A. Schilpp, ed., *Albert Einstein: Philosopher-Scientist* (New York: Tudor, 1951).

or normative interpretations of religious experience governing theory-building?[37]

The debate on pluralism must challenge every simplistic or reductionist model of classical theism, by drawing on neglected resources in the tradition. Certain moments in the Patristic development of trinitarian doctrine could prove fruitful. In relation to STR the dialectic between unity and trinity implies a system less enclosed than classical theism appreciated. For example, the split between East and West symbolized by the *filioque* insertion in the Nicene-Constantinopolitan Creed was a question of which pole (oneness or threeness?) one takes as starting-point, how one articulates the analogue model of tri-unity. The result was a pair of complementary theologies East and West coexisting in tension, isomorphic in christology, and unresolved on pneumatology. This instance recalls Gödel's Theorem that no logico-deductive formal system can be both complete and consistent. Similarly, the ambiguity of religious language requires an appropriate formal calculus to account for levels of usage. Such a system of coordinates was attempted by both Arius and Athanasius, if in differing ways. Here, then, is a case study in relational or differential theory.

GENERAL THEORY: GLOBAL THEOLOGY

Can Christian special theory advance to general theory? Does it have resources that make for a leap beyond the exclusivist-inclusivist dialectic? This might be a hidden christocentrism, as in the "christology from below" of Schillebeeckx and Rahner. That is, knowledge of Jesus as the Christ is inductive, based on human experience of transcendence, and dependent on the contingent conditions of human being: where we are born, our cultural milieu, and so on. This approach is open to the fact that a variety of responses to the phenomenon of Jesus of Nazareth

---

37. Cf. W.H. Austin, "Waves, Particles, and Paradoxes" *Rice University Studies*, 53.2 (Spring 1967). Note that his "paradox of the religious ultimate" (p. 45) remains within Christian parameters.

is possible, besides the orthodox doctrine of the Christian community. For the ecclesia, faith means "union with Christ," a definition that requires unpacking in terms of the nature of such *unio mystica*, and so of its Object.

Others are engaged in a "theocentric" model of theological reflection (e.g. Robert Jenson in theology, James Gustafson in ethics) with potential for a revision of classical theism along relativity lines. For instance, one may imagine a development of Logos doctrine that includes links with Sophia or Pneuma, with the Sophiology of some Easter Orthodox theologians, or the Pneumatology left underdeveloped after the Nicene era. This might be pursued even further, relating to the principle of Dharma or of Tao, a genuine step into the thicket of religious pluralism. This kind of move could explore as archetypal analogue *revelation through Word*—invisible (Judaism), visible (Christianity), audible (Islam), inaudible (mysticism), iconic (Hinduism). And following the traditional coupling of Word and Spirit, it could link with theories of Spirit: where christology divides, pneumatology may unite.

A neglected dimension in Patristic teaching may be of great moment, namely the development of Logos christology.[38] The concept of *logoi spermatikoi* had helped Justin Martyr to a positive appreciation of extra-Christian knowledge of God. Subsequent reflection led to Chalcedonian christology, whose definition by negations poses a classic recognition that mystery is preserved more through negative than positive theology. This apophatic turn is expressed in the asymmetrical model of christology in which *logos asarkos* is greater than *logos ensarkos*, that is, disincarnate Logos remains greater than the enfleshed Word. The twin concepts *anhypostasia* and *enhypostasia* spell things out: the humanity is enhypostatic within the personal union named Jesus the Christ; but the Christ or Logos remains outside the incarnate form, or *anhypostatic*.[39] This means that the eternal Logos is patient

---

38. See chapter 8 below for development of themes in this paragraph.
39. E.g. at Second Constantinople, 553; cf. K. Barth, C.D. 1.2, 161ff: "a doctrine unanimously sponsored by early theology in its entirety".

of assuming many forms, of relating to possible worlds besides our own planet. I have noted this point above (chapter 3). Here it signifies simply the capacity of classical christology itself to adventure into a pluralist context in positive and constructive ways. This ancient idea was revived in the sixteenth-century Lutheran-Calvinist debate on the ubiquity of Christ's bodily presence, when the Lutherans nicknamed the anhypostastic thesis "extra Calvinisticum." Reprising the Augustinian distinction *totus/totum* (Logos is "in" Jesus the Christ truly but not completely), Calvin and notably Peter Martyr Vermigli taught a more open christology that could be developed in pluralist context.[40]

Here is a divine presence that includes the incarnate Word but is not exhausted by it. It has been traditionally articulated in a global way, but could become truly universal, relevant to every possible field of religious phenomena, just as the cosmic Logos is relatable to every conceivable life-form in the universe. Ironically, as noted above, the conservative C.S. Lewis saw the point in his science fiction trilogy starring a space traveller appropriately named Ransom.[41]

UNIFIED THEORY: MODAL THEOLOGY

A perspective on world religions that will be properly "universal" demands a theory able to include possible data from extra-terrestrial sources. A universal theory of revelation and salvation (or their analogues) must account for such *cosmic possibilities* as hypothetical

---

40. Martyr: *Dialogue on the Two Natures in Christ*, 1561 (trans. J.P .Donnelly, Peter Martyr Library Vol. 2, Kirksville MO: Sixteenth Century Essays & Studies XXXI, 1995); cf. E.D. Willis, *Calvin's Catholic Christology* (Leiden: E.J Brill, 1966, 67); T. F. Torrance, "The Problem of Spatial Concepts in Reformation and Modem Theology" in *Space, Time and Incarnation* (London/New York: Oxford University Press, 1969), 22ff.

41. C.S. Lewis, *Out of the Silent Planet, Perelandra (Voyage to Venus), That Hideous Strength*. See Chapter 3 above. But Lewis himself maintained an exclusivist Christology: "Since our Beloved became a man, how should Reason in any world take on another form?" (*Perelandra*, 54).

rational creatures outside our galaxy. The modern problematics of otherness or "alienation" are best approached through such theory. Although statistical probabilities suggest that such lifeforms exist, the argument does not rely on existential data. It runs: *if* aliens exist they exist *necessarily* in relation to Transcendence. This compares with the "many worlds hypothesis" in quantum physics, potential states that imply probabilities among compossibles.[42] If our epistemology and soteriology are limited to the planet earth, they cannot claim genuine universalizability, the criterion for unified field laws.

For medieval theologians, angelic being functioned as a test case and limiting concept for epistemology and soteriology. So we may test our theory (as its principle of falsifiability) by the imaginative construct of extra-terrestrial life-forms: what would revelation/knowledge (necessarily) of transcendence and salvation (possibly) mean for them? Any theism that fails to account for not merely extra-Christian but extra-terrestrial beings fails the test of coherence. For unless we can relate the Transcendent to such creaturely forms, we construct theories of merely geocentric or anthropocentric relevance. Our cosmic model therefore offers an argument *a fortiori*—the universal context provides a limiting-concept (*Grenzfall*) for theories of human knowledge of God and atonement. It therefore functions to regulate merely global questions of otherness/alienation. "Pluralism" that refers to extra-Christian religion but not to extra-terrestrial is opting for less than universality. This line of thought explains in part Einstein's rejection of "anthropomorphic" ideas of God.

Although not all physicists accept Stephen Hawking's thesis of a Grand Unified Theory uniting the four forces of physics, it offers an isomorphic model for relating the data of religious pluralism.[43] We

---

42. Cf. Raschke, *Theological Thinking.*, esp. Ch. 4: e.g., are religions "conjugate variables" that reflect differing choices of identical pairs, or more like a series of prior forks in the road of possible relationships to transcendence?

43. S. W. Hawking, *A Brief History of Time* (New York: Bantam Books, 1988).

noted above that the relation of science to religious studies is not inferential but analogical. Thus UFT has strong links with Heidegger's "field theory" of human being, as well as T. F. Torrance's idea of the topological language of scripture, a field of intersection requiring relational models.[44] My argument is that we tend to jump from Copernicus to Hawking without going through Einstein. That is, we equate relativity with relativism and therefore regard the latter as the leading (or only) alternative to the traditional christocentric paradigm. We need to ponder the significance of *field* as the key to understanding reality, as if not space itself but inbetween spaces constitute the possibility of knowledge.[45]

A theory of relativity for religious pluralism, therefore, is not an alternative theory of relationship among world religions. Rather, it offers an alternative analogy with scientific method that illuminates prior questions of coordinates in establishing "truth-claims," and of the fields to be subsumed under universal laws. Have we yet reached a proper stage of general theory in religious studies? Do we know how to proceed towards a unified field theory? If pluralism knows the proper question, neither inclusivism nor relativism is quite the answer.

---

44. E.g. *Torrance, Space, Time & Incarnation*, 80ff; cf. Iain Paul, *Science, Theology and Einstein* (Belfast/Ottawa: Christian Journals, 1982); *Science and Theology in Einstein's Perspective* (Edinburgh: Scottish Academic Press, 1986).

45. Cf. Einstein and Infeld, *The Evolution of Physics: From Early Concepts to Relativity and Quanta* (New York: Simon and Schuster, 1938). This idea resembles the "negative theology" of deconstructionists such as Jacques Derrida—e.g. "Différance," in A. Bass, ed., *Margins of Philosophy* (Chicago: University of Chicago Press, 1972); Mark C. Taylor, *Deconstructing Theology* (New York: Crossroad, 1982).

6

DOGMA AND ICON

There is an ancient quarrel between philosophy and poetry.
— Plato[1]

We have seen that modernity tended to exhaust its theory of knowledge based on the paradigm of natural science. Thus *imagination* was excluded, even though the consciousness that the human mind reasons by means of *images* is a commonplace, at least since Aristotle's concept of the phantasm as the mind's mirror image of reality. Was Nietzsche correct in his thesis that the original Dionysian energetics were sublimated in Apollonian rationality? Can the Dance of Life be reduced to analytic description rather than performance? Would you ask Pavolva what her dancing "means?"[2]

So the role of the *imagination* remains problematic, perhaps the key to the *problématique* of the theory of knowledge inherited from the Enlightenment. In our quest for the modal nature of doctrine we note an irony of our modern academic scene: while teachers of theology and/ or religion argue about how to get started on God-talk, the sciences carry on with concepts of analogy, paradigm, model, archetype, and

---

1. *Republic*, 607.
2. She was in fact so asked, replying: "If I could say it, do you think I should have danced it?"—see McLelland, *The Clown and the Crocodile* (Richmond: John Knox Press, 1970) "The Dance of Life," 71ff.

so forth. We seem forgetful of the rich heritage in which it was theologians who hammered out precise definitions for these very terms. One example of gross negligence is the popular assumption that when Aquinas talks about "analogy" he means analogy of being (which he sometimes does) rather than analogy of proper proportionality (which he prefers).[3] Another assumption is that when natural and social sciences develop their concepts of types and models they are speaking a different language from that of historical theology. Perhaps what is missing is the recognition that there is a "practical" intellect as well as a "speculative" one, and that the former "also has its ways of approach towards God."[4] So the point of this chapter is to sketch not only the striking similarity of language, but the "family resemblance" that cuts across disciplines and demands our attention. In particular, in our quest for modal theology we now turn to analogies with the arts.

IMAGE AND/AS ICON

Among the arts which should we choose as paradigm? Now the *dance* has been known since the classical age as the key to life's mystery: "most people say of those who reveal the mysteries, that 'they dance them out'" (Lucian). And Plato acknowledged that "the gods had pity on us, and gave us Apollo and the Muses to be our playmates and leaders in the dance."[5] This liturgical dimension is clear in the evolution of "things acted" (*drama*) from "things done" (*drōmena*) of primitive religion, perhaps the threshing-circle where Thespis is said to have turned from his fellow worshippers to face the spectators. Both tragedy and comedy embody the deepest symbols into which the Mysteries initiated their disciples.[6] In one sense theatre rather than dance provides the best analogue for religious

---

3. See James F. Anderson, *The Bond of Being: an Essay on Analogy and Existence* (London: Herder, 1949).
4. Jacques Maritain, *Approaches to God* (London: George Allen & Unwin, 1955), 68.
5. Plato, *Laws*, II.653.
6. See McLelland, *God the Anonymous*, 4ff: "Mystery and Tragedy."

symbolism. Both are liturgical, a shared spectacle, motions of doom and renewal: "Agon, Sacrifice, Feast, Marriage, Komos" (Frances Cornford). Again, while tragedy may seem the more "serious" art, it is comedy that acknowledges the supreme motion of grace, the finale of revelation and ultimate meaning. Tragedy speaks of *gravitas*, the weight of human fault and of divine glory, but comedy unveils *levitas*, the lightness of being and the way upwards. Accordingly, religion provides Act Five for the human drama, its revelation (*anagnôrisis*) discloses the ultimate mystery: "the dark is light enough" (Christopher Fry).[7]

Western "classical theism" posited two reasons why the Transcendent is elusive: "sense" and "sin." That is, as sensible creatures we gain immediate knowledge only through the senses; all else—abstract concepts, values, truth itself—are mediated through sense perception, dependent on signs and symbols. Secondly, this situation is further complicated by the "fault" that lies in human being, an error or transgression that affects both body and mind, darkening the significance of the signs of transcendence.[8] The latter means that theory of knowledge alone will not explain the human condition; only a theory of fault and its cure will provide the complete answer. This is why Paul Ricoeur begins his phenomenological study of human being with "the language of avowal," *l'aveu*, which "speaks of fault and evil to the philosopher."[9]

---

7. See McLelland, *The Clown and the Crocodile* (Richmond: John Knox Press, 1970), 79ff, "Beyond Tragedy-The Comic Vision," and 87ff, "The Masks of Drama and the Face of Truth." For Augustine, "my weight is my love," whether up or down, each "to his own place." (*Conf.* XIII.9).

8. The biblical statement in *Romans* 1:18–23 posits a universal revelation: "what can be known about God is plain to them, because God has shown it to them," qualified by the "darkening of their minds" that leads to a perversion of such natural knowledge.

9. Ricoeur's philosophy of the will moves from the initial voluntary and involuntary (establishing a free but conditioned willing) to the second stage, "empirics" entitled *Finitude et Culpabilité*. First is *L'Homme faillible* (1965) analyzing the language of avowal to show the possibility of evil, followed by *La Symbole du Mal* (1967) on the reality of evil as expressed in symbol and

Academic studies tend to ignore soteriology and concentrate on epistemology. For Western religion at least (ever since the classical Mysteries), this distorts the reality of transcendent knowing: one cannot apprehend the divine without being changed, reborn or "twice-born," i.e. *communication entails communion.* When sign and symbol are treated as simply a problem about knowing, they function in a context devoid of authentic religious (i.e. transcendent) meaning. With symbolism in mind, let us now turn to the aesthetic realm in search of analogues for Christian theology—will *icons* enlighten *dogma*? Is it perhaps the case, as Elizabeth Sewell contends, that "the Orphic voice" is the clue to holistic thinking, since poetry is "a form of power," as the old myth recounts? If so, then "Poetry, metaphor, mythology are highly realistic and down to earth. It is logic and mathematics which are the imaginative and fantastical exercise."[10] She means that the former are self-involving while the latter abstract from the *Lebenswelt*. The mode of *poiêsis* is a labour of love, "a choreography of language and mind" as John Henry Newman put it. His category of "illation" was a form of inference that sublimates mere demonstration in probing the sublime and transcendent objects that inspire our trust or faith.[11]

Consider some theories of "art and the sacred." Symbols are judged by whether they communicate religious meaning rather than whether they make for change in the reader/viewer. For instance, the idea that "God" has disappeared from the postmodern intellectual horizon was loudly proclaimed by Nietzsche; it has been an assumption for art critics ever since.[12] Whereas former ages would have attributed this change to a deepening of the fault in human being, now the very concept of "the

---

myth.

10. Sewell, *The Orphic Voice: Poetry and Natural History* (New York: Harper Torchbooks, 1971 [Yale, 1960]), 39.

11. J.H. Newman, *Essay in aid of a Grammar of Assent*, 1870; Sewell, 34.

12. E.g. Jane Dillenberger, "The Appearance and Disappearance of God in Western Art," in *Image and Spirit in Sacred and Secular Art*, ed. Diane Apostolos-Cappadona (New York: Crossroad, 1990) 93–107.

sacred" is in dispute, the iconic realm has been emptied of higher meaning. Jean-Luc Marion is one who sees the problem. Beginning from a critique of the Cartesian immanentist ego and a positive regard for Patristic thought, he distinguishes between idol and icon. The former remains within the worldly "visibility" established by consciousness, while the latter is given, a different mode that "sees" the invisible.[13] With such modality we are able to recognize the transcendent power of iconic being.

One could approach "the arts" in several ways; literature has been the obvious favourite for Western scholars. Paul Ricoeur has noted that the very word "fiction" implies the re-shaping or re-making of reality, echoing Nelson Goodman's "reality remade."[14] Images in both literary and plastic arts are productive, they augment reality. Some would claim (C. S. Lewis for one) that all stories reflect the one Story that constitutes human being in all its grandeur and misery (Pascal), that ours is a "story-shaped world" (Brian Wicker). Whereas plastic images may copy some phenomenon and so refer to what is absent, fictive images have no such referent; they intend nothing simply or merely "real." Marianne Moore's famous remark that poetry creates "imaginary gardens with real toads in them" points to the power of the image and why it functions realistically, even at times as "magic realism."[15] While art is often considered a "work" and so patient of ergonic categories, when viewed as *play* it opens up the field of *homo ludens* (Johan Huizinga), both play and contest, *paideia* and *agōn*, the ritual acting-out and dancing-out of Mystery. All modes of creative artistry participate in this

---

13. J-L. Marion, *God Without Being*, trans. T. A. Carlson (Chicago: Chicago University Press, 1991)

14. Goodman, *Languages of Art: an approach to a theory of symbols* (Indianapolis: Hackett, 1976); Ricoeur, "That Fiction 'Remakes' Reality," unpublished paper; he refers to F. Dagognet, *Ecriture et Iconographie* (Paris: J. Vrin, 1973). Cf. Ricoeur's thesis that "La symbole donne à penser" in *The Symbolism of Evil* (Boston: Beacon Press, 1967).

15. Marianne Moore, *Collected Poems*, 41.

playful remaking of reality, and so function as witnesses to the sur-real as home of Beauty. They remind us that "There is nothing that does not participate in beauty."[16] And play allows the imagination to sport with images of the happy turning, such as Aristotle's *eutrapelia*, characteristic of one who has attained *theōria*, and Tolkien's *eucatastrophe*, the good crisis, and so to secure the transcendent dimension of being human.[17]

Western art remains problematic when taken to be "religious." Martin Heidegger described the work of art (*Kunstwerk*) as one that establishes a world, that preserves reality, "the becoming and happening of truth."[18] Art is a modality in which there occurs a peculiar "openness of being," and therefore an authentic dis-closure of Truth; herein lies its relevance to theological dogmata. Here also is an illustration of his basic thesis of "the rootlessness of Western thought" which begins when Roman thought appropriated Greek terms without their meaning, namely "the basic Greek experience of the Being of beings in the sense of presence"— philosophy is displaced by metaphysics. Hence the combination of subject and predicate does not necessarily mirror the structure of the thing, its union of substance and accidents.[19] For Heidegger the Sacred manifests itself in the artwork as a worldly phenomenon that is not in itself a presence. But through it "the *world worlds*" to gain surer purchase on being and create space for the world of truth. The familiar thought-path (*Denkweg*) of Heidegger tries to open itself to Being by "a radical questioning about art," rather than reducing the artwork to an aesthetic object. "The real thinker thinks Being while the real poet names the Holy."[20] The poet Hölderlin serves the un-concealment (*a-lêtheia*) of

---

16. Thomas Aquinas, *De div. nom.*, 4.5.

17. I have treated these themes in *The Clown and the Crocodile* (Richmond: John Knox Press, 1970).

18. M. Heidegger, "The Origin of the Work of Art" (*Der Ursprung des Kunstwerkes* (lecture 1935–36) in *Holzwege* 1950), trans. A. Hofstadter in *Poetry, Language and Thought* (New York: Harper & Row, 1971), 17–87.

19. Heidegger, "Origin," 153, 170, 183f.

20. See C. Nwodo, "The Role of Art in Heidegger's Philosophy," in *Philosophy Today*, 21/3 (Fall, 1977), 294–304.

Being—so the artist is inspired by Being. "All art as the letting-come-to-pass of the advent of the truth of beings as such, is in essence poetry."[21] Through surrender to the call of Being, the artist participates in the revelation of Being.

Paul Tillich's aesthetics resonates with Heidegger's. He provides some typologies in his analysis of the artwork.[22] His theory of symbols attempts to rescue the transcendent from reduction to phenomena: the very idea of symbol posits something more, a surplus of meaning beyond every immanent definition. Everyone has an "intuition" of The Ultimate, but since it is apprehensible only through myth or symbol, it is easily reduced or buried in the Unconscious. One thinks of Jung's aphorism: "the stars have fallen from heaven; symbolism has waned." Tillich notes the familiar distinction of subject matter as *form* and *style*. Every style points to self-interpretation and so to ultimate meaning. He notes Dilthey's "stylistic keys:" idealistic, realistic, subjective and objective. While all four are present in the artwork, one or more predominates. The twentieth century saw a break with classic style and the rise of Expressionism. He thinks that the expressive style "dominates in all periods in which great religious art has been created."[23] The artwork intends "to express the realness of the real in the object rather than to grasp its form."[24] Thus it expresses not so much the content (*Inhalt*) as in cognition, but the very "import" (*Gehalt*) of reality.

---

21. Heidegger, *Holzwege* 59; cf. "Hölderlin and the Essence of Poetry," in *Existence and Being*, ed. W. Brock (Chicago: Henry Regnery, 1949), 293ff.

22. P. Tillich, "Protestantism and Artistic Style," *Theology of Culture*, trans. R. C. Kimball (New York: Oxford University Press, 1959); "Existentialist Aspects of Modern Art," in *Christianity and the Existentialists*, ed. C. Michalson (New York: Chas. Scribner's Sons, 1956); *Masse und Geist* (1962) GW 2, 35–90.

23. Tillich, "Protestantism and Artistic Style," 74.

24. R. P. Scharlemann, "Tillich and the Religious Interpretation of Art," in J.L. Adams, ed., *The Thought of Paul Tillich* (New York: Harper & Row, 1985), 160.

PLURALISM WITHOUT RELATIVISM

For Tillich, "religion is the substance of culture; culture is the form of religion."[25] When culture ("the arts") offers us form without transcendent religion it becomes *autonomy*; when religion offers us substance without aesthetic form it becomes *heteronomy*. These two alienating cases form a polarity of credulity and scepticism. *"Theonomy"* reconciles the two in a dynamism where culture and religion are harmonized, communicating truth. From this basis Tillich offers various typologies of artworks. If one regards surface and depth as form and content one may distinguish "profane" or secular styles in which impressionism and realism dominate, from "religious" art exemplified by romanticism and expressionism (depth prevailing over natural forms); and also from "classical" where depth and appearance are balanced.[26] Thus the true object of our "unconditional concern" shows Itself through those aesthetic symbols that express the substance of that Ultimate Concern termed "God." The transparency of religious art, particularly the liturgical arts, unite religious style and content that together are expressive of transcendent Reality.

SEEING AND HEARING

Perception, in Western epistemology, tends to begin with the eye, from classical times to John Locke.[27] Sight, says Plato, is our greatest blessing, without which we would not reach philosophy.[28] Theological treatises on light investigated sensible light as symbolic of "the invisible

---

25. Tillich, "Existentialist Aspects of Modern Art," in *Christianity and the Existentialists*, ed. C. Michalson (New York: Charles Scribner's Sons, 1956).

26. Scharlemann, "Tillich and the Religious Interpretation," 162. See 173, fn 12 for four typologies developed by Tillich.

27. See K. H. Tachau, *Vision and Certitude in the Age of Ockham* (Leiden: E.J. Brill, 1988); J. Locke, *An Essay Concerning Human Understanding* (1690), II.IX, 9: "Of Perception:" the simple ideas received by sight, "the most comprehensive of all our senses," are basic in epistemology. Richard Rorty notes that "ocular metaphors" are as dominant before the 17th century as after: *Philosophy and the Mirror of Nature* (Oxford: Blackwell, 1980), 12f.

28. Plato, *Tim.* 47B.

light with which God illuminates every man."²⁹ Optics functions as the primary way of apprehending reality: *theōria* means beholding, a reflection that applies to that deeper in-sight of "enoptics" or "epoptics" dear to the Mysteries. Similarly, the mirror image of the *speculum* refers to inner speculation, contemplation. This image presents a puzzle (strikingly presented by Magritte) inasmuch as it affords a glimpse of both identity and otherness. The Renaissance emblematist Alciati put it: "What is a picture? A false truth." The *veritas falsa* belongs to the logic of representation, positing the very dilemma of "picturability" that besets modern science in its search for proper models, as noted above. It is "the sadness of Narcissus" as he mistakes image for reality. Because he does not *know* what he *sees*, Narcissus represents the ultimate alienation, and finally disappears, leaving behind only a flower to bear his name. ³⁰

Martin Buber thought that the Greeks "established the hegemony of the sense of sight over the other senses, thus making the optical world into *the* world," into which "the data of the other senses are now to be entered." ³¹ There were dissenters, of course, notably William Blake. He prefers "double vision," and prays, "May God keep / From single vision and Newton's sleep!"³² Blake—according to Frye's interpretation—

---

29. Gilson, *History* 341. cf. T. F. Torrance, "The Theology of Light," in *Christian Thought and Scientific Culture* (Belfast: Christian Journals, 1981), 75ff.

30. Pierre Legendre, *Lecons III: Dieu et Miroir: étude sur l'institution des images* (Fayard, 1996) 14; cf. IV: "L'au-delà logique de l'image . . ." 111ff. See Ovid, *Metam*. III, 434

31. Buber, *The Eclipse of God* (1952), 40, quoted in T. F. Torrance, *Belief in Science and in Christian Life* (Edinburgh: The Handsel Press, 1980) 22. Cf. John Macmurray, *The Clue to History* (1938). See T. F. Torrance, *Intuitive and Abstractive Knowledge: From Duns Scotus to John Calvin* (Rome: Studia Scholastica, 1963).

32. In a poem incorporated in a letter to Thomas Butts (22 November 1802)—see Northrop Frye, *Double Vision: Language and Meaning in Religion* (Toronto: United Church Publishing House, 1991), 22f.

wishes to add the human dimension to all perceived reality, and so to enlarge the world with an added dimension. His vision of "fearful symmetry" entails the method of anagogy, a study of ritual and myth, supplying "the missing piece" by which thinking may restore the "whole pattern."[33] Such a *Gestalt* may well be the clue to proper rationality, one that sees through the superficial rationalism of prosaic utterance. The third eye of in-sight allows us to see *through* rather than merely *at*, so that the depth of meaning in metaphor, even of oxymoron, is rendered visible to the mind.[34]

The Christian East took a decisive turn in producing an image that functioned as *icon*, that is an integral part of worship. Indeed, "the icon belongs to the *esse* or essential being of the church; it is a vital part of that general order of human activity within the church that serves to express Christian revelation."[35] Etienne Gilson has noted the difference between East and West in declaring that Bernard of Clairvaux attempted a third theology, "a new theology which unites the Greek theology, based upon the relation of image to model, with the Latin theology based upon the relation of nature to grace."[36] For Bernard, the action of grace effects union with Christ or *unio mystica*, with the human Jesus as Exemplar. Bernard's sermons to his community illustrate his striking understanding of religion as a pilgrimage through the moments of Christ's life, replicating each stage.[37] This bears strong resemblance to Gregory of Nyssa's teaching on the Christian life as the true *askēsis*, a toilsome

---

33. Frye, *Fearful Symmetry: A Study of William Blake* (Princeton: Princeton University Press, 1947), 425.

34. E.g. T. W. Organ, *Third-Eye Philosophy: Essays in East-West Thought* (Ohio University Press, 1987), Ch 1: "Oxymorons as Theological Symbols."

35. L. Ouspensky, "Icon and Art" in B. McGinn & J. Meyendorff, eds., *Christian Spirituality: Origins to the Twelfth Century* (New York: Crossroad, 1988) 382.

36. Gilson, *History of Christian Philosophy in the Middle Ages* (New York: Random House, 1955), 164.

37. See "Of those in whom Christ's mysteries are not as yet fulfilled," in *Bernard of Clairvaux: Selected Works* (New York: Paulist Press, 1988).

ascent (*anabasis*) whose itinerary involves both knowledge and virtue, and whose goal is that knowledge of truth which is also knowledge of being (*gnōsis tōn ontōn*).[38]

The long Iconoclastic controversy among Eastern theologians has been well documented, notably by Jaroslav Pelikan.[39] Since Byzantine thought "specified the content of theology as doxology," images were acceptable insofar as they promoted devotion.[40] What the word is to hearing, the image is to seeing. In a similar distinction to that of Tillich's, the iconoclastic struggle was solved by distinguishing the mode of representation from the subject: sacred art not only depicts a holy subject, it renders it in a way appropriate to devout meditation. The final settlement by the Seventh Ecumenical Council reads: "The honour rendered to the image passes to its prototype, and the person who venerates an icon venerates the person (*hypostasis*) represented in it."[41] Orthodox theology is famous for its emphasis on the Transfiguration of Christ.[42] Here the Uncreated Light enlightens the Son while the Word of the Father pronounces a blessing. Transfigured humanity is the goal of creation; if there were no need of atonement the Transfiguration would have been the Eschaton, at least the fulfilment of the creation of the human species. It may be the case that seeing and hearing each yields an alternative perspective on reality. Sight is relatively passive, it implies "speculation" or contemplation. This is clear from the mystical tradition where in-sight is rewarded by "showings" of in-visible or transcendental reality. For that exemplary mystical theologian Richard of St. Victor, for instance, as the novice progresses in *askēsis* he moves

---

38. See W. Jaeger, *Two rediscovered works of ancient Christian literature: Gregory of Nyssa and Makarios* (Leiden: E.J. Brill, 1954), 77.

39. Jaroslav Pelikan, *The Spirit of Eastern Christendom (600–1700)* (Chicago: University of Chicago Press, 1974), Ch. 3, "Images of the Invisible," 91–145.

40. Pelikan, *op. cit.*, 131.

41. NPNF 14:549ff.

42. So much so that Father Florovsky is reported to have warned his students: "We were saved not on Mount Tabor but on Mount Calvary."

through imagination and intellect to "understanding," where reason is surpassed and Showing happens.⁴³

PERCEPTIONS OF SPIRIT

What of the hearing of *music*? Is not the religious inspiration for great sacred music of moment as well as that of sacred art? In particular one thinks of Mozart, the favorite musician of Karl Barth and worthy of treatment by Hans Küng. For Barth, Mozart is simply the best, worthy of "a place in theology" because "he knew something about creation in its total goodness." In face of "the problem of theodicy" he did not respond with a *Candide* (the Lisbon earthquake continued its philosophical reverberations during his lifetime), but "had the peace of God" allowing him to see "the whole context of providence."

> As though in the light of this end, he heard the harmony of creation to which the shadow also belongs but in which the shadow is not darkness, deficiency is not defeat, sadness cannot become despair, trouble cannot degenerate into tragedy and infinite melancholy is not ultimately forced to claim undisputed sway. ⁴⁴

This reflects Barth's own "theodicy" in the chapter entitled "God and Nothingness," in which the negative is always with the positive—"in their inequality [Mozart] heard them both together."

Küng shares Barth's assessment of Mozart's genius in reconciling positive and negative moods, in its "lofty art" of "transcending musical categories, of the bounds and genres and modes in the most subtle of all

---

43. Richard of St. Victor (d. 1173), *Benjamin Major (The Mystical Ark)* in *Richard of St. Victor*, ed. G. A. Zinn (New York: Paulist Press, 1979); cf. the *dilatio*, *sublevatio* and *alienatio* of the mind. In *The Mystical Ark* the three levels are symbolized by the wood of the ark, its gilding, and the pure gold of the propitiatory (e.g. Ch. 4).

44. Karl Barth, *C.D.* III.3, 298; cf. Barth, *Wolfgang Amadeus Mozart* (Ev. Verlag Zollikon, 1956) and the four essays in W. Leibrecht, ed., *Religion and Culture: Essays in Honor of Paul Tillich* (London: SCM, 1959), 61–78.

spiritual arts." He notes that "An abstract masterpiece can speak the truth in the pure language of sound . . . and in the end say something inexpressible, unspeakable: in the midst of music the 'ineffable mystery.'" Such music shows "how wafer-thin is the boundary" between music and religion.[45] Of course, Augustine would share this opinion but qualify it by warning of the dangers of music. Just as Plato and Aristotle identified "ethical melodies," so Augustine recalled his own experience in letting the music obscure the words in worship.[46] This caution reflects the debate as to whether to allow music in worship at all. The conclusion is significant:

> Not the voice, but the desire; not the tune, but the heart; not being noisy but loving, sounds in God's ear.[47]

So the aesthetic analogue to theology is to be taken with care, lest another alien autonomy rob the dogma of its rights.

Any schema of theological science and aesthetics remains problematic, but serves to introduce the distinction between alternative languages nevertheless subject to similar method and model-building. For instance, Calvin Seerveld begins his "modal aesthetic theory" with an "opening hypothesis," that "the nuclear moment" of artworks is "a matter of 'allusiveness' or 'nuancefulness.'" Such allusiveness replaces traditional definitions of "the *qualifying* function of art" through the beautiful or the harmonious. In a close historic study, he notes the heuristic nature of all theory, and the need to recognize "aesthetic concepts" as *sui generis*. His hypothesis of "symbolical objectification"

---

45. Hans Küng, *Mozart: traces of transcendence* (Grand Rapids: Eerdmans, 1992), esp. "Theme 7 and Finale: Traces of Transcendence," 29ff.

46. Plato, *Rep.* III.398Dff; Aristotle, *Pol.* VIII.7, 1341B33ff; Augustine, *De Musica, Conf.* IX.7, 15 (PL 32,770); see McLelland, "Music and Songs," *Peter Martyr Reader*, ed. Donnelly, James & McLelland (Kirksville, MO: Truman State University Press, 1999), 167–72.

47. Gregory of Rome, Synod of Rome decrees, dist. 92, cap. *Cantantes* (PL 187, 429).

runs close to the idea of "expressive form" in Cassirer and Langer. Such modal aesthetics breaks through the premature closure of theories of art as "personal preference, dilly-dally trivia or adiaphora," and describes an area cleared for imaginative play.[48] The "symbolic form" of Cassirer sought to probe the "secondary meaning" of human artefacts, the forming of images with oblique meaning.[49] Seerveld attempts a further step, perceiving the allusive nature of the artwork as "one kind of real, functionally coherent way-of-being-there."

Let us consider[50] the way in which the medieval worldview was formed by visual images of proportionate beauty. Geometry was the "canon of proportion" or "true measure" in planning a cathedral. "With but a single basic dimension given, the Gothic architect developed all other magnitudes of his ground plan and elevation by strictly geometrical means, using as modules certain regular polygons, above all the square."[51] Indeed, Francesco di Giorgio developed a ground plan of a church corresponding to the proportions of the human figure, strikingly similar to the modular figure of Le Corbusier in our own day. Obviously the elegance and simplicity for which scientists seek in developing their models is not so new.

THE POETICS OF SPACE

An excursus on space or topoanalysis is called for. Suffice it to say that the recovery of *time* as a spatial dimension reminds us that we can no

---

48. C. Seerveld, "Modal Aesthetic Theory, Preliminary Questions with an Opening Hypothesis," in *Rainbows for the Fallen World* (Toronto: Tuppence Press, 1980) 131ff. Cf. Seerveld, *A Christian Critique of Art and Literature* (Toronto: Association for the Advancement of Christian Scholarship, 1977).

49. E. Cassirer, *An Essay on Man. An Introduction to a Philosophy of Human Culture* (New York: Doubelday Anchor Books, 1944), 92ff.

50. The original lecture used visual aids from this point on.

51. Otto von Simson, *The Gothic Cathedral* ("Origins of Gothic Architecture and the Medieval Concept of Order"), Bollingen Series 48/1962 (Princeton NJ: Princeton University Press, 1988) 14.

longer say simply that someone "is" without identifying the space-time location. Probably the French novelists and philosophers have pondered best this life-grid or interface that holds us. "Je suis ou je suis" (Noël Arnaud). To be is to remember where you are, not only what time it is but what time is, as Bergson and Proust showed. And if time moves us with it, through memory and hope we penetrate its shape, we discover its circularity. In that odd book *The Poetics of Space*, Gaston Bachelard has discussed "the phenomenology of roundness." For Van Gogh (as for Karl Jaspers), "Life is probably round."[52] For after all, in being-there, you cannot separate the *being* from its *there*. So perhaps this puzzle, this quest for roundness echoes the discovery of the new dimension, the participation in the common field of human being, of transcendence.

Henry Moore's sculptures are relevant. Moore does not explore or interpret the surface of the human body, or its skeletal form. He seeks a depth analysis of that "form" which participates in the creative mystery of Being. He is an image maker but his model is one whose depth is not the orderly bone and muscle that served the apprenticeship of Da Vinci and Michelangelo. Moore has been schooled in a discipline in which dissonance and disorderliness must find expression. For him the "negative spaces" are eloquent of true being, for non-being threatens us and the environing world has recovered its primitive mystery, its *mana-tabu* duality. Humanity will survive, and this *sur-vivre* is our unique measurement. So we move from gentle experiment with the mother-and-child motif beloved of Moore to those solid and recumbent figures that bend our seeing to their own elusive perspective.[53]

Cézanne, like the medievalists, accepted geometrical proportion; but unlike them he followed his imagination in constructing a world in which cube and cone were allowed free play, to heighten and to

---

52. Bachelard, *The Poetics of Space* (*Poétique de l'espace*) trans. Maria Jolas (Boston: Beacon Press, 1994).

53. Illustrated by his *"Three Piece Reclining Figure" (1961–62)* in front of the National Bank of Canada, Montreal, which I used to pass daily on my way to and from the Métro.

define. The problem—or mystery?—of perspective had concerned artists for centuries. The *Opticorum libri sex* of Francisco Aguiloni (1613) included seven illustrations by Peter Paul Rubens; one is a "geometrical analysis of the figure of Hercules." Here is the familiar blocked forms of analytical cubism.[54] Cézanne was liberating space; Picasso set time free also. Picasso's breakthrough—for artists as well as scientists, paradigm shift proves a traumatic experience and a personal crisis—was a structural one, in that he accepted the temporal relativism of perspective, and allowed all aspects of his subject to make themselves visible at once. Thus the "real" object, as distinct from that which inhabits our merely visual field, is on view. This attempt to disclose the depth or essence of things, showing their dynamism or energy, is the more remarkable when we think that his experimental manifesto, *Les Desmoiselles d'Avignon*, dates from 1907, when Max Planck's quantum theory was just stirring its major controversy, its paradigm crisis. Indeed one can see in the development from Impressionism to Cubism (Van Gogh's universe of radiant light and energy for example) a striking parallelism to the shift in scientific models then underway. Thus the method of abstraction and fragmentation was a way of penetrating the dimension of depth, not only accepting but welcoming the resulting distortion.

THE DREAM AND TRUTH OF PICASSO

Modern drama is said to have begun in 1950 with Beckett's *Waiting for Godot*—significant because his two clochards are "killing time." Similarly, modern painting began with Picasso's *Les Desmoiselles d'Avignon* (1907). Both the play and the painting are famous for their sparse lines, their reduction of objects to almost painful simplicity, their distortion of reality to convey more than meets the senses. More than any other painter, perhaps, Pablo Picasso embodies the turmoil of our times and

---

54. See M. Kemp, *The Science of Art: Optical themes in Western art from Brunelleschi to Seurat* (New Haven: Yale University Press, 1990), 101. The work is in London's Courtauld Institute, No. 427v.

the quest for ultimacy in a world without God, or a supposed Godot. In a series of cartoons he depicted Franco as a repulsive polyp; the title was "The Dream and Lie of Franco."

Picasso has been analyzed *ad nauseam*—his roots in primitive Iberian and African art, Fauvism and Surrealism, and of course the *corrida* (a late series of sketches features Tauromachy, with Christ as Matador). The point here is his Cubist method, the way it illustrates the nature of dimensionality. Put simply, cubism attempts to display round objects on flat surfaces, and even four-dimensional subjects/objects. We could call it "transcendental painting." Its origins include Cézanne and Seurat, van Gogh and Gauguin. As for the name, when Georges Braque's canvases submitted for the 1908 "Show of Independent Artists" were rejected, Henri Matisse was on the jury and described them as "entirely constructed of little cubes." In 1907 Picasso began work on a canvas called "the first Cubist painting." Of his new style he said, "In my case a picture is a sum of destructions."[55] The notorious *Desmoiselles* exhibits dissonance—incompatibility—within its own frame, the three figures on the left showing Iberian motifs, the two on the right, African, not to mention the simultaneous back and front poses. Later paintings show a developing abstraction; one might compare his two portraits of Ambroise Vollard his agent, one "straight" and one cubist, to see his deconstructive intention.

Picasso challenges our way of seeing. Apollinaire termed his work "mystical naturalism," since "everything enchants him."[56] Recall Thomas Kuhn—learning "to see a new gestalt . . . a revolutionary transformation of vision?" Here we are again—it's not simply depicting three dimensions in two, otherwise plastic arts would do a better job, though Henry Moore shows that this is far from simple. Picasso is after that *in-seeing* praised by Rimbaud, or what Origen of Alexandria called "enoptics." One might say: *one eye for sight, two for depth,*

---

55. Quoted in *Picasso and the Cubists* (New York: Jupiter Art Library, n.d.), 5.

56. *Apollinaire on Art* (New York: Viking Press, 1972), 13.

three for in-sight. "Third-eye theology" (C. S. Song) is not only Eastern, particularly in Buddhism, but Western too. This shift in modalities is hindered by the dominance of ocular imagery in Western epistemology, which has privileged simple optics at the cost of audition. We note Franz Rosenzweig as a leading dissenter here: his "speech-thinking" challenges traditional formal logic, its insight deriving from the Jewish-Christian dialogue to which he was committed, as well as his passion for the poetry of Judah ha-Levi.[57] A related movement was that of the Patmos Circle, with which Barth was associated, and Martin Buber in particular. We might say: seeing as such is never believing, but hearing puts us in the picture.[58]

It has been said, "Picasso makes us see." He himself has stated: "Nature and art are two different things. In art we express our conception of what is not visible in nature." Jacques Derrida has fastened on the phenomenology of sight, quoting Picasso: "Painting is a blind man's profession. He paints not what he sees, but what he feels, what he tells himself about what he has seen." Derrida comments, "*Idein, eidos, idea*: the whole history, the whole semantics of the European idea, in its Greek genealogy, as we know—as we see—relates seeing to knowing."[59] For instance, it took decades before astronomers could begin to "see" the planet Uranus, because their accepted paradigm could admit only star or comet. They weren't truly seeing what they were looking at. Is it a similar case with our God-models? If so, then we need self-critical experimentation, in the cubist style, until we learn to see through the pictures to That which lies waiting in their depths.

---

57. See *Franz Rosenzweig's "The New Thinking,"* ed. & trans. by Barbara Galli (Syracuse, New York: Syracuse University Press, 1999).

58. See H. Stahmer, *"Speak That I May See Thee!"* (New York: Macmillan, 1968), 121ff.

59. Derrida, *Memoirs of the Blind* (Chicago: University of Chicago Press, 1993), 12; *Picasso on art: a selection of his views,* compiled by Dore Ashton (New York: Viking Press, 1972).

So, through analytic cubism to synthetic, and beyond to surrealism and abstraction, but always an exploration of the depth in human being, the field of relations that make him lover or victim or clown or matador or dancer—Picasso surely guides us in the art of paradigm shift, the aesthetic model which discloses authentic human being. His subjects range from *commedia dell'arte* to victims of modern warfare in Guernica and Korea. He uses the "lies" of art to unmask the truth about human being, about being human. The *Guernica's* tortured figures, both human and animal, mount an apocalyptic protest at the bombing of the Basque town as modern Fascism came to power. Of this work he said, "The bull is not Fascism, but it is brutality and darkness . . . the *Guernica* mural is symbolic . . . allegoric . . . The mural is for the definite expression and resolution of a problem, and that is why I used symbolism."[60] Such protest led Paul Tillich to call it "a great Protestant painting . . . not the Protestant answer, but rather the radicalism of the Protestant question which one can find in Picasso's masterpiece."[61] Perhaps the true significance of Picasso is his grasp of the *brokenness* of human being—in both laughter and tears we "break up," as his portrait "Weeping Woman" shows so vividly. And in the broken and tortured images of *Guernica* we see the dreadful destructive power of evil: a grayish world, lightened only with a passing glance and a meager lantern.

REMAKING REALITY

If there is a moral to this collage of word and picture, of science and art, it is that analogue models are by nature tentative, in flux, ever in search of new truth. Whether we learn from this something about revelation, about divine-human engagement, about a critique of our ideas

---

60. Quoted in T. Hilton, *Picasso* (New York: Oxford University Press, 1975), 241.

61. Tillich, "Protestantism and Artistic Style," in *Theology of Culture* (New York: Oxford University Press, 1964), 48.

of God, will depend on several things. In this chapter we have isolated only a few, chiefly implicit, ways in which doctrine resembles aesthetic modes—they could suggest a study of theological models in terms of the scale/analogue distinction, or the paradigm shift category, or perhaps even, thanks to Picasso, the question: is this or that doctrine classical, baroque, cubist or abstract?

If we take the Christian doctrine of the Trinity as a case study, we may see the point of the above sketch of the function of analogue models. The idea of God as tri-unity is under a constant temptation to be taken as a scale model, constricted within the logic appropriate to determinate dimensions and interpreted as an authentic and absolute picture of what God "really *is*." Yet was it not, in the Patristic period at least, a breakthrough paradigm necessitated by the anomalies of that special case, Jesus of Nazareth? And did it not precipitate a crisis in that it postulated a historical drama as analogue for what God "really is *like*"? Is not there a perennial warning in that beautiful theme of Byzantine theology ever since Origen and the Cappadocians, that every cataphatic statement is a kind of parenthesis within the ultimate apophatic context of God-talk?[62]

The analogy with Cubism is apt: the Tri-unity as cube *in re* is apprehensible only in distorted perspective *in intellectu*. Even the simpler triangle offers modalities in which the ratio of hypotenuse to longer and shorter sides recalls the subtle teaching on subordination and procession. Similar analogies could be drawn from mathematics, where exponential numbers allow a descent to roots, the fundamentum, including "radical" deity. Irrational numbers, like most square roots, and complex numbers which involve imaginary parts, remind us that in this most esoteric discipline, which is also the most reliable, our mental journey involves necessary distortion. Whenever "infinity" is on view (Origen considered this a fruitless subject for meditation) we fall into *aporia*, put classically by Zeno, whose paradoxes can never be terminated. But aporetics are not solved by saying that Achilles and the tortoise simply converge in the

---

62. See Chapter 8 below on "Nicene Theology."

finite. The theoretical point is to make us aware that everything that rises, or extends, does not converge, that there is an endless number of endlessnesses, as Georg Cantor's theory of "transfinite numbers" holds. There is Mystery, witnessed to analogically in metamathematics. Heinrich Scholz, author of *Mathesis Universalis*, declared that "natural numbers reflect the good God; all else is human work."[63] The Romantic poet Novalis has a beautiful insight about the perpetual play of threefold infinity, a parenthesis in a mathematical fragment: "God is sometimes $1 \times \infty$, sometimes $1/\infty$, sometimes 0." In the first two, Barth states, "is contained the whole ideology of Romanticism, while 'sometimes 0' contains its problem."[64]

THE SUR-REAL AND THE SUPER-NATURAL

What does an artwork *signify*? Is the *Kunstwerk* worthy of Heidegger's confidence in its revelatory power, a sort of aesthetic *a-letheia*? Does it show its own "world of the text" as Gadamer and Ricoeur contend? And is there some correlation or compatibility between artwork and human knowledge of transcendence? If so, analogies from this field of human endeavour might function better than the complex and ambiguous scientific analogies noted above. Before looking at Surrealism we should note the stream of similar forms of literature and art. Flannery O'Connor's grotesques are a good example. She once remarked that we regard evil as grotesque ("unnatural") but must learn to see good in the same way, since "in us the good is something under construction."[65] Thus her "saints" are fanatics, prophets burdened by truth. As *Kulturkritik*, Colin Falck provides a salutary challenge by inviting us to

---

63. Scholz, *Der Gottesgedanke in der Mathematik* (1934), 293ff. He contrasts God's gifts with human works.
64. K. Barth, *Protestant Theology in the Nineteenth Century*, 363. This relates to Isaac Asimov's remark that "Infinity is not an integer . . . It is a quality, the quality of endlessness."—*Adding a Dimension* (New York: Lancer Books, 1969), 40.
65. Flannery O'Connor, Introduction to *A Memoir of Mary Ann*, 1961.

re-consider Romanticism as heir to the search for Transcendence: the proper "scriptures" authentic for our time "may be the poetry or literature to which our own culture gives us access."[66] Nietzsche may have been correct in discerning that Greek religion ultimately sublimated the Dionysian within the Apollonian, but the real "tragedy" lay in the suppression of the Dionysian *élan* in subsequent ages. Blake sought to raise awareness to "perceive the infinite," but when the Infinite has landed, so to speak, transcendence is in jeopardy: "This *is* my body." Reason and fantasy need each other like lovers.

The movement called Surrealism (its initial exhibition was 1925 in Paris) makes a similar point about in-seeing and aesthetics. Picasso never joined the group, although he shared in some of their exhibitions and wrote poetry on their (automatic writing) principles. The idea of *sur-réalité* owes most of its conceptual formulation to André Breton and Apollinaire. It was the latter who first used the name—in program notes to Diaghilev's ballet *Parade*, with music by Erik Satie, decor and costumes by Picasso![67] Apollinaire drew on recently revived traditions, notably Hermeticism and Orphic *surnaturalisme* to develop an iconography influential on the Parisian circle.[68] Its original spokesman, André Breton, stated its creed: "I believe in the future resolution of these two states of dream and reality, seemingly so contradictory, in a sort of absolute reality, of surreality." He declared "the omnipotence of the dream in the free-wheeling play of thought," but qualified this by adding that some "control by reason" is in order regarding the products of the imagination.[69] Dreaming was important, guided by Freud, with his

---

66. Colin Falck, *Myth, Truth and Literature: Towards a true post-modernism* (Cambridge: Cambridge University Press, 1993), xvi.

67. He wrote of "a kind of surrealism, which I consider to be the point of departure for a whole series of manifestations of the New Spirit that is making itself felt today" (*Apollinaire on Art*), 452.

68. A. Hicken, *Apollinaire, Cubism and Orphism* (Burlington, VT: Ashgate, 2002). Iris Murdoch remarked that under Breton Surrealism became "a curious revolutionary enterprise." (*Sartre*, 345).

69. Breton, *Manifesto*, 1925, in Ferdinand Alquié, *The Philosophy of Sur-*

DOGMA AND ICON

interest in the Uncanny (*unheimlich*). Oscar Dominguez produced a set of surreal playing-cards, with the suit of spades named "dreams" and its master card "Freud, Magus of Dreams."[70] Nietzsche thought dreams significant for understanding the work of the Dionysian imagination, and cited Wagner's Hans Sachs, *die Meistersinger*: "this is the poet's task, to mark his dreams and interpret them."[71]

Surrealism seeks the free play of thought, approaching the dream-state. It thus shifts modalities from "clear and distinct ideas" to "psychic automatism," invoking images of juxtaposition, puzzles and palindromes, biomorphic shapes. They are disturbing, shocking— none more so than on film, notably the "shock-montage" of *Un Chien Andalou* (1928) of Luis Buñuel and Salvador Dali, with its gripping opening scene of a razor slicing an eye.[72] Dali, while differing from Picasso politically, was a master of the surreal mode; his canvases are mystifying, teasing, playful. They symbolize not just a distance from classical tradition but the shift in modalities we are discussing. Goya understood clearly that "the sleep of reason brings forth monsters."[73]

A similar play on infinity and closure is offered by that intriguing book *Gödel, Escher, Bach*. Gödel's indeterminacy, Escher's infinity, Bach's fugue—all display the profile of the surreal. (A fugue is a segue with attitude). All three, attending to such different subjects, converge in their knowledge of the limits of human experience and knowledge, and at this edge they lead us to peer into the abyss where

---

realism (University of Michigan, 1969), 179.

70. Celia Rabinovich, "The Surreal and the Sacred: Archaic, Occult and Demonic Elements in Modern Art, 1914–1940," McGill Ph.D. thesis, 1984, unpublished.

71. "das grad'ist Dichters Werk, dass er sein Träumen deut' und merk'"— Nietzsche, *The Birth of Tragedy*, I.

72. See U. M. Schneede, *Surrealism* (NY: Harry N. Abrams, 1974), "Films —The Principle of Shock—Montage," 38ff.

73. "El sueño de la razon produce monstruos," in the series *Disasters of War*. Cf. the Compline hymn *Te lucis ante*: "Let dreams depart and phantoms fly, / The offspring of the night."

authentic sight—*theōria*—recovers the mystery of being. A striking instance is afforded in the case of Bach. Whereas Mozart died in 1791 while composing his great and incomplete Mass, in the middle of the movement *Lacrimosa dies illa*, for Bach it is his "Art of the Fugue" that ends the chase dramatically. Its last page has a note by his son C.P.E.: "N.B. In the course of this fugue, at the point where the name B.A.C.H. was brought in as countersubject, the composer died."[74] Let every player tremble at this bizarre example of closure!

---

74. Douglas R. Hofstadter, *Gödel, Escher, Bach: an eternal golden braid* (New York: Vintage Books, 1980), 80.

7

COMPARING THE INCOMPARABLE

Modalities of Knowing and Being

> *I call this a society of explorers. In a society of explorers man is in thought.*
> — Michael Polanyi[1]

If we are to be or become *Savants*, we must act as explorers, ever searching for the magnetic pole that attracts our mental compass. Humanists too are driven by heuristic models—all the more so in religious studies, where our subject involves ideas of transcendence. In this chapter I raise two questions. One is whether the categories under which our "normal" study of religion proceeds, particularly the *compatible*, the *commensurable* and the *comparable*, are stronger than the modality of their opposites: the incompatible, the incommensurable, the incomparable (the happy ambiguity of the last term should not be missed). I ask also whether it is valid to argue that some form of "unitary field laws" applies in religion as in science. I trust the result

---

1. *The Tacit Dimension* (New York: Anchor Books, 1967), 83.

will assist our interdisciplinary task of religious studies.

CATEGORY MISTAKES

Today's central issue of "pluralism" refers to the situation in which various cultural and religious traditions cohabit the same space. This has always been true of global history, of course; Jaroslav Pelikan illustrates how the problem of "finality *versus* universality" concerned Christians from earliest times. His case-studies from the third century (Tertullian to Eusebius) show the understanding of finality as *eschaton* and of universality as *imperium*.[2] In recent decades, however, particularly since 1945, the issue has moved into more general consciousness, and not only for Christians. The topic is well explored by now, and the resulting dialogue among world religions. For instance, Hilary Putnam sees relativism as having failed, and offers a "transcendental" argument, that rationality is transcultural.[3]

Comparative study is based on the assumption that there is a unified field called Religion, a genus to which world religions belong as species, and that we can formulate universalizable propositions about it. A famous statement of the case was F.C.S. Northrop's *The Meeting of East and West* (1946), in which a "grand synthesis" is possible once you determine the most abstract principles of a culture, then deduce details. Some dissenting voices may be heard, not least Antonio Gualtieri and Willard Oxtoby.[4] Before them, Wilfred Cantwell Smith had cautioned us to take care in drawing comparisons—e.g. is the Qur'an comparable to the Christian Bible, or Muhammad to Jesus? (No and no: the Qur'an is like the Christ, and Muhammad like Paul). Moreover, Smith's early

---

2. J. Pelikan, *The Finality of Christ in an Age of Universal History* (Richmond, VA: John Knox Press, 1965), 6.

3. Putnam, *Reason, Truth and History* (Cambridge University Pres, 1981) in Owen C. Thomas, "Religious Plurality and Contemporary Philosophy: a Critical Survey," in *HTR* v. 87 (April 1994), 200f.

4. A. Gualtieri, "What is Comparative Religion Comparing?" in *JSSR* (1967) VI/1; W. Oxtoby, "*Religionswissenschaft* Revisited" in *Numen* 1967.

principle remains fundamental: "that the study of religion is the study of persons."⁵ This alerts us to the danger in our analytic of religious data, namely that where these are conceptual or abstract, we are apt to reify and codify and so to betray the human subject of study. Our method must steer between the poles of *an objectivity that distorts* and *a subjectivity that coerces*.

Our present question concerns the very theory of universal theory, the thesis that we can refer religious data to a theoretical or abstract unity called Religion—or religious experience, God-consciousness, etc. Recall Wilfred Smith's view that "theology" is one; it may be pursued by Christians and others but cannot be "Christian theology" except in a secondary meaning. That is, various individuals and groups may "do" theology from their perspectives; it is natural for each devotee to claim an absolute role for a certain deity or Idea; comparing such existential roles, however, is best done by seeking to articulate a "world theology" embracing the "ultimate concern" of all. Such is the reasoning of scholars such as Smith, Leonard Swidler, John Hick and Ninian Smart. But Masao Abe puts the critical question starkly: "There is no common denominator for world religions;" he qualifies it by asking about "the positive meaning of this negative statement."⁶ He thinks that both positive and negative answers imply a false dualism which must be overcome in favour of a *neither-nor* position: "nondualistic unity thoroughly allows the distinctiveness or uniqueness of each religion without any limitation—through the realization of 'zero' or emptiness."

The debate on pluralism suffers, I believe, from some category mistakes concerning the nature of the comparable. G. E. Moore warned

---

5. Smith, "Comparative Religion: Whither—and Why?" In Eliade & Kitagawa, eds., *The History of Religions* (Chicago: University of Chicago Press, 1959), 34.

6. "'There is no common denominator for world religions:' the positive meaning of this negative statement," *Journal of Ecumenical Studies* 26:1 (1989), 72–81.

us that "good" is indefinable, like "yellow:" it is a quality that the world has, independent of its being known.[7] This sort of modern Cambridge Platonism opposes naturalism in value-theory; it also suggests that indefinables object themselves to our apprehension in ways that defy simple comparison or categorization. In religious studies it seems easy to move from absolutism to relativism: all religious phenomena are comparable, given their categorization as concepts of or ways to the Absolute. Look at the three terms mentioned above. "Commensurable" (Latin *commetior/ mensus*) means to measure by some standard; "compatible" (*compati*; cf. *compassio*) means to feel pity, hence of like feeling; "comparable" (*comparo*) means to put together, hence sharing characteristics. The negative of all three indicates lack of common standard—of measurement, affection or characteristic. "Incomparable" has, of course, a secondary meaning of beyond comparison and therefore peerless. George Lindbeck uses the term "unsurpassability" to make the point.[8] The conundrum of comparativism is part of the heritage of Modernism, as is clear from its thesis on justice, for instance. The question of "Whose Justice?" as formulated by Alisdair MacIntyre is taken up by John Rawls as part of the problem of pluralism.[9] Rawls wishes to replace the dominant (Kantian) solution of a common rational consensus by the criterion of "reasonableness," in turn queried by Charles Taylor as assuming a "liberal" orientation.[10] Must justice, too, suffer the uncertainty of postmodern relativism?

Thus mere definition tells us that while such data show themselves to have—or else we assume or judge there to be—something in common, it also warns us that the terms are not thereby identical. In comparing two

---

7. G.E. Moore, *Principia Ethica* (1903).

8. George Lindbeck, *The Nature of Doctrine* (Philadelphia: Westminster Press, 1984) 3: "Many Religions and the One True Faith," 46ff.

9. A. MacIntyre, *Whose Justice? Which Rationality?* (Notre Dame, IN: University of Notre Dame Press, 1988) J. Rawls, *Political Liberalism* (New York: Columbia University Press, 1993).

10. C. Taylor, "Justice After Virtue," in *After MacIntyre: Critical Perspectives on the Work of Alisdair MacIntyre*, ed. J. Horton and S. Mendus (Notre Dame, IN: Notre Dame University Press, 1994).

religions, for instance, what is incommensurable may be compatible, as we will see in Panikkar's analysis. We may take as an example: Christianity begins with original sin, and Buddhism with "original suffering" as it were; these seem to lack common measure, yet this does not prevent common feeling for the human condition. Hans Küng presses this point to posit a common feeling for "Humanum" as what remains essential for all cultures.[11] Again, if "salvation" is taken as measure, the claims of Jesus as the Christ on the one hand and Krishna as the Lord on the other may be commensurable and therefore incompatible.[12] That is, how is the Christian to understand *bhakti* and *moksa*?

In all comparison or analogical reasoning, one begins from a hunch or expectation, the Stoic *prolêpsis*. All theology faces a dilemma—both Greek and Christian pursued theology through the middle way of *the concept of analogy* in steering between affirmation and negation, anthropomorphism and agnosticism. The dilemma is: "G-d" is completely incommensurable with the created order, and therefore *beyond* every human attribute; yet religious language ascribes to God intelligence, will and even emotion. Such attribution can be neither univocal nor simply equivocal. Analogies of attribution compare terms, analogies of proportionality compare relations. Both move beyond simple constructs (A:B::A:C) to posit a similarity of proportion (A:B::C:D), that is, the modes of attribution on both sides enjoy *a likeness of relation*. The problem with analogy is getting started. Some metaphysical structure must be in place to provide the terms and relations in the first place—*analogia entis* or *analogia fidei* for instance. While theological formulae may be enlightened through analogical predication, we lack the confidence of former generations in such movement between creation and Creator, or finite and infinite. This is a chief reason why

---

11. H. Küng, "The *Humanum* as a General Ethical Criterion," in Swidler, *Towards a Universal Theory*, 239ff.

12. See Ninian Smart on such incompatibility: "Truth and Religions" in John Hick, ed. *Truth and Dialogue in World Religions: Conflicting Truth Claims* (Philadelphia: Westminster, 74), 50ff.

analogy has become displaced by "the rule of metaphor" these days. We resort to more imaginative and more tentative ways of attribution

A CAVEAT FROM KARL BARTH

Karl Barth advanced an unpopular thesis: "The Revelation of God as the Abolition of Religion." He sees revelation as "the judging but also reconciling presence of God in the world of human religion, that is, in the realm of man's attempts to justify and to sanctify himself before a capricious and arbitrary picture of God." In short, "religion is unbelief . . . the one great concern of godless man . . . He does not believe. If he did, he would listen; but in religion he talks . . . in religion he takes something for himself . . . he ventures to grasp at God."[13] Now this does not mean that the Christian religion as such is "the fulfilled nature of human religion," for divine revelation is a judgment on *all* religion. "Religion is always self-contradictory and impossible *per se* . . . Therefore revelation denies that any religion is true . . . it can become true only in the way in which man is justified, from without . . . " And this applies equally, for "whatever we said about the other religions affected the Christian similarly." It too, "stands under the judgment that religion is unbelief, and that it is not acquitted by any inward worthiness, but only by the grace of God, proclaimed and effectual in His revelation."[14] Thus Christianity is also "relativised," dependent on divine grace for its faith.

What are we to make of this strange thesis? It is not exclusivist since it includes Christianity among the religions being denounced. Indeed, Barth is clear that one cannot make a sacred/secular distinction, since all we have is "non-religious language" so that "the Christian community . . . cannot, then, escape being secular."[15] He also warns that one may be deceived when "he adjudges his fellow man a non-Christian," a statement akin to Rahner's concept of the "anonymous Christian." We have judged

---

13. Barth, *C.D.* I.2, §17, 280–361, esp. "2. Religion as Unbelief," 297ff.
14. *Ibid.*, 302, 325.
15. *C.D.* IV/3.2 (1962) 735.

that view to be implicitly exclusivist, but with Barth it reflects his caution about any sort of pride, his critique of Christianity itself as not even the "true religion," but only a witness to a Gospel beyond all religiosity.[16]

Barth admits as "the most adequate and illuminating heathen parallel to Christianity . . . the two related Buddhist developments in 12th and 13th century Japan," namely Yodo-Shin & Yodo-Shin-Shu. (He does not consider Bhakti as so significant).[17] "It is only the 'Japanese Protestantism' of Genku and Shinran which calls for serious consideration." Whatever we may think of this modest venture into comparative religion, we should note that Barth's definition of religion flows logically from his rejection of natural theology, while his concept of divine revelation demands a different approach to the question of Christian exclusiveness. M.M. Thomas has noted the similarity in Iqbal to Barth, as well as to Bonhoeffer"s "religionless Christianity:" "In Islam prophecy reaches its perfection in discovering the need of its own abolition."[18] Here again, Wilfred Smith's idea of the ambivalent "end" of religion proves relevant too. For "a task of the modern religious reformer is to help men not to let their religion stand between them and God." Smith cites Barth (along with Brunner, Tillich and others) as supporters of his own thesis that the concept "religion" is inadequate and misleading. God "does not reveal a religion, He reveals Himself; what the observer calls a religion is man's continuing response . . . The observer sees the movement; the participant sees what it signifies."[19]

---

16. CD IV/3.1 (1961) 365.

17. *Ibid.*, 340ff. Writing in 1948, Barth acknowledges (281) that he is following Chantepie de Saussaye's *Lehrbuch der Religiongeschichte* (1925).

18. M.M. Thomas, *Man and the Universe of Faiths* (Madras: Christian Literature Society, 1975), 107f.

19. W.C. Smith, *The Meaning and End of Religion* (New York: The Macmillan Co., 1962), 129. See 125, 302ff for his positive response to Barth.

PLURALISM WITHOUT RELATIVISM

WHAT TO COMPARE?

Comparison, therefore, is a risky business, especially in our scientific age. Extreme caution is required in comparing "science and religion," drawing parallels in method or theory between disciplines such as physics and religious studies. We have already discussed the notorious "paradigm shift" described by Thomas Kuhn as a phenomenon in the history of science. Note was taken above of the important symposium edited by Hans Küng and David Tracy which applies it to the history of theology; our critique argued that the examples from church history are not paradigm shifts at all, but merely shifts within the Incarnational paradigm of Christian theology. By "paradigm shift" Kuhn means that "normal science" undergoes crisis when a new way of seeing is breaking through, entailing "revolutions as changes of world view." Similarly, those who advance "parallels" and "relationships" between science and religion may be guilty of the fallacy of misplaced concreteness (Whitehead)—or of "misplaced abstractness"?

A properly Copernican shift would qualify the trinitarian paradigm itself: e.g. must the Nicene-Constantinopolitan creedal interpretation of the scriptural data remain normative? Could not some "heretical" christology prove complementary? What of the "anti-Nicene" stance developed by Radical Reformers in the 16thC, preferring an "ante-Nicene" softer christology that avoids the Middle Platonic categories of subsequent development of doctrine? What of the "pneumatic" christology recently explored by David Newman and others?[20] Are such models capable of being developed into genuine paradigms to displace and to limit the orthodox paradigm of classical theism?

The confident, even sometimes arrogant, quest for unified theory is predominantly Western. Certainly it is popular these days to develop comparisons between Western physics and Eastern mysticism. Our students love books with titles such as *The Tao of Physics* or *The Dancing*

---

20. See the next Chapter.

Wu-Li Masters.[21] For such works, the "new physics" and the mystical East meet like longlost lovers. To be sure, there are formulations in Chinese, Hindu and Buddhist religions that echo the dynamism of 20thC physics, with its relations, energies and quantum leaps. (I remember when it was fashionable to ridicule the "mysterious universe" of Sir James Jeans.) The monumental work of Joseph Needham observed something the same without claiming as much, although physicist David Bohm saw the world as a unified Whole, and related this explicitly to the teaching of Jiddu Krishnamurti.[22]

Raimundo Panikkar has raised important objections against a universal theory of religion.[23] He sees the enterprise as the product of a specific anthropology and metaphysics, rooted in a "Western syndrome," a drive towards universality in physics and religion and politics. This assumes that the true and the best are identical, and must be exportable, *universalizable*. "The 'once and for all' of the Christian event (see Heb. 7:27) and its claim to universality are perhaps the clearest manifestation of this spirit." Against the domination of *logos* he sees pluralism as entailing "the dethronement of reason and the abandonment of the monotheistic paradigm." Pluralism arises "when we are confronted with mutually irreconcilable worldviews or ultimate systems of thought and life." He distinguishes *relativism*, which destroys itself in its very affirmation, and *relativity*: Truth is essentially relational and cannot be ab-solute. Panikkar's alternative is a "cosmic confidence in reality" recognizing a dimension incommensurable

---

21. Frithjof Capra, *The Tao of Physics: an Exploration of the Parallels between Modern Physics and Eastern Mysticism* (NY: Bantam Books, 1977); G. Zukar, *The Dancing Wu-Li Masters: an overview of the new physics* (NY: Perennial Classics, 2001).

22. J. Needham, *Science and Civilization in China* (Cambridge: Cambridge University Press, 1954), 6 vols. David Bohm, *Causality and Chance in Modern Physics* (London: Routledge & Kegan Paul, 1957).

23. R. Panikkar, "The Invisible Harmony: a Universal Theory of Religion or a Cosmic Confidence in Reality?" in L. Swidler, ed. *Toward a Universal Theory of Religion* (Maryknoll, NY: Orbis Books, 1987), 118ff.

with *logos*. This involves a softer form of comparison, "homeomorphic equivalents." He notes cogently that "Religions may be incommensurable with each other despite some possible common traits." But this does not preclude one religion's being "a dimension of the other in a kind of trinitarian *perichoresis* or *circumincessio*."[24] The latter is a significant advance in revising classical theism, extrapolating intratrinitarian relationships to include other theologies.

One of Panikkar's examples is this: "Brahman" and "God" have similar functions but not meanings in their respective universes [sic] of discourse. We cannot compare, but we may "impare" to use his neologism. Such an "imparative" method resembles the search for isomorphic resemblances in scientific models. His conclusion is that a "concordant discord" (offstage voices of Heraclitus, and now Zaehner) must replace universal theory. Stanley Samartha has also noted the ambivalence in Hindu theology. He thinks that Brahman as *sat-cit-ānanda* and the concept of a triune God "could be regarded as two responses to the same Mystery in two cultural settings." But he warns that "One cannot be used as a norm to judge the other."[25]

Respondents to Panikkar's thesis in the Swidler symposium include Bibhuti Yadav, offering a critique from the Buddhist stance of Chandrakirti. The latter was "obsessed with the measurability principle" and committed to rational logic: "a methodology of arriving empirically at universal propositions . . . celebrating the virtues of objectivity and self-criticism." He has "no theory of reality and no methodology of arriving at universally true propositions."[26] This caveat from India rejects Panikkar's starting-point as merely Western guilt-complex (irony: Panikkar accuses the drive for universalisability as "Western"), yet indirectly acknowledges

---

24. Panikkar, "The Jordan, the Tiber, and the Ganges," in *The Myth of Christian Uniqueness*, 112.

25. S.J. Samartha, "The Cross and the Rainbow," *The Myth of Christian Uniqueness*, 76.

26. Bibuhti S. Yadav, "Anthropomorphism and Cosmic Confidence," in Swidler, *Towards a Universal Theory.*, 175ff.

his point that universality is hardly possible in face of such theoretical negation.

Peter Slater has made a significant contribution, first by analysis of George Lindbeck and John Hick, then by citing the work of the Kyoto school (e.g. Kitaro Nishida and Masao Abe), heir to the Nishida-Tanabe philosophy which posited an original "pure experience" as perspective. The latter insists on ultimate non-dualism, leading to what Slater terms a "cognitive pluralism." This is a move beyond the two Christian theologians' sort of pluralism to denote the "background of meaning whereby we know that different religious language-games are religious." If praxis or commitment forms a test of authenticity, as Lindbeck and Hick assert, then we need "more than ontological coherence theories and epistemological correspondence theories if we are to do justice to the liberating visions which inform authentic religious developments, within and across the boundaries of space and time."[27] We are reminded here of Mark Heim's view noted earlier, that there may be a "practical incompatibility," deriving from two valid testimonies to "different conditions of religious fulfilment."[28] Thus the question of unifying theory remains open.

FROM GUT TO TOE: PROBLEMS WITH UNIVERSAL THEORY

The thesis at play here is the question, *Can we assume that a universal theory is possible?* In science the debate on this issue continues. Ever since Plato, western thought has sought the One behind the Many. Plato attempted a synthesis of Parmenides and Heraclitus in ontology, much as Kant attempted to unite Descartes and Hume in epistemology. Hegel was not the first to subsume everything under a System. Middle and Neo-Platonists tried it, as did Church Fathers, Scholastics, Renaissance and Reformation heroes and villains. Whether in the guise

---

27. P. Slater, "Towards a responsive theology of religions," *SR* 6/5 (1976).
28. Heim, "Many True Religions."

of philosophy of history (the Renaissance "Polybian norm" of objective truth) or of metaphysics ("ontotheology"), the grand designs and chains of being share one significant notion: they all *assume* that a unifying theory is possible.

The notorious example of the formulation of Laplace some two centuries ago is a warning: the method of an impersonal science can provide universal knowledge, provided an intelligence knew "all the forces by which nature is animated and the respective positions of the entities which compose it . . . nothing would be uncertain for it, and the future, like the past, would be present to its eyes."[29] Related to this issue is the nature of theory itself. The "observational vocabulary" privileged in scientific theorizing must be severely qualified by what Carl Hempel calls "*hypothetical, or theoretical, entities,* i.e., presumptive objects, events, and attributes which cannot be perceived or otherwise directly observed by us."[30] He concludes that observable terms are not sufficient for inductive systematisation; the "theoretician's dilemma" is that if he attempts to make do with observables only, he "starts with a false premise." The movement toward more general theory, in either science or religious studies, must acknowledge this mixture of induction and deduction, observation and interpretation.

Modern names from Einstein to Hawking show that philosophers of science assume a Grand Unified Theory (GUT) or Theory of Everything (TOE) to be possible, and work towards it. Einstein embarked on the quest for unified theory as soon as his General Theory was completed, publishing a preliminary paper extending his mathematical foundations to the electromagnetic field in 1923. By 1928 his wife could write, "He has solved the problem whose solution was the dream of his life." But it became more like the nightmare of his final years as colleagues such as Niels Bohr argued that quanta are governed by mere probability, and that

---

29. See M. Polanyi, *Personal Knowledge*, 139ff.
30. Hempel, "The Theoretician's Dilemma," in D. Shapere, *Philosophical Problems of Natural Science* (New York: Macmillan, 1965) 34.

faith in some deeper level of unity is a chimera.[31] Other dissenters reject the assumption on behalf of the growing edge of science itself. One need mention only the name of Karl Popper, who warns that experience yields singular, not universal, statements, and that the advance of empirical science cannot be logically mapped or replicated.[32]

The question for us is whether this scientific debate supplies a valid analogy in religious studies. Its data are the four elemental forces hypothetically split by the Big Bang and now in need of a unifying theory of explanation. So far the gravitational and electromagnetic fields are linked, but attempts to subsume the third "weak" force have failed, while a fourfold unification to include the "strong" force seems even more remote. Current speculations on "supersymmetry" and "superstring" reinforce the multidimensional nature of our universe, but are more interesting than productive. Data from chaos theory also question the assumption. It refers to the unstable behaviour of nonlinear dynamical systems, ignored while determinism held sway in philosophy of science. It calls for open possibilities, for synchronic rather than diachronic approach, in short for theoretical denial of unified theory. Whether chaos theory (an oxymoron?) is relevant remains moot. F.L. Shults has argued that "the new science of chaos" which examines the universal nature of systems sits well with the idea of contingency in terms of God's relation to the world. He argues that "systems that appear disorderly may be explained by higher forms of order," offering an analogy to theology's reflection on the ultimate rationality behind the order of the universe."[33]

Classical science relied on axioms or *principia* that knew where to start and where to end. This produced the *quaestio* as the way formal logic, with the art of distinguishing (*ars diiudicandi*) operating in

---

31. R. W. Clark, *Einstein: the life and times* (New York: World Publishing Co., 1971), 404ff.
32. K. Popper, *The Logic of Scientific Discovery* (New York: Harper, 1968).
33. F. LeRon Shults, "A Theology of Chaos: An Experiment in Postmodern Theological Science," *SJT* Vol. 45, 223ff.

solving problems. But modern physics is seized with the problem of "the logic of discovery," the heuristic model that expects novelty, discontinuous with past knowledge. This art of discovery (*ars inveniendi*) no longer assumes that we know what something is (*quid sit?*); our first question is always "what's it like?" (*quale sit?*)—not quiddity but quality.

KNOWING ABOUT KNOWING

Aristotle outlined formal logic with precision, but he also acknowledged symbolic logic, the unchartable waters of "If." Consider, for example, his distinction between demonstration and dialectic, with syllogism as logical instrument for the former and enthymeme for the latter.[34] Here is a distinction *within reasoning* that contradicts every superficial rationalism, alerting us to the complexity of decision-making—the ultimate test of freedom and selfhood. "The starting-point of demonstration is not demonstration."[35] Everything depends on where we begin: either axiom or leap.

Aristotle's ten predicaments or categories identify the elements of composite statements. Immanuel Kant's table of twelve categories is also intended to describe the "pure conceptions of the understanding," the *a prioris* of all possible judgments and so the stuff of "universalizable" propositions.[36] Our major question obviously requires an accounting of their claim to universality—"the forms in which the mind grasps and shapes reality."[37] Maurice Boutin has argued that the very question of divine "existence" needs to be brought under a threefold logic: of perfection, causation and eventuality, in order to explore these variant modalities of knowing.[38]

---

34. Aristotle, *Top.* I.1,100a27ff, *Rhet.* II.21.
35. *Meta.* IV.5,1011a8ff.
36. Aristotle, *Categ.* 4, *Topics* I.9; Kant, *Critique of Pure Reason*, B106.
37. P. Tillich, *ST* 1, 192.
38. M. Boutin, "Conceiving the Invisible," in *The Three Loves*, 2ff. Boutin examines Kant's Table of Categories in 4ff, "Existence and Reality."

Like many things, our "modern" epistemology was anticipated by premodern modernities. Take the radical realist Duns Scotus. The Thomist system had operated on the virtual identity of knowing and being—as Hegel would later agree, to be is to be intelligible. But Duns—that canny Scot—the *doctor subtilis* (with his *Quaestiones subtilissimae in Metaphysicam*), anticipated a certain metaphysical barber named Occam: abstractions grow quickly and need constant clipping: "Entities are not to be multiplied without necessity" (*Entia non multiplicanda praeter necessitatem*). Scotus held that philosophy's object is being, while theology's is God not as God but only as the most perfect concepts we can form about divinity, that of 'infinite being'. Infinity is a mode of being that precedes Aristotle's (and Kant's) distinction of categories. This means beginning not from act but from possibility (which includes act); acts imply contingency but "the possible" implies necessity. Divine willing possesses an intrinsic liberty that resists formalization. Gilson remarks that the "honeymoon of theology and philosophy" ended with Duns Scotus. A crucial instance of incompatibility is before us: two disciplines that seem to seek the same ultimate Object but which in fact operate with different modalities.

It seems that there are two kinds of knowing, both equally "rational" but attending to different objects or fields. Aristotle distinguished the soul's "two parts which grasp a rational principle," yielding scientific/technical or calculative/humane reasoning.[39] Thanks to the new discipline of biomedical ethics, the distinction between demonstration and persuasion has been revived with much fruit (even if "phronetic" reasoning has a distinctly odd ring to it). Immanuel Kant recognized the distinction in his critiques of pure and practical reason, while Polanyi supplies his own spin of proximal/distal or focused/peripheral.[40] Here is where the debate over Thomas Kuhn's thesis fits; he defends his position against the charge of subjectivism as follows: "the

---

39. Aristotle, *Nic. Ethics*, 1139a7ff.
40. M. Polanyi, *Personal Knowledge*, 123ff, *The Tacit Dimension*, 9ff.

criteria of choice . . . function not as rules, which determine choice, but as values, which influence it." Values may be "an insufficient basis for a *shared* algorithm of choice. But they do specify a great deal: what each scientist must consider in reaching a decision, what he may or may not consider relevant."[41] Since none of us occupies the universal fulcrum of Laplace's superpower, we must make do with hypothetico-deductive models, with persuasive arguments and value-judgments. No doubt in our study of the religious dimension of persons, our algorithms approach a "universalizability" less absolute than that of Kant, but they may yet produce an elegant method and credible results.

Nonetheless we still seem to prolong the obsession with epistemology bestowed on subsequent generations by Immanuel Kant: first ask how we know, then what we know, since "objects conform to the mind." Bernard Lonergan didn't fall for that one; reprising our theme in the previous chapter, he insisted that epistemology is compromised when *seeing* is taken as its model: "The myth is that knowing is like looking;" this misses "the world mediated by meaning."[42] Despite his penchant for mere logic, Bertrand Russell even reversed the process: "It has been common among philosophers to begin with how we know and proceed afterwards to what we know. I think this is a mistake, because knowing how we know is one small department of knowing what we know."[43] This relates to the axiomatics of our discipline, but also to what may be called its aporetics, our calculus of probabilities, which must allow the *aporias* of human knowing to have their place, without premature closure, which may prove impossible.

The premises of empirical science are now in question, having proved as unproveable as those of other disciplines. Perhaps here is where we

---

41. T. Kuhn, *Structure*, 389.
42. B. Lonergan, *Method*, 238.
43. B. Russell, *Our Knowledge of the External World* (New York: New American Library, 1960); Russell regards logic as " the essence of philosophy;" he is supposed to have remarked about Wittgenstein: "Poor Ludwig—he gave up logic for common sense."

must introduce a logic not of discovery but of negation. I have in mind the gift of Eastern thinkers to Western logic. Hindu logicians also debated the nature of words as referring to the universal or the particular. The Nyaya school developed a comparative theory of meaning linked to negation. Buddhist thinkers, particularly of the Dignāga school, somewhat like Western nominalists, interpreted the theory of inference as *apoha*, differentiation or exclusion.[44] The metaphysical nature of Negativity differs from East to West, according to Masao Abe. Let Paul Tillich represent the occidental tradition: "Thought must start with being; it cannot go behind it." "Being precedes nonbeing in ontological validity." "Being 'embraces' itself and nonbeing."[45] Eastern logic, however, particularly Taoist and Buddhist, posits nothingness as ultimate: "that which is neither being nor non-being." In the West, nonbeing is *me on* or *privatio*; absolute *ouk on* is unthinkable. In the East, *anatman* or *Sunyatta* offers a neither-nor view of ultimacy. Abe cites the Japanese terms *u* and *mu* as "of completely equal forces in relation to one another."[46] This Middle Path between and beyond affirmation and negation could be compared to Dante's way of the affirmation and negation of images, or to the cryptic rune of John of the Cross, *todo y nada*. Perhaps Karl Barth's thesis helps too, that "God" is a term that precedes the theism/atheism split.

KIERKEGAARD AS ARISTOTELIAN

For Aristotle, *motion* is king, as both Hegel and Kierkegaard saw, though with differing results: this challenges a traditional interpretation of Aristotelianism as merely static. It sees that being is "determinate" only in its "indeterminateness"—as the given, it is "indeterminate immediacy" (Hegel). Motion is a transition from potency to act, from

---

44. See R. Hayes, *Dignāga on the interpretation of Signs* (Boston: D. Reidel, 1987).
45. Tillich, *ST* I, 163, 189.
46. M. Abe, "'There is no Common Denominator for World Religions:' the Positive Meaning of this Negative Statement," in *JES* 26:1 (1989).

the "not yet" to the "already." If God is *actus purus* or *perpetuum mobile* then no concept can be formulated to express this What? (*Enter Kierkegaard, with irony*).

Everyone knows of Kierkegaard's enchantment with Socrates, his model for the concept of irony and the maieutic method. But after his magisterial thesis devoted to the subject[47] he turned to Aristotle. It was 1842; he was in Berlin, hearing Schelling lecture. He soon determined that the Hegelian "System" was flawed in its foundation, since the concept of *Aufhebung*, mediation or sublation, was a category mistake with fateful consequences. His own concern with "stages on life's way" convinced him that the transition between life's existential life-styles (*Stagen*) was not a matter of mediation but of dynamic change, from one modality to another. He found in Aristotle's notion of *kinēsis* the right category, helped by Trendelenburg's analysis of Aristotle's modal logic.[48]

Kierkegaard's "philosophical works," the brief *Philosophical Fragments* (*Smuler*, "Crumbs") and its huge *Concluding Unscientific Postscript to the Philosophical Fragments*, show philosophy seeking to advance beyond itself—for, as S.K. says, to do something Socratic means to go beyond Socrates. The *Fragments* propose a *Tanke-Experiment* or "thought-project" (with Lessing in mind): "How does that which comes into being change? Or, what is the nature of the change involved in becoming (*kinēsis*)? . . . This change is clearly not a change in essence, but in being; it is a transition from not being to being." He faults Aristotle for assuming that everything necessary is possible, whereas "possibility cannot be predicated of the necessary," since "becoming takes place with freedom, not by necessity." [49]

---

47. *The Concept of Irony with Special Reference to Socrates*, 1841.

48. Kierkegaard, *Philosophical Fragments*, "Interlude" on "Becoming;" *Concluding Unscientific Postscript* 100, 267n; Cf., A. Come, *Trendelenburg's Influence on Kierkegaard's Modal Categories*, ed. A. T. McKinnon (Montral: Inter Editions, 1991).

49. *Fragments*, 60f.

In the *Postscript* Kierkegaard expounds a bold thesis: "a logical system is possible" but "an existential system is impossible."[50] In constructing a logical system, one cannot include "anything which is subject to an existential dialectic." "Nothing must then be incorporated in a logical system that has any relation to existence, that is not indifferent to existence." The Hegelian System cannot include motion, dynamism, change within its straitjacket. Formal logic deals with abstractions, the static formulations of its objective method. The speculative philosopher does not deal with possibility, the possibly new or different (that which may exist in the realm of the excluded middle). As S.K. says: "The theory of true and false propositions, e.g., Epicurus, tends only to confuse the issue here, since it is essence and not being which is reflected upon, so that in this way no help is afforded with respect to a determination of future being."[51] Kierkegaard follows a different scent; he is after the wild game of actuality, existence, warts and all. He condemns modern philosophy: "not that it has a mistaken presupposition, but that it has a comical presupposition, occasioned by its having forgotten, in a sort of world-historical absent-mindedness, what it means to be a human being."[52] When S.K. states that "subjectivity is truth" he is not settling for the isolated self of subjectivism, but for "subject-being," or Heidegger's *Subjectität* (*nicht Subjectivität*).

Before leaving Kierkegaard we might note that the religious concept of the "twice-born" supports his category of the leap, those who have made the transition from one mode of being to another, through an experience that marks the incommensurability of the two spheres. For "what is born of the flesh is flesh, and what is born of the Spirit is spirit" (*John 3:6*). One can "describe" life in each stage—Kierkegaard did so brilliantly in his depiction of the three existence-spheres—but one cannot describe the motion from one to the other; only "indirect communication" will make do. Hence the need for philosophical midwives

---

50. *Postscript*, 99.
51. *Fragments*, 61.
52. *Postscript*, 109.

to assist at new birth—not concepts but *conceptions*. And for different modalities of knowing what and how to communicate. Indirect communication of non-universalizable categories: as noted above, is this not what constitutes *aesthetics*?

CONCLUSION

It seems that all our models these days express the loss of the Cartesian self—Ego as Cogito—a substantive core capable of interacting with external reality. Like the solid particles of classical physics, this has given way to an open-ended model of dynamic fields of energy. Selves do not touch in contiguity so much as intersect in magnetic fields of force. Their interplay resembles the game of chess when a third dimension is added: the depth allows new definitions of space, new rules governing the moves possible for the various chessmen (not "chesspersons" since it comes from the O.E. *meyne*). Geometry is a familiar example of how adding a dimension creates a shift in modality: from plane to solid changes the rules, while the fourth dimension of time adds further complexity. So also with subjectivity: *Ego* now is more like *Amo*, denoting a desire to find and to meld, to share in the Platonic mode of participation, *methexis*. Michael Polanyi, once again, warns that exploration entails an attitude of "indeterminate commitments;" modal thinking recalls us to the indeterminacy of knowledge, of special import in religious studies.

We began with talk of universal theory, with how everything fits together. Does this leave us with "pluralism *as* relativism"? Like Donne, must we lament "'Tis all in pieces, all coherence gone"? Let us end rather in the mode of Franz Rosenzweig.[53] Writing painfully because of his paralysis, his last words were: " . . . and now it comes, the point of all points, which the Lord has truly revealed to me in my sleep: the point of all points for which there . . . " It was December 9, 1929, the last day for the great "speech-thinker" whose kind of word-therapy gave out at the

---

53. See Barbara Galli, *Franz Rosensweig's "The New Thinking"* (New York: Syracuse University Press, 1999).

last. Or perhaps—as with all analogies, metaphors and playfulness—it broke down in order to hold up (as with Bach's fatal closure, as we saw). For the modality of dialogue is expressible not in concepts but in coinherence.

8

MODES OF CHRISTOLOGY

... the word "Godhead" signifies an operation and not a nature.

— Gregory of Nyssa[1]

THEOLOGY AS CHRISTOLOGY

Pluralism is not new, but what is different is our new awareness of its impact and demand on human relations. What used to be settled by "arms and the man" requires acceptance, coexistence, and dialogue. Religious pluralism involves similar shift from debate to dialogue, from imperialist monopoly to common enquiry. For Christian theology, traditional christology poses not only the obvious central point of conflict with other types of faith, but suffers from its development in an absolutist-exclusivist era. This assumed that identifying Jesus of Nazareth with the Second Person of the Trinity entailed a unique, unrepeatable and absolutely universal role for the incarnate Son of God, both revelatory and salvific. And this ideological absolutism was reinforced by the power granted an established religion. Therefore, as M.M. Thomas notes, one is "risking Christ for Christ's sake" in

---

1. "On Not Three Gods," quoted in Hick, *God and the Universe of Faiths*, 150.

PLURALISM WITHOUT RELATIVISM

engaging in genuine interreligious dialogue.[2]

The logically contradictory position to exclusivism in religious debate is that of historicism or relativism. This asserts that revelation and salvation are in principle to be found in every religion, and are of equal validity and truth. This may or may not involve a reductionist relativism of values. Current dialogue on religious pluralism seeks a third option, called inclusivism, which will relate positively to the plurality of religious experience and interpretation. The "theory of relativity" outlined above provides critique of this development. I consider the situation to be more complex than the relational models assume; their "paradigm-shift" does not break through the impasse of a normative christology.[3]

Our approach here is that trinitarian theology involves christology as its decisive theoretical moment. A different approach would be to compare trinities found in other religions; this gambit has a long history, comparing "ethnic trinities" to the Christian.[4] Augustine's famous search for analogues in human nature was helped by his Platonic anthropology. One might also note the philosophical fascination with threeness, *Triplizität*, as evident particularly in Immanuel Kant's works.[5] The issue has been sharpened by the debate initiated by *The Myth of God Incarnate* and its rejoinder, *Incarnation and Myth*.[6] As noted above, John Hick, editor of the former volume, has laboured valiantly over the years to develop an alternative paradigm that could break the absolutist/relativist deadlock. A crucial work in this regard is his *God and the Universe of Faiths*, which turns on the analogy with the Copernican revolution. Just as the geo-

---

2. M.M. Thomas, *Risking Christ for Christ's Sake: towards an ecumenical theology of pluralism* (Geneva: WCC Publications, 1987).
3. See chapter 3 above.
4. See L.L. Paine, *The Ethnic Trinities and their Relation to the Christian Trinity* (Boston: Houghton Mifflin, 1901). This includes the formulation of Plotinus: the One, the Monad, the Soul (*to hen, ho nous, he psyche*).
5. C.G. Jung and others would "complete" the triadic form in a mandala.
6. John Hick, ed. *The Myth of God Incarnate* (London: SCM, 1977); M. Goulder, ed. *Incarnation and Myth: The Debate Continues* (Grand Rapids: Eerdmans, 1979).

centric worldview was displaced by the heliocentric, so the "new map of the universe of faiths" must shift from a Christianity-centered to a God-centered picture of the universe of faiths.[7] Such enterprise entails displacing the static categories of Platonic-Nicene theology by the action-based categories preferred, for example, by Gregory of Nyssa. Before turning to this point, let us look more closely at the fruits and fallout of Nicaea.

NICENE THEOLOGY

Trinitarian theology was formulated during a period when the worldview of Christian Fathers was largely Middle Platonist, with Augustine's Neoplatonism an outstanding and influential exception.[8] Harry Wolfson, however, warned us not "to dress them up in the uniform of the Academy or the Lyceum or the Porch, to march them under the school banner of Plato or of Aristotle or of the Stoics, and to make them sing their school songs."[9] Yet it is true that the Niceno-Constantinopolitan Creed[10] operates with categories developed from Platonism, in which the tendentious concepts of "person" and "nature" function in peculiar, perhaps singular, ways. Of this "hybrid deity" and "tangled web" of doctrine (Colin Gunton), one historian states: "Trinitarian theology was superimposed on philosophical conceptions

---

7. J. Hick, *God and the Universe of Faiths* (New York: Macmillan, 1973, 1988), 148.

8. See J. N. D. Kelly, *Early Christian Doctrines* (London: Adam & Charles Black, 1958), 10f, 375ff on the significance of "the Platonic doctrine of real universals."

9. H. A. Wolfson, "Arianism and Apollinarianism," in *Religious Philosophy* (New York: Atheneum, 1965), 36.

10. The Nicene Creed was produced at the Council of Nicaea, 325; the Council of Chalcedon in 381 probably produced the final composite document, read out formally at the Council of Chalcedon in 451. See J. B. Walker in *The Dictionary of Historical Theology*, ed. Trevor A. Hart (Grand Rapids, MI: Eerdmans, 2000), 396ff.

of God."¹¹ Another asks: "Does it make sense to speak of pre-Nicene orthodoxy?"¹² This is not to agree wholeheartedly with Harnack's charge that "the Nicene doctrine of the incarnation was the result of a Hellenizing process through which Greek metaphysical concepts and categories were imposed inappropriately on Christian faith."¹³ To be sure, discursive theological thinking involved conceptual tools quite different from ours today; for example, the status of universals, the nature of substance and of person, and the correlation between being and value (the better the more real). The idea of Tri-unity worked out in such terms, and faced with the subtle contrary reasoning of "heresies" (i.e. minority "opinions"), yields the foundational documents of this Creed and its refinements at subsequent councils, notably Chalcedon in 554, where the relationship between the two natures in Christ was further defined.¹⁴ It is significant that the christological "description" consisted of four adverbs, each beginning with an alpha-privative (*asynkhytos, atreptos, adiairetos, akhoristos*), providing negations or boundaries rather than positive attributes and so disallowing "how" questions.¹⁵ These conciliar statements

---

11. J. J. O'Donnell, S.J., *Trinity and Temporality: the Christian Doctrine of God in light of Process Theology and the Theology of Hope* (London: Oxford University Press, 1983), 44. Colin Gunton, *Act and Being; Towards a Theology of the Divine Attributes* (London: SCM, 2002), chapters 1 and 2.

12. R. Williams in *The Making of Orthodoxy*, ed. R. Willliams (in honour of Henry Chadwick) (Cambridge University Press, 1989), 1–23.

13. Harnack, *History of Dogma* (London: Williams & Norgate, 1898), IV, 98. Harnack's view is that "the so-called Creed of Constantinople (381) can in fact be taken simply as a formula of union between orthodox, Semi-Arians, and Pneumatomachians."cf. Alan Torrance, "Being of One Substance with the Father," in *Nicene Christianity*, ed. C. Seitz (Cumbria, UK: Paternoster Press, 2001), 50.

14. See J. W. C. Wand, *The Four Great Heresies* (London: A.R. Mowbray, 1955).

15. See J. R. Wright, "The Meaning of the Four Chalcedonian Adverbs in Recent Ecumenical Agreements," *St. Nersess Theological Review* I/1, 1996, 43–49. Bonhoeffer used to warn against the falsity of *Wie-Fragen*.

MODES OF CHRISTOLOGY

were taken as standards attesting to the final and absolute truth of Jesus as the Christ; hence the peculiar phenomenon of creedal anathemas.

The historical context does not simply relativize such documents, however. It suggests, rather, a more open interpretation both of terminology and of intention. Despite the limitations of time and place, and the politicization of theology in the Roman Empire, the Church Fathers attempted a theology that would honour the transcendent otherness of divinity. And despite the subtle philosophical concepts available to them, neither the Cappadocians in the East nor the Augustinians in the West were able to solve the problem of tri-unity by logic, that is the relation beween *ousia* and *hypostasis*, or between Trinitarian parity and the Father as "fount and origin of all divinity," *fons et origo totius divinitatis* (Council of Toledo).[16] If *ho theos* refers properly only to the Father or Ground, it is difficult to refute Origen's argument for subordinationism in both christology and pneumatology.[17] Some have suggested an alternative "theocentric" approach as more appropriate.[18] Maurice Wiles advocates a more radical revision yet, to overcome the "contradiction" of the claim that the Incarnation is "unique, final and unrepeatable," with special reference to Rahner's Christology.[19]

The doctrine of Tri-unity seeks to preserve the equality of its "persons" by describing a process of mutual indwelling (*circumincessio*), corresponding to mutual delight (*perichōrēsis*, lit. "dancing around"). Given such subtle categorization, Karl Barth was disturbed by the very word "person," with its modern meaning of "self-consciousness."

---

16. Joseph T. Lienhard compares the "two traditions" of "dyohypostatic" and "miahypostatic" formulations, each with strengths and weaknesses: The 'Arian' Controversy: some categories reconsidered, in *Theological Stuuies* 48/3 (1987) 415–37.

17. J.J. O'Donnell, *Trinity and Temporality* (NY: OUP, 1983), 40ff

18. E.g. Jas. F. Gustafson, *Ethics from a Theocentric Perspective* (University of Chicago, 1981) 2 vols; Robt Jenson, *Systematic Theology 1* (New York: Oxford University Press, 1997).

19. M. Wiles, *Christian Theology and Inter-Religious Dialogue* (London: SCM, 1992), esp. 4: "A Theology for Dialogue."

His alternative is three "modes of being," the danger of modalism or Sabellianism notwithstanding. Indeed, Barth was accused by Vladimir Lossky of standing in a Western tradition that reduces trinitarian dogma to a non-trinitarian modalism.[20] Yet Georges Florovsky's account of St. Gregory the Theologian (4thC) summarizes his concept of hypostasis: "The hypostatic names express the mutual relationship of the persons, *schēseis*. The three persons are three modes of being, inseparable and yet not confused, each 'existing independently.'"[21]

Now there is no doubt that the kernel of Christian theology is christology. The great book by Donald Baillie on the subject spoke of "the central paradox . . . the paradox of Grace," the paradigmatic Event that echoes Kierkegaard's Absolute Paradox, "the God in time."[22] Like Kierkegaard's Socratic paradox—the basic wonder at any relation between the human and eternity—Baillie identified an initial paradox arising from Christian experience that the good "is somehow not wrought by himself but by God," a sort of prelude and analogatum of the Absolute.[23] Baillie notes two trends of Trinitarian thought, one in Karl Barth, with his category of "modes of being" and the other in Schleiermacher and Ritschl. Schleiermacher's "avowed Sabellianism . . . may sound 'modalistic' but it is not Modalism in the heretical or Sabellian sense."[24]

---

20. Lossky, *La procession du Saint Esprit dans la doctrine trinitaire orthodoxe* (Paris, 1948). K. Barth, *Church Dogmatics* I.1, 400. Barth points to the difficulties in both the Eastern term *hypostasis* (even if safer than *prosôpon*) and the Western *persona* (even if safer than *substantia*).

21. G. Florovsky, *The Eastern Fathers of the Fourth Century* (Büchervertriebsanstalt, 1987), 134.

22. See J-P Sartre on "The Singular Universal" in *Kierkegaard: a Collection of Critical Essays*, ed. J. Thompson (New York: Anchor Books, 1972), 230—65.

23. D.M. Baillie, *God Was In Christ: an Essay on Incarnation and Atonement* (London: Faber & Faber, 1948), 114. "This is the deepest paradox of our whole Christian experience, and it runs right through it, woven into its very texture" (117). S. Kierkegaard, *Philosophical Fragments* (1848).

24. Ibid., 133ff; Barth, *C.D.* I.1, 407: "we prefer to say the three 'modes of being' in God."

MODES OF CHRISTOLOGY

The Fathers did not consider their formulae to encapsulate absolute Truth, nor to be themselves irreformable. An outstanding witness here is Augustine. He declares that "the absolute transcendence of the supreme Trinity defies comparison," since the term "person" is merely a necessary convention (*consuetudo loquendi*). And in a striking passage he can declare: "When the question is asked, What three? . . . the answer is given 'three persons,' not because the phrases are adequate but because they are only an alternative to silence."[25] This echoes Anselm's "ineffable plurality" of the "three I know not what."[26] Such caution reminds us that development of doctrine reflects development of piety, as it were: the *lex orandi* dictates the shape of the *lex credendi*.[27] Tillich puts it baldly: "Christology is a function of soteriology."[28]

Progress in doctrine is on view in the series of conciliar decrees after Chalcedon. Christology continues to develop for another two centuries, notably in the twin doctrines of *anhypostasia* and *enhypostasia*, enunciated by Leontius of Byzantium and John of Damascus for example, and encoded at the Second Council of Constantinople in 553.[29] H.M. Relton considers the *anhypostasia* to be meaningless, while *enhypostasia* connotes no independent humanity, but "being personal in the Logos", "in-personal" (*enhypostatos*).[30] Thus the mystery of *theanthrôpos* was safeguarded on both sides, still in the spirit of the earlier Chalcedonian negations. This history reminds us that Logos doctrine insists on an asymmetrical christology: the deity is always more than

---

25. Augustine, *De Trin.* V.9,10 and XV.43,23. *Verius enim cogitatur Deus quam dicitur et verius est quam cogitatur.*

26. *ineffabiliis pluralitas, tres nescio quid*—Anselm, *Monol.* 38, 79.

27. See Maurice Wiles, *The Making of Christian Doctrine* (Cambridge University Press, 1967), 68ff.

28. Tillich, *S.T.* II, 150.

29. See Barth, *C.D.* IV.2, 49f, 91; Baillie, *God Was in Christ* 85ff: "Critique of Christologies."

30. Relton, *A Study in Christology* (London: SPCK, 1929). A.B. Bruce thought that the "hypostatic union" is greater than the distinction—*The Humiliation of Christ* (Edinburgh: T & T Clark, 1895), 64f.

the humanity; the latter is contained within the former (*ensarkos*) but not vice versa (hence *asarkos*)— Donald Baillie's monograph took up this point; his intention was to signal the end of docetism, the modern shift to "take the full humanity of our Lord more seriously than has ever been done before by Christian theologians."[31] He noted that *anhypostasia*, in which the divine person assumes humanity, entails "the impersonal humanity of Christ," according to Cyril of Alexandria. The latter was in controversy with Nestorius who rejected the title *Theotokos*, though perhaps anticipated by Apollinarius.[32] For Cyril there is no independent human nature, only *anhypostatos*. But is he *Man* without being also *a man*? Leonard Hodgson states: "the Incarnation is to be thought of as the entry upon experience of such a life by the divine Logos"—i.e. the *nous* or *pneuma* remains Logos, as with Apollinarius.[33] T. F. Torrance sums up by noting that the twin terms rule out adoptionism on the one side and monophysitism on the other.[34]

Athanasius, hero of the anti-Arian controversy, remarked of the Incarnation: "the flesh has become logified (*sarkos logotheisês*)."[35] The Cappadocian Fathers, seeking to define the sort of Mystery declared at Nicaea, opposed their Arian opponents by stating that "you cannot apply dialectics to the mystery of the Trinity." Their theological spin on the philosophy of being led to "a special term, for all practical purposes new, . . . the *theoprepês*," that is, what is "fitting" for Divinity.[36] But they insisted equally that such definition must come through liturgy and mystical theology, a sort of "Liturgical mysticism."[37] The true theologian is

---

31. D. M. Baillie, *God Was in Christ*, 11.
32. *op.cit.*, "Critique of Christologies," 85ff.
33. Hodgson, *The Doctrine of the Trinity* (London: Nisbet & Co., 1943), 68; cf. 71ff on the Logos doctrine.
34. Torrance, *The Christian Doctrine of God, One Being, Three Persons* (Edinburgh: T. & T. Clark, 1996), 160.
35. Athanasius, *Oratio contra Arianos*, III, 33.
36. J. F. Callahan, *Augustine and the Greek Philosophers* (Villanova, PA: Villanova University Press, 1967), 13. The term was coined by Stoics.
37. E. Gilson, *History of Christian Philosophy in the Midddle Ages* (New

engaged in a process of sanctification, *theôsis*, which gives entrance to a life of contemplation, *theognôsia*.[38] Colin Gunton says that Arianism is "the perennial problem . . . perhaps the twentieth century's favourite heresy, and it is among the most appealing."[39] His point is well taken: modernity (and postmodernity, naturally) rejects the very idea of a "generated" Logos who subsequently unites with a human being, *pace* Origen who could defend the eternal generation without committing himself to an unambiguous incarnation.[40] A significant by-product of anti-Arian orthodoxy is its emphasis on the divinity of Christ to the virtual exclusion of his humanity; this has been remarked by Josef Jungmann and Thomas Torrance.[41]

"MODES OF BEING"

The figure of Karl Barth (1886–1968) looms large once again on the stage of modern theology. His forceful rejection of natural theology belongs to his development of a theology without presuppositions.[42] We have noted his notorious call for the "abolition" of religion. More important for our purpose here, as stated in earlier chapters, is T. F. Torrance's thesis that in fact Barth displaced traditional natural theology as an independent prologue to theology with a new natural theology

---

York: Random House, 1955), 53. See especially the fine summary by Georges Florovsky, *The Eastern Fathers*.

38. See W. Jaeger, *Two Rediscovered Works of Ancient Christian Literature: Gregory of Nyssa and Macarius* (Leiden: E.J. Brill, 1954), 23, 77.

39. C. Gunton, "And in One Lord, Jesus Christ, Begotten, Not Made," in *Nicene Christianity*, ed. C. Seitz (Grand Rapids, MI: Brazos Press, 2001), 35.

40. See McLelland, *God the Anonymous*, "Analogy and Incarnation," 107ff.

41. Jungmann, *The Place of Christ in Liturgical Prayer* (Collegeille, Minn.: Liturgical Press, 1989); T. F. Torrance, "The Mind of Christ: the Problem of Apollinarianism in the Liturgy," in *Theology in Reconciliation* (London: Geoffrey Chapman, 1975), 139ff.

42. See Rolf Ahlers, *The Community of Freedom: Barth and Presuppositionless Theology* (New York: Peter Lang, 1993)..

consistent with positive theology. Barth's pilgrimage from the liberalism of his teacher Harnack, through Kierkegaard and Schleiermacher, Anselm and Heppe, has been well documented. Its stages have also been well debated. The "eggshell" thesis of Hans Urs von Balthasar is the most familiar, offering a model for interpreting Barth's development in two stages, from liberalism to dialectics and then through Anselm to analogical method. He also suggests that the *Christian Dogmatics* was not so much replaced by the *Church Dogmatics*, but rather forms a logical progression towards analogy.[43] The Balthasar thesis has been challenged by Bruce McCormack, who offers an alternative paradigm in which dialectical theology is Barth's constant goal, developing through four stages.[44] The first two are echatological, the third pneumatological and the final a christocentrism, informed chiefly by the anhypostatic-enhypostatic categories just noted. Eberhard Jüngel approaches Barth through his category of "God's being is in becoming," and notes that Barth's critique of any trinitarianism based on classical theism's dictum that divinity cannot suffer reflects his "opposition to every form of natural theology "in "perhaps its most extreme formulation."[45]

One important question being debated about Barth is the role of Holy Spirit in his trinitarian formulation. McCormack's third stage features a strong role for Holy Spirit. This has been the topic of a monograph by John Thompson, who sees Barth not as purveying a new Spirit-christology but as remaining true to his christological focus: the Spirit is always anonymous, pointing to the Christ.[46] This relates to another

---

43. Hans Urs von Balthasar, *The Theology of Karl Barth: Exposition and Interpretation*, trans. E.T. Oakes, S.J. (New York: Holt, Rinehart & Winston, 1971).

44. B. McCormack, *Karl Barth's Critically Realistic Dialectical Theology: Its Genesis and Development 1909–1936* (New York: Oxford University Press, 1995).

45. E. Jüngel, *The Doctrine of the Trinity: God's Being is in Becoming* (Grand Rapids, MI: Eerdmans, 1976), 84.

46. J. Thompson, *The Holy Spirit in the Theology of Karl Barth* (Pickwick Publications, 1990).

significant development in Christian theology, a Spirit-christology that privileges pneumatology: "The Lord is the Spirit" (2 Cor. 3:17). This rather ambiguous phrase is related by Piet Schoonenberg to 2ndC Spirit christology, for instance in the *Shepherd* of Hermas: "the Holy Spirit is the Son of God" (9:1). Schoonenberg compares Spirit and Logos christologies, concluding that they are equivalent but not identical; he remains "sympathetic" and open to the view of Harry Wolfson and other scholars who regard them as identical.[47] The alternative has been explored in functional terms, a sort of theological pragmatics.[48] It has been related to the search for a "pneumatological theology of religions" by conservatives seeking to move away from the soteriological approach to a more general one.[49] It has also been espoused by John Hick, developing the christologies of Donald Baillie and Gregory Lampe.[50]

Karl Barth's preferred term for trinitarian relations, "modes of being,"[51] sounds like the ancient heresy of Modalism, but Barth is explicit in rejecting this interpretation: "The doctrine of the Trinity means, as the denial of modalism, the expressed declaration that those three elements are not foreign to the Godness of God . . . not an economy foreign to His essence . . . Modalism in the last resort means

---

47. P. Schoonenberg, "Christ and the Spirit: an Essay in Spirit Christology," in *Schola* (Hales Corners, WI: Sacred Heart School of Theology) Vol. 1, 1978, 29–49.

48. Paul W. Newman, *A Spirit Christology: Recovering the Biblical Paradigm of Christian Faith* (New York: University Press of America, 1987), esp. 181ff, "Functional or Ontological Presence of God."

49. e.g. Amos Young, *Beyond the Impasse: Toward a Pneumatological Theology of Religions* (Baker Book House, 2003), in dialogue with Clark Pinnock, Stanley Samartha, etc.

50. John Hick, "An Inspirational Christology for a Religiously Plural World," in S. Davis, ed. *Encountering Jesus* (Philadelphia: Fortress Press, 1988). See also G. Lampe, *Exploration in Theology* 8 (London: SCM, 1981), Ch. 3 "What Future for the Trinity?"

51. Karl Rahner suggested the alternative "manner of subsistence"—*The Trinity*, E.T. J. Donceel (New York: Herder and Herder, 1970), 303ff.

the denial of God."⁵² In modalism "we have to do not with a God as he is, but only with a god as he appears to us ... modern Sabellianism must become idolatry."⁵³ The heresy of monarchianism or modalism was widespread in the ancient church, driven by the twofold conviction of "the oneness of God and the full deity of Christ."⁵⁴ The objection to the Logos doctrine, by Noetus and his followers, was that it seemed to split Father and Son not only verbally or nominally but in reality. The view that the Word has no independent substance has as corollary "patripassianism," that the Father himself suffered.⁵⁵ Barth's thesis is that orthodox trinitarianism constitutes a denial of subordinationism on the one hand and modalism on the other.⁵⁶ By honouring "the contours of his being" the conciliar development shows "a kind of circular course among the three modes of existence, like Augustine's *unitas, aequalitas, connexio*.⁵⁷ Now Barth is correct to distinguish parts of a whole (aliud, aliud, aliud) from persons-in-relation (alius, alius, alius), but he follows by accusing the

---

52. Barth, *C.D.* I.1, 438f; cf. D.M. Baillie, *God Was in Christ*, 136ff.

53. Barth, *C.D.* I.1, 9, 405. Barth thinks that Schleiermacher followed in the "footsteps" of modalistic monarchianism.

54. J.N.D. Kelly, *Early Christian Doctrines*, 119. There was also "dynamic monarchianism" or adoptionism, beginning with Novation (c. 250) and associated chiefly with Paul of Samosata, condemned at the Synod of Antioch in 268. He reserved the term "God" for the Father, denying that the Word was a substance (*ousia*): 115ff. See H.A. Wolfson, *Philosophy of the Church Fathers* (Cambridge: Harvard University Press, 1956), I.589ff.

55. This was developed by Sabellius, excommunicated by Pope Callistus (ca 220). Sabellianism sees Godhead as a monad ("Son-Father") expressing himself through modes of Son and Spirit. See Epiphanius, *haer.* 62, 1, 4ff. cf. Tertullian, *Adv. Praxeam* 5ff. (Note that modern theology has modified the traditional doctrine of divine impassibilty, at least since the nineteenth century. The idea of "the crucified God" has been popularized by Jürgen Moltmann and others, although within a trinitarian schema, relying on a sort of *sympatheia* between Father and Son—J.K. Mozley, *The Impassibility of God* (Cambridge University Press, 1926); Moltmann, *The Crucified God* (London: SCM, 1973).

56. *C.D.* I.1, 431ff.

57. *C.D.* I.1, 425ff; Augustine, *De doct. chr.* I.5.

Monarchians—"in whose footsteps Schleiermacher and his school have walked in modern times"—of taking the three persons as "phenomenal forms under which God's real single essence was concealed as something different and higher."[58] Thus he denies all attempts to identify a divine essence beyond Trinity in the search for possible points of contact with world religions in their theology.

THE "EXTRA CALVINISTICUM"

One dimension of Logos christology with much relevance to our modal thesis was advanced by Calvinists in their sixteenth-century debates with Lutherans on the ubiquity of Christ's body; the latter dubbed the opponents' doctrine "extra Calvinisticum".[59] The difference stems from the implication of *kenosis*: as William Temple put it starkly: "What was happening to the rest of the universe during the period of our Lord's earthly life?"[60] The classical formulation that external acts of the Trinity are one (*opera Trinitatis ad extra sunt indivisa*), does not much help the thorny issue of dual personality in the Christian form of incarnation. The question remains: what is the difference between the modes of Logos enfleshed and unfleshed (*ensarkos, asarkos*)? Luther's theology of the cross posited a Christ fully identifiable by manger and cross, and so he balked at Calvin's stress on an ascended Lord, which Luther considered an implicit theology of glory.

We mention this debate because it is an excellent commentary on the crucial text, "The Word was made flesh" (John 1:14). While the Reformation issue concerned the kind of presence of Christ in the Eucharist, the question is as old as the search for proper definition of the hypostatic union. Indeed, the debating partners summoned up the

---

58. *C.D.* I.1 405.
59. See the excellent monograph on the topic by David Willis, *Calvin's Catholic Christology: the function of the so-called Extra Calvinisticum in Calvin's Theology* (Leiden: Brill, 1966), p. 1. See Chapter 3 above, "Test Cases."
60. William Temple, *Christus Veritas* (New York: Macmillan, 1954), 142f.

ghosts of Christmas past, as it were, in appealing to the ancient creedal formulations: the Lutherans called Calvinists "Nestorian," and the latter retorted with "Eutychian."[61] Augustine had spoken of "Christ everywhere whole but not wholly," a distinction between *totus* and *totum* central to his letter to Dardanus, which "served as the classic patristic text in the controversy over the ubiquity of Christ's risen body."[62] The Conciliar distinction between Logos *asarkos* and *ensarkos* proved relevant, as did the scholastic distinction between Christ's presence *totus* and *totum*.[63] Calvin and his colleagues concluded that the Son continued an existence beyond the flesh. Calvin writes, "we do not imagine that [the human nature] was an enclosure;" thus "deliberately following the early Church in the rejection of any receptacle notion of space" according to T. F. Torrance.[64] Their position provoked the Lutherans to dub it "that Calvinistic `beyond'" (*illud extra Calvinisticum*). Theodore Beza stated: "Because of that union, it is not necessary nor does it follow to say that wherever the Word is, there also is his humanity."[65] For Luther, the entire Word became Jesus of Nazareth; for Calvin, the human Jesus did not include the entire Word. The debate took a peculiar turn through the doctrine of

---

61. See J. P. Donnelly, *Dialogue on the Two Natures in Christ* Peter Martyr Library Vol. 2 (Kirksville, MO: Sixteenth Century Essays & Studies XXXI, 1995). The Dialogue is Martyr's way of rebutting the christology of John Brenz, e.g. *De vera maiestate Christi ad dextram Dei Patris sui omnipotentis* (Tubingen, 1954).

62. Donnelly, *op.cit.*, 14n; Augustine, *Ep. 187, ad Dard.* (PL 33, 839); Lombard, *Sent.* III, dist. 22 (PL 21, 367). Peter Martyr printed the letter as an appendix to his *Treatise on the Eucharist* (Oxford, 1549): see McLelland, *The Oxford Treatise and Disputation on the Eucharist* (Peter Martyr Library Vol. 7; Kirksville: Sixteenth Century Essays & Studies LVI, 2000), 109.

63. Peter Lombard, *Sent.* III, dist. 22,3; Aquinas, *S.C.G.* IV.43; cf. Calvin, *CO* 9:194f.

64. Calvin, *Inst.* II.13.4; T. F. Torrance, *Space, Time and Incarnation* (London: Oxford University Press, 1969), 31f.

65. Beza's remarks at the Colloquy of Montbéliard (1586): Willis, op.cit., 16ff.

ubiquity, the "everywhereness" of Christ's body.[66] Lutherans stressed the "real presence" of Christ in the elements, while Calvinists stressed the *sursum corda*: "lift up your hearts" to the risen and ascended Christ. The latter was viewed by the Lutheran opposition as a denial of Christ's presence, a sort of "real absence" theory.

Peter Martyr Vermigli's contribution was to take up the philosophical burden of proof. The Reformed party was accused of using spatial categories (like Aristotle!), as if "heaven" is a place or locality. He replied: "if you define such a place with reference to the daily revolution of the earth, then your absurdity needs no answer." He argues that "God's right hand" is "a term with several meanings," invoking his familiar appeal to polysemy, notably forms of metaphorical speech.[67] We must not make too much of this category for the Reformers themselves. While it suggests a certain ambiguity about their christology, an attempt to maintain the "absolute being of the Logos asarkos"[68] rather than an exclusive revelation in Jesus Christ, it allows us to experiment with a more nuanced christology that bears on the issue of pluralism. That is, a Logos christology has a dimension outside the Incarnation, a potential that relates to those outside the historical revelation in Jesus Christ. This is adumbrated in the Bible itself, in its universal references and intention, not least in the Book of Revelation: by the light of the *shekina* "shall the nations walk; and the kings of the earth shall bring their glory . . . the glory and honour of the nations."[69]

---

66. See McLelland, *The Visible Words of God* (Edinburgh: Oliver & Boyd, 1957), 103ff and Ch. 8: "The Eucharist and Ubiquity;" also "Lutheran—Reformed Debate on the Eucharist and Christology" in Empie & McCord, eds, *Marburg Revisited* (Minneapolis: Augsburg, 1966), 39–69.
67. *Oxford Treatise*, 109ff, Donnelly, *Two Natures* 118ff.
68. Alexander Schweizer, quote in Willis, op.cit., 2.
69. Rev. 21: 24, 26.

PLURALISM WITHOUT RELATIVISM

CHRISTOLOGIES AND THE CHRIST

We may conclude that modern christology must begin with traditional formulations, but need not hesitate to explore further development of doctrine. We should remember the "ante-Nicene" Radical Reformers of the 16th century who foreshadowed our contemporary "christology from below". They tried to reopen the concepts with which classical theism had related trinity, christology and incarnation, relations which are not fixed dogmata. A new age in christology is often said to have begun with Karl Rahner's thesis in 1960 that the immanent Trinity in God's pretemporal eternity is identical with the economic Trinity: "the Trinity of the economy of salvation *is* the immanent Trinity and vice versa."[70] It is most significant that Rahner is attempting to correct the fact that "Christians, for all their orthodox profession of faith in the Trinity, are almost always just 'monotheists' in their actual religious existence." The paradox is that this divine oneness is not incarnational but undifferentiated, concerned with "the grace of the *Dei-hominis*, not as the grace of the Word incarnate as Logos."[71] This may be related further to Barth's insistence that Christian theology has to do neither with pure deity nor pure humanity, ruling out mere theology and anthropology in favour of a "theanthropology." The dynamics of such "Christology" therefore ought to avoid all speculation that leads to abstraction. This theme is echoed by Emil Brunner: the Bible "contains no doctrine of God as he is in himself [*Gott-an-sich*], none of man as he is in himself [*Menschen-an-sich*]. It always speaks of God as the God who approaches man [*Gott-zum-Menschen-hin*] and of man as the man who comes from God [*Menschen-*

---

70. Karl Rahner, "Remarks on the Dogmatic Treatise 'De Trinitate,'" *Theological Investigations* Vol. 4 (Baltimore: Helicon Press, 1966) 87; see also W. Pannenberg, "Father, Son, Spirit: Problems of a Trinitarian Doctrine of God," *Dialog* 26/4.

71. Ibid., 81. He sees the problem largely beginning with the replacement of Lombard by Thomas, so that now *De Deo Uno* precedes *De Deo Trino*, throwing the latter into "a splendid isolation."

von-Gott-her]."⁷² Here again a fruitful line of revision is suggested, even though it seems to emerge from a simply exclusivist position. Yet it reflects that classical sort of universalism according to which the Logos became *Man* while also becoming *this* man. This is a "singularity" not yet given its due.

Finally, there is the tentative nature of theological formulae: talk of the Transcendent is not transcendent talk—"le Dieu defini est le Dieu fini." The gap between human speech about the divine informs all great theology: we know only in part through the gracious condescension of the Mystery itself (*anabasis, accommodatio*), allowing us to witness to the Presence, but only in correspondingly broken speech, what Calvin dubbed "impropriety." A comment by Wittgenstein is apt: "There is one thing and only one thing in the world of which it makes no sense to say that it is a metre long, and that is the standard metre in Paris." That is, one measures metres by this rule, but the rule itself is what "one metre" means. If this is related to the Christ-event, we might say that to call Christ "divine" has things the wrong way round. An independent definition of divinity is impossible for the Christian; rather, "Jesus the Christ" is what "divine" means.⁷³

The way in which such christology may be related to those scriptures which show a universal intention has always been moot. One early and valiant attempt to explicate this positively was that of Prosper of Aquitaine, Augustine's defender, in the first work of Christian literature dedicated to the question of the salvation of the heathen, *De vocatione omnium gentium*. Prosper's distinctions *ante legem, sub legem, sub gratiam* led him to posit universal salvation as part of faith, relying on the distinction between general and particular grace.⁷⁴

---

72. Brunner, *Truth as Encounter* (London: SCM, 1964), 87.

73. I owe this use of Wittgenstein to my friend Alistair McKinnon, in an unpublished paper "The Meaning of Religious Assertions."

74. Prosper of Aquitaine, *De vocatione omnium gentium* (formerly attributed to Leo the Great): Migne, *PL* 51, 547ff. See I.12 and II.2, 663ff, 687f.

Modernity, of course, is shaped by Descartes and Kant more than by Church Fathers. One may venture to say that "classical theism" came to an end with Renaissance-Reformation, running into the dogmatisms that sparked the Cartesian scepticism (or what William Temple dubbed "the Cartesian faux-pas"). For Kant, Jesus Christ is "archetype," a concept within human reason that acts as arbiter for rational theology. The latter supplies the "pure idea of the understanding" which enables reason to judge the content of external revelation. Thus rational religion provides "the substratum and foundation of every investigation," so that "religion within the limits of reason alone" issues in *"a service of the heart* (in spirit and in truth)."[75]

Kierkegaard brings a critical insight to the Kantian problematics, replacing archetype by "prototype," thus allowing a "contemporaneity" for later disciples:

> Christ came into the world with the purpose of saving the world, also with the purpose—this in turn implicitly in his first purpose—of being the prototype, of leaving footprints for the person who wanted to join him, who then might become an imitator.[76]

The shift from Kantian and philosophical admiration of Christ the archetype to a theological appreciation of prototypical Exemplar and Saviour recalls us to the classical debate in which the arbiter is not reason but conscience. Indeed, Kierkegaard's critique of Luther is in large part because the Reformer resisted the emphasis on prototype in favour of Christ as Atoner, an extreme grace bordering on antinomianism.[77] If this chapter has suggested the possibility of deriving a more open

---

75. I. Kant, *Lectures* 161; *Religion Within the Limits of Reason Alone*, trans. T. Green & H. Hudson (New York: Harper Torchbook, 1960), 180.

76. See Kierkegaard, *Practice in Christianity*, trans. and ed. by Hong and Hong (Princeton, NJ: Princeton University Press, 1991) 238. See Jas Farris, "Christ as Prototype," *Toronto Journal of Theology*, 8/2 (1992) 288–96.

77. See Kierkegaard, *Journals and Papers*, trans. and ed. W. & E. Hong (Bloomington IN: Indiana University Press, 1967), V, 324f.

christology from historical Christian theology itself, it will have been enough to introduce further exploration of other christologies in the next chapter. For if, as Athanasius is reported to have said, in the Old Testament epiphanies "the Logos was learning to become incarnate," a para-incarnational modality is as logical as any pre-incarnational mode.[78]

---

78. The quotation is ascribed to C.C.J. Webb in Kenneth Cragg, *The Christ and the Faiths* (Philadelphia: Westminster Press, 1986), 227; cf., "Is Christ Multiplied?" 175–96.

9

INCARNATION IN HINDUISM AND ISLAM

> *H (Hindu): I suspect that C (Christian) is going to be under fire from two directions. On the one hand, there are those like the Muslims who repudiate the very notion that a human can be divine, can literally be God. For this is blasphemous from his point of view. On the other hand, there are those who feel, as did Gandhi, that the very uniqueness of the Incarnation constitutes a stumbling-block.*
> — Ninian Smart[1]

THEOLOGY WITH OR WITHOUT CHRISTOLOGY: HINDUISM

Trinitarian Analogies

Trinitarian analogies are found not only in the psyche, as Augustine held, but in many articulations of religious experience. The vexed question of defining religion is best approached in the almost universal self-description of various faiths as "the Way" (*Hodos, Via, Dharma, Rta, Tao,* etc). What Western scholars dub "religions" are not

---

1. *World Religions: A Dialogue* (Penguin Books, 1966), 90.

phenomena in themselves, but modes of being through which people see and experience the world in certain ways: "seeing-as", "experiencing-as."[2] And W.C. Smith's warning should be a constant guide, that the very names for world religions are forms of reification (mostly given by outsiders), and that the problematics of religious studies are chiefly the product of Western academics.[3] Some Hindu scholars claim that "Hinduism" is but a name invented by Europeans for the convenience of the discipline of "comparative religion."[4] Smith also speculated what Christian christology would be like if Paul had gone east instead of west, perhaps to encounter the relationship of complementary yin/yang rather than the dichotomy of eternity/time of Western classical theism. This theme is taken seriously by Jung Young Lee: the bipolarity of nature represents a kind of opposition "necessary but also complementary to each other."[5] C.S. Song has explored similar questions in his *Theology from the Womb of Asia*, including the Korean theology of *Han*.[6] Rather than pursue such speculation, let us concentrate on two "religions" where

---

2. L. Wittgenstein, *Philosophical Investigations*, trans. G.E.M. Anscombe (Oxford: Basil Blackwell, 1968), XI.193 on "two uses of the word 'see'" showing two kinds of "object" (cf., the duck-rabbit figure, 194).

3. W.C. Smith, *The Meaning and End of Religion* (New York: Macmillan, 1962), Ch. 2, "'Religion' in the West."

4. E.g. it is rather "a tolerant Indian umbrella under which sects and sub-sects, opposite and opposed" have lived and live—P.K. Najhawan quoted by Hans Staffner, S.J. in *Jesus Christ and the Hindu Community* (Anand, India: Gujarat Sahitya Prakash, 1987); D.S. Sharma calls it "more a league of religions than a single religion with a definite creed" (87). Cf., H. von Stietencron, "'Hinduism:' a European Term," *Christianity and the World Religions*, H. Küng et. al. (Garden City, NY: Doubleday, 1986), 138.

5. J.Y Lee, *The Trinity in Asian Perspective* (Nashville: Abingdon Press, 1996), 24. He uses the trigrams of the *I Ching* to interpret the three Persons in dynamic terms.

6. C.S. Song, *Theology from the Womb of Asia* (Maryknoll, NY: Orbis Books, 1986), 70ff; Cf., Suh Nam Dong, "Towards a Theology of *Han*," in *Minjung Theology*, ed. Kim Yong Bok (Singapore: Christian Conference of Asia, 1981), 51-61.

christology is a vital issue.

Beyond the Indus valley we find a vast land of long history and manifold experience, offering alternative ways to escape suffering and to experience the essence of Absolute Being at the self's centre. The broad reach of Hinduism suggests its peculiar richness: both theism and non-theism, both one and many, both personal and impersonal. The earliest Veda says: "The Real is One, though sages name it variously."[7] Vedanta teaches that the One is Brahman (as distinct from Brahma), a powerful sort of monistic ontology. Yet even this "socalled 'acosmism' of Shankara," according to Hugo Meynell, is compatible with the Christian doctrine of creation. Further, he argues, the idea of Brahman as sole reality can be "one very forceful way of affirming the metaphysical uniqueness of God."[8] *Tat tvam asi*—"That art thou"— reflects a sense of oneness with the Ultimate not restricted to the experience of "unitive mysticism" analyzed by Westerners.[9] This Way may be described as a form of *Dharma*. Its tension with Christianity derives from the latter's singular form of *sādhana dharma*, a specific way of salvation. Yet attempts at a synthesis have been made, for instance in South India by Mahadeva Aiyer in the movement to maintain the Hindu *samaj dharma* while adopting the Christian *sādhana dharma*.[10]

There are parallels or analogies between the two, particularly the Hindu trinity (*Trimūrti*). Siva, the "three-formed" great god (Mahadeva) is creator, preserver and destroyer: Brahma, Vishnu, Rudra. Again, Animananda spoke of Brahman by the compound Sanskrit term *Saccidananda*, Being-Consciousness-Joy, with the Logos as *Cit* (Intelligence). Vivekananda taught that Jesus was an *Avatara*, and V. Chakkarai

---

7. *Rg Veda* 1.164.
8. H. Meynell, comment on R. V. DeSmet's "Origin: Creation and Emanation," in *Person and God*, ed. G. F. MacLean and H. Meynell (Lanham, MD: University Press of America, 1988), 221.
9. R.C. Zaehner, *Hindu and Muslim Mysticism* (New York: Schocken Books, 1960).
10. See Staffner, *Jesus Christ and the Hindu Community*, 36–57.

developed "the most comprehensive Indian treatment of Christology."[11] In Saivism all three cosmic operations are united: creation, conservation, consummation.[12] There is also a parallel with the silent and spoken Logos (*endiathetos/prophorikos*) in Brahmanism (*nirguna/saguna*), somewhat like the immanent and economic Trinity. Karl Rahner has noted the irony in the approach of Church Fathers, including Augustine, who sought as many parallels as possible to the Trinity in Jewish and pagan literature, whereas modern Roman Catholic scholars adopt an opposite view.[13]

Incarnational Analogies

It is in Vaishnavism that we approach our subject more nearly, through the divine "descent" (*avatara*).[14] Unlike the Vedas and Upanishads, the "Great Epic" (*Mahabharata*) introduces a personal deity, revealed in different forms, appropriate for different ages and needs. Its famous section the *Bhagavad-Gītā* is familiar as the articulation of Krishna's manifestation to Arjuna. The god's descent is motivated by grace and justice:

> Whenever there appears
> A languishing of Righteousness (*dharma*)
> When Unrighteousness (*adharma*) arises
> Then I send forth [generate] myself. (4:7f)

---

11. See R.H.S. Boyd, "Indian Christian Thinking in Relation to Christ," *SJT* 19/4 (6/6 1966), 456-63.

12. A. Sharma, *A Hindu Perspective on the Philosophy of Religion* (Basingstoke: MacMillan, 1990), 21. Cf., G. Parrinder, *The Christian Debate: Light from the East* (New York: Doubleday, 1964) on Hindu trinities and their contrast with monism, e.g. Sankara, and the "modified nondualist" Ramanuja.

13. Rahner, "Remarks on the Dogmatic Treatise 'De Trinitate'" in *Theol. Inv.* IV (Baltimore: Helicon Press, 1966), 86.

14. See G. Parrinder, *Avatar and Incarnation* (London: Faber & Faber, 1970), Chapters 2 and 3.

Only by love can men see me, and know me, and come unto me. (11:54)

The spirituality of such personal faith (*bhakti*) is sublime, and close to (although distinct from) the Christian notion of justifying faith. Arjuna responds to the incarnate revelation:

> I bow before thee, I prostrate in adoration; and I beg thy grace, O glorious Lord! . . . As a father to his son, as a friend to his friend, as a lover to his beloved, be gracious unto me, O God. (11:44).

Arjuna is called to raise himself to the level of Vibhuti, in imitation of the unique manifestation of Krishna, a "Yogi of union," in whose heart the god dwells through mercy (10:11). This avatar is taken more "realistically" by modern commentators (Aurobindo, Radhakrishnan) than by earlier (Sankara).[15] Such "redeeming power of the love of God" inspired, among others, the exalted theology of Ramanuja and the love verses of the Marathi poet Tukaram.[16] In this regard, we must recognize in modern India the whole dimension of iconoclasm, a reforming program that attempted to displace idolatry with transcendent worship, belying Western assumption and demanding a better interpretation of Hindu "idols."[17]

The notorious difference between incarnations pits the unique and unrepeatable (*einmaligkeit*) Christian form against the multiform

---

15. I. Vempeny, "Avatara and Incarnation in the Bhagavadgita and in the N. T." in *Krsna and Christ* (Pune, India: Ishvari Kendra, 1988), 233–53; A. Casu, "Sri Aurobindo on Christ and Christianity" in Sharma, ed., *Neo-Hindu Views of Christianity* (Brill, 1988), 182-212. Cf. Staffner, "The Message of the Bhagavad Gita," *op.cit.* 135ff.

16. See Staffner, *op.cit.*, "The Bhakti Movement: the God of Love is our Salvation," 150ff. Also S. Kulandran, *Grace: A Comparative Study of the Doctrine in Christianity and Hinduism* (London: Lutterworth, 1964), Section Two.

17. See N. Salmond, *Hindu Iconoclasts: Rammohun Roy, Dayananda Sarasvati and Nineteenth-Century Polemics Against Idolatry* (Waterloo, ON: Wilfrid Laurier University Press, 2003).

Hindu.[18] Yet the reception of the Christian message in India, as elsewhere, is never an either/or decision (that is, as missionaries seek). We find evidence of an "Asian Christ" incorporated in Eastern religions.[19] Keshub Chandra Sen, for one, could embrace Jesus Christ as another avatar, "a devout Yogi and loving Bhakta."[20] The Ramakrishna Order associated with Swami Vivekenanda included worship of Jesus within its spiritual experience. For example, a Vedanta guru holding Christmas celebration said: "Meditate on Christ within, and feel his living presence." One of his disciples reports: "For the first time I realized that Christ was as much our own as Krishna, Buddha, and other great illuminated teachers whom we revered."[21]

A Problem with History

Such an "Oriental Christ" is interpreted through a form of demythologization (that is, presuming a prior mythologization) to become a spiritual Exemplar.[22] This is seen not only in the Ramakrishna movement but with scholarly attention in the impressive philosophical theology of

---

18. See K. Cragg, *The Christ and the Faiths* (Philadelphia: Westminster, 1986), "Christologies and India," 75ff; cf. the debate between Brian Hebblethwaite and John Hick on the uniqueness of the Incarnation, in M. Goulder, ed., *Incarnation and Myth: the Debate Continues* (Grand Rapids: Eerdmans, 1979), 6: "Christ and the Claims of Other Faiths," 197ff.

19. See R. H. S. Boyd, "Indian Christian Thinking in Relation to Christ," in *SJT* 19/4 (1966), 446-63.

20. See David Kopf, "Neo-Hindu Views of Unitarian and Trinitarian Christianity in Nineteenth Century Bengal: the Case of Keshub Chandra Sen" in Sharma, ed., *Neo-Hindu Views*, 106-19, and M. M. Thomas, *The Acknowledged Christ of the Indian Renaissance* (London: SCM, 1969). Hans Staffner uses the work of Sen to begin his case for a possible synthesis of Hinduism and Christianity (*op.cit.*, 5-21).

21. H. W. French, "Reverence to Christ Through Mystical Experience and Incarnational Identity: Sri Ramakrishna" in Sharma, ed. *Neo-Hindu Views*, 66. The disciple was Swami Prabhavananda, his master Swami Brahmananda.

22. See the typology in *Any Room for Christ in Asia?*, ed. L. Boff and V. Elizondo (Maryknoll: Orbis Books, 1993–Concilium 1993/2).

Sarvepalli Radhakrishnan. He contrasts Hindu tolerance—"the hospitality of the Indian mind"—with Christianity's "disease of dogmatism." The latter reflects "the Semitic creed of the 'jealous God' in the view of Christ as 'the only begotten Son of God' and so could not brook any rival near the throne."[23] His solution is to seek "the generic tradition" from which our isolated traditions have sprung, binding them together "as varied expressions of a single truth." For him, the essence of religion is not revelation attained by faith but our attempt "to unveil the deepest layers of man's being and get into enduring contact with them."[24]

This raises two questions. Can we reconcile the God of theism—however we interpret the divine "wrath"—with a religion of introversion? And, is it self-evident that we are dealing with the same *kind* of event (to be recovered through common ancestry), as if the problem is one of absolute and relative incarnations? Christian orthodoxy interprets the incarnation of the Logos as unrepeatable, unique. It is clear that quite different ideas of *history* cast the two in contradictory roles. Certainly the Early Church was clear that its *theôria* depends ultimately on the *historia* of the biblical witnesses.[25]

East and West are separated by their sense of the historical. It is not so simple as linear versus cyclical, or "the moving image of eternity" versus *maya*, Brahma's dreaming. For it engages the difficult question as to which is to determine which, why the human story is cast in such different modes that in turn inform the stance called faith. Westerners have tended to consider their worldview superior because it takes history to be the decisive form of human being. Indeed, Ernst Troeltsch saw the "background of the problem of the absoluteness of

---

23. S. Radhakrishnan, *Eastern Religions and Western Thought* (London [s.n.] 1940), 324f. See Ishwar Harris, "Radhakrishnan's View of Christianity" in Sharma, ed., *Neo-Hindu Views*, 156-81.

24. op. cit., 347.

25. See K. Froehlich, ed., *Biblical Interpretation in the Early Church* (Philadelphia: Fortress Press, 1984), 1–29. Also Chapter 6 above on incommensurability.

Christianity" as modernity's "development of an unreservedly historical view of human affairs," whose "idea of history" forms the "matrix out of which all world views take shape."[26] Hence Christian faith, centred on an incarnate Lord, was thought to relativize the diffuse and apparently abstract theology of the religions of India. In modern times the contrast between West and East has been termed "thisworldly and otherworldly", and more recently "anxiety and tranquillity."[27] But what if this begs the question, a Western form of *petitio principii*? The argument seems circular: taking history decisively is better because history is decisive. This begs the question as to *why* history is thought to be decisive.[28] The Western view of human decision-making produced classical theatre, the tragedies of ancient Greece. But India produced nothing similar: "men could be under the grip of fate, but never of tragedy."[29] So a phrase such as "divine purpose" makes little sense to the Hindu ear.

Christology, therefore, stands in dialectic with history. If the human story begins and ends in (and with) time, it is logically coherent to claim that Jesus as the Christ is history's centre.[30] For the Hindu, however, such a philosophy of history is reductive, simplistic. It misses the very Transcendent which it thinks to protect, producing a spirituality often materialistic, even hedonistic. This critique is evident in Arvind Sharma's categories. He notes that such distinctions as myth/history or docetic/real

---

26. Troeltsch, *op. cit.*, 45f. See Ch. 4 above, "Troeltsch's Dilemma."

27. A. Schweitzer, *Christianity and the Religions of the World* (New York: H. Holt & Co., 1939); J. Arapura, *Religion as Anxiety and Tranquillity* (The Hague: Mouton, 1973).

28. N. Smart, *World Religions*, 90ff. Vivenanda once replied to a missionary's claim that the Scriptures' historical character makes them true: "Yours are man-made and mine are not; their non-historicity is in their favour" (Sharma, ed. *Neo-Hindu Views*, 99.

29. Radhakrishnan, quoted by M.M. Thomas, *Man and the Universe of Faiths* (Madras: Christian Literature Society, 1975), 44.

30. See W. Pannenberg, "Eternity, Time, and the Trinitarian God" in C.E. Gunton, *Trinity, Time, and Church: a Response to the Theology of Robert W. Jenson* (Grand Rapids, MI: Eerdmans, 2000), 62ff.

are themselves matters of faith. He thinks it better to consider propositional and non-propositional views of revelation. For they address the final question of authority, whether textual or experiential. What requires further exploration is "the convergence between the non-propositional view of revelation and the Hindu view of incarnation."[31]

Beyond scholarly exploration, of course, is the pursuit of dialogue, which seeks to transcend theology by probing "more deeply, towards spirituality." This was the experience of Klaus Klostermaier in his sojourn in Vrindaban, where dialogue led from academic theology into "the real life of the mind."[32] It reminds us that the nature of transcendence is always to go beyond phenomena and their concepts. Perhaps this is why the historical *Jesus* has had greater impact on India than the *Christ*. Ghandi, most famously, synthesised the spirituality of the *Gîtâ* with that of the Sermon on the Mount: *Satyagraha* reworks *ahimsa* in light of *agapê*.[33]

The remarkable career of Raimundo Panikkar, with feet in both camps, as it were, brings a distinct challenge. His "solution" to the relation between the two religions is "interpenetration, mutual fecundation—and a mutation in the self-interpretation of these selfsame religious traditions."[34] Whether there be "doctrinal parallelisms" is less important than a genuine "encounter" in which the Christ and "the existential dharma of Hinduism" meet in openness.[35] Panikkar provides a "christological commentary" based on *Brahma-Sūtra* I,1,2: "That from which all things proceed and to which all things return and by which all things are." Here is a distinction within deity that provides

---

31. A. Sharma, *A Hindu Perspective*, 67ff.
32. K. Klostermaier, *Hindu and Christian in Vrindaban* (London: SCM, 1969), 83, 99.
33. Thomas, *op. cit.* 79.
34. R. Panikkar, *The Unknown Christ*, 35.
35. Panikkar, *op. cit.* 50ff. In fact he does assign privilege to "Christ, the Meeting Place," although in his own particular sense that Christ is already present in Hinduism as light of the world: "Christ is already present in every form of worship, to the extent that it is adoration directed to God" (49).

contact with Logos christology, namely "Isvara, God the Son, the Logos, the Christ." Here also is a reality that "connects the two poles" of divine and human.[36]

THE QUESTION OF BUDDHISM

Among world religions Buddhism remains a question rather than an affirmation. Given that Theravāda Buddhism has no concept of a saving god, nor is Gotama an object of worship, should it even be classified as a religion? Neither trinitarian nor incarnational analogies seem present when one passes from Hinduism to early Buddhism. The Buddha's own prescription for "salvation" resembles the Socratic way of overcoming ignorance rather than the Christian victory over sin. Gotama's struggle with Māra is like the temptation of Jesus through Satan in the wilderness, but it does not imply a like doctrine of sin and Saviour. Gotama becomes enlightened; Jesus resolves his vocation. The Buddha's "prescription for liberation from the world's ills" is hardly comparable to Christian atonement.

One noted scholar who seeks complementarity between Buddhism and Christianity is Ninian Smart, whose Gifford Lectures propose a theory of "transcendental pluralism."[37] He admits that Buddhism "remains a difficult case for those who seek formal point of contact between theologies."[38] He notes the theistic advance in Mahâyâna developments: "the cult of Bodhisattvas and celestial Buddhas made these beings, phenomenologically considered, divine."[39] More significant is

---

36. Panikkar, *op. cit.* 155ff.
37. *Beyond Ideology: Religion and the Future of Western Civilization* (London: Collins, 1980), 14.
38. Ninian Smart, *The Yogi and the Devotee* (London: George Allen & Unwin, 1968), 21.
39. Smart, "The Work of the Buddha and the Work of Christ" in Brandon, ed. *The Saviour God*, 160ff. See, e.g., Smart, *Doctrine and Argument in Indian Philosophy* (London: Geo Allen & Unwin, 1964), *The Religious Experience of Mankind* (New York: Charles Scribner's Sons, 1969), 77ff, "The Buddha." Also

the development in Mahayana of the *Trikaya* or "Three Bodies" concept expressing the devotion of *bhakti*. The numerous "Lords Buddhas" of the *Lotus Sutra* constitute the blissful body, contrasted with the body of Manifestation, the historical Buddha; behind all is the absolute *Dharmakaya* or eternal Buddha, the "Truth-Body."[40] Certainly the process of "crossing over" is governed by Bodhisattvas, "dependent on a perfectly enlightened Buddha—the Buddha Amitâbha." Yet "they operate strictly within the law of *karma*, and their power to do good is based on the tremendous amount of 'merit' (*punya*) they have accumulated."[41] Such a treasury of merit resonates with the later medieval Christian concept, one that sparked Martin Luther's revolt on behalf of free grace. It may also suggest a similar tension between faith and works, two ways of spirituality in various religions. This dimension relates to another concept, Buddhist messianism, the expectation of "the coming of a new Buddha, the last Buddha Maitreya," who "will renew the Dharma and usher in the Buddhist world order."[42]

Any rapprochement between Buddhism and Christianity, or indeed other religions, turns on its mystical dimension, according to Smart.[43] He contrasts the numinous (judging Otto's category to be too narrow) and the mystical. The latter has certain defining characteristics: it purifies consciousness, transcends the subject-object distinction, is

---

L. P. Barnes, "Light from the East: Ninian Smart and the Christian-Buddhist Encounter," *Scottish Journal of Theology*, 40.1 (1987), 67–83.

40. Smart, *The Religious Experience of Mankind* (New York: Charles Scribner's Sons, 1969), 103ff.

41. E. Conze, "Buddhist Saviours" in Brandon, ed. *The Saviour God*, 70ff.

42. M. M. Thomas, "Buddhist Messianism and Existential Suffering," pp 81-95 of *Man and the Universe of Faiths* (Madras: Christian Literature Society, 1975). The quotation (81) is from the Convocation of the Sixth Buddhist Council in Rangoon.

43. See Smart, "Interpretations of Mystical Experience," *Religious Studies*, I (1965), 75–87.

timeless and "unutterable."[44] To define the mystical is to ask for trouble, as we will suggest in the next chapter. There is the obvious contradiction in articulating an ineffable experience. There is also the question whether Smart is correct in positing a common Transcendent beyond such experiences, placing division or pluralism as belonging to the realm of interpretation. No doubt this is what every attempt at solving the problem of pluralism does: the classic formulation of Denis the Areopagite has negative theology qualifying positive, with a crowning unity beyond both.[45]

Whatever we think of the cognitive value of mystical experience, it remains true that we must follow Smart in according genuine knowledge of the Transcendent to forms of religious experience that receive different—even contradictory—doctrinal interpretation. Perhaps nowhere is this more poignant than in the religions of the Indian subcontinent, with their wild variety of experiential data. And here, as with Hinduism, those such as Thomas Merton who claim to live in both sets of experience, may provide better signs of the future than our academic debates.[46] There is also Karl Barth's recognition of the challenge facing Christian theology from "evangelical" Buddhism, while C. S. Song has noted that "Bhakti religion and Shin Buddhism" (in 1549 Frances Xavier dubbed the latter "the Lutheran heresy") raise deeper questions than other forms.[47]

"CHRISTOLOGY OUTSIDE THEOLOGY:" ISLAM

The phrase is Kenneth Cragg's, in his sympathetic treatment of Islam.[48] This is a stance in marked contrast to Jacques Ellul's estimate of

---

44. Smart, *Beyond Ideology*, 133ff.
45. See chapter 10 below.
46. *Thomas Merton on Zen* (London: Sheldon Press, 1976), "A Christian Looks at Zen," 91ff. Cf. Geo Siegmund, *Buddhism and Christianity: A Preface to Dialogue* (University of Alabama Press, 1980), esp. 152ff, "Buddha and Christ."
47. Barth, *C.D.* I.2, 340; Song, *Third-Eye Theology* (New York: Orbis Books, 1979), 88ff. See ch. 7 above, "A Caveat from Karl Barth."
48. K. Cragg, *Jesus and the Muslims* (London: Allen & Unwin, 1985), 61ff.

Islam as "the subversion of Christianity." The latter declares, "I believe that in every respect the spirit of Islam is contrary to that of the revelation of God in Jesus Christ."[49] Ellul blames Islam for the mysticism which invaded Christian Europe, and even for the Crusades in which Christians invaded the Muslim lands. Cragg, on the other hand, pays attention to what the Qur'an says about Jesus.

Jesus in the Qur'an

> People of the Book, do not go to unwarranted lengths in your religion and get involved in false utterances relating to God. Truly Jesus, Mary's son, was the messenger of God and His word—the word which He imparted to Mary—and a spirit from Him. Believe, then, in God and His messengers and do not talk of three gods. You are well advised to abandon such ideas. Truly God is one God. Glory be to Him and no 'son' to Him whose are all things in heaven and the earth, their one and only guardian. (*Surat* 4:171f)

Cragg's thesis is that Islam is one of three religions that look back to Abraham: Judaism as its seed, Islam as its founding idol-breaker, Christianity as its prologue to suffering.[50] "Those who believe" (*muslims*) in the Qur'an include Jews, Christians and Sabaeans (2:62, 5:69). One is reminded of Lessing's *Nathan the Wise*, where three rings are given to the three sons, but so mixed that one cannot tell which is the original and authentic ring of the father.

An important point to note at the very beginning of the Muslim critique of Christian trinitarianism is the differing concepts of *person*. Western theory developed from Greek metaphysics through Boethius and Augustine to posit a rather substantive idea of human being. On the contrary, the Muslim word for person, *shakhs*, does not appear in the

---

49. J. Ellul, *The Subversion of Christianity* (Grand Rapids: Eerdmans, 1986), 98.
50. K. Cragg, *The Privilege of Man* (London: Athlone, 1968), 55ff.

Qur'an itself; the preferred term is "spirit" (*naf,* cf. Hebrew *nephesh*).⁵¹ Such basic cognitive dissonance between the two faiths helps explain one contradiction that requires preliminary attention in dialogue. Soul and body may unite (through *hulûl*) but Divine and human cannot do so without dividing the divine essence. This was a point that the great Al-Ghazâlî (1058-1111) sought to prove in his "Excellent Refutation of the Divinity of Jesus Christ according to the Gospels."⁵² Even Sûfî mystical teaching on the closeness if not "identification" of mystic and God does not imply a genuine incarnation in the Christian sense.⁵³

As to the person of Jesus, there is a kind of "soft christology" within the Qur'an, beginning with the positive treatment of Mary (3 and 19, Sura Mariam) and continuing with Jesus, "a word from God . . . the servant of God:"

> We have granted Jesus, Son of Mary, the elucidations and have fortified him with the Holy Spirit. (*Surat al-Baqara* 2:87)
>
> [Mary and Jesus] have been made an *aya*, a sign for humankind.(*Surat al-Mu'minum* 23:50)⁵⁴

Thus the holy pair are signs giving knowledge of something unknown, a revelation indeed. This christology is symbolized in the Qur'an by the Virgin Birth of Jesus at the beginning and his peculiar role of Judge at the End. It accords to Jesus a unique place, existing in a sort of dialectic with that of Muhammad.⁵⁵ The vexed question of the Qur'an's dismissing the

---

51. See A.H. Khan, "The Idea of Person with Reference to Islam," *Harvard Islamics* 13/2 (1990).

52. See Parrinder, *Avatar and Incarnation* (London: Faber & Faber, 1970), 192ff: "Incarnation in Islam?" Ghazâlî stresses the Gospel witness to the humanity of Jesus, and interprets other verses metaphorically.

53. See Parrinder, *Avatar and Incarnation*, 198: "Sûfî Beliefs." He reviews the ideas of al-Hallâj, Rûmî and Ibn ʿArabî in particular.

54. See K. Cragg, *The Christ and the Faiths* (Philadelphia: Westminster, 1986), 29ff, "Theologies of the Magnificat."

55. See G. Parrinder, *Jesus in the Qur'an* (London: Faber, 1965).

crucifixion as a kind of misunderstanding, an "illusion" ("so it seemed to them," *Surat Nisa'* 4:157), is receiving more positive treatment today.[56] Moreover, there is a kind of Assumption linked to the End:

> God raised him to himself . . . And before they come to die, the people of the Book, to a man, will believe on him. On the day of resurrection he will be a witness against them. (*Surat* 4:159)

Yet none of this should lead Christians to an overly-confident stance: in this "reduced" material "the Christian observer has detected meanings that were never intended."[57] A related topic, of course, is the Shi'a emphasis on Ali's sacrificial death, reflecting what Montgomery Watt calls "the Muslim yearning for a Saviour."[58] There is also the general Muslim regard for Abraham as not only the "idol-breaker" but himself a figure of trial and suffering celebrated in the Festival of Sacrifice, the *'Id al-Adha* commemorating the offering of Ishmael.[59]

The Qur'an as the Christ

What Christians often miss, however, is the sort of "christology" attributed to the Book itself. As Wilfred C. Smith used to insist, in order to "compare" Islam and Christianity, one must grasp the proper analogues: the Hadith (Tradition) is like the Bible, Muhammad is like Paul—it is the Qur'an that resembles Christ.[60] For the Qur'an is Word

---

56. See Mahmoud Ayoub, "Divine Revelation and the Person of Jesus Christ," Hartford Seminary, *Newsletter of Christian-Muslim Concerns*, 43 (July 1990).

57. Josef van Ess, "Islam and the Other Religions: Jesus in the Qur'an," in Küng, *Christianity and the World Religions*, 99.

58. M. Watt, "The Muslim Yearning for a Saviour: Aspects of Early 'Abbâsid Shi'ism" in Brandon, ed., *Saviour Gods*, 191ff.

59. *Genesis* 22 and *Surat* 37; The Qur'an does not name the son, but Tradition replaces Isaac by Ishmael. The story is the Jewish *Akeda* that is focus for much discussion on the problem of suffering in light of the Holocaust.

60. W.C. Smith, "Is the Qur'an the Word of God?" in *Questions of Religious Truth* (New York: Charles Scribner's, 1967), 39ff.

of God (*Kalâm Allâh*), the "recitation" which claims to be verbally revealed, not merely in its "meaning and ideas," and therefore "pure Divine Word."[61] Thus we face a radical monotheism which purifies the concept of God from every hint of "association," *Shirk*. The Christian doctrine of Trinity must appear to such singular purity as polytheism, a corruption like that from which Muhammad saved his people in the first place. The *Shahâdah* puts it beautifully: "There is no God but God." As a warning against idolatry it means "No God unless God." Cragg terms this "non-generic singularity," since "Allah" is not a species of "ilahah."[62] And in terms reminiscent of the Ontological Argument, *Allâhu Akbar*, "Greater is God!" is logical partner to Anselm's "than which nothing greater can be conceived" (*ens quo nihil maius cogitari potest*).

God's relationship to his creatures is accomplished through a "sending down" (*Tanzil*) accommodated to the hearers of the divine Word given through his Prophets. Tanzil rejects incarnation as an improper modality of divine presence which would displace the spoken Word enshrined in the Qur'an. This Word is the only medium that guarantees genuine Transcendence, so that to say "God is the Third of Three" is illogical (*Surat* 5:78).

The Hadith includes sayings from Jesus, usually admonishing us to distance ourselves from the world. Al-Ghazâlî (1058-1111) is familiar with them, indeed he includes forty-seven from the one he calls "Prophet of the Heart."[63] His "Refutation of the Divinity of Jesus Christ" is also noteworthy in its critique, which turns on the metaphorical interpretation of sayings by and about Jesus.[64] Such tropical exegesis recalls us to

---

61. F. Rahman, *Islam* (Chicago: University of Chicago Press, 1979), 30ff. Cf. Josef van Ess: "completely inimitable" in *Christianity and the World Religions*, ed. Küng, 16.

62. K. Cragg, *Jesus and the Muslims*, 33.

63. Most are in his *The Revival of the Sciences of Religion*; see Tarif Khalidi, *The Muslim Jesus: Sayings and Stories in Islamic Literature* (Cambridge, MA: Harvard University Press, 2001). Khalidi calls the collection "the Muslim gospel."

64. F. Shehadi, *Ghazali's Unique Unknowable God* (Leiden: Brill, 1964); G.

the theological foundation of Islam which makes Incarnation unthinkable. Still, in the Arabic Muslim literary tradition Jesus emerges as "a major figure . . . both apocalyptic and 'biblical,'" indeed "a model ascetic figure."[65]

The *Shi'a* tradition (followers of Alî) introduces a different idea: the "divine indwelling" (*hulûl*) explains the phenomenon of the Imam. He shares a communion with God something like that of Jesus. Isma'ili scholars speculate about this analogue to incarnation, although they reject extremists such as the Druzes, calling them *hulûlîya* like the Christians. In Sufi mysticism the influence of Plotinian emanationism as well as Hindu monism strengthens the idea of union with God, *ittihâd* or "becoming one."[66] The Persian mystic-poet Rumî (d. 1273) teaches divine manifestations in every age: "the Loved One assumes a new garment." These include Jesus, Muhammad, Alî and Hallaj the Crown of the Mystics, executed in 922 for the heresy of *Shirk*. Finally, Ibn 'Arabi (d. 1240) is an extreme monist with a Plotinian Logos (*kalima*). The God beyond properties is patient of human participation or "identification."

Jesus occupies a peculiar role in Islam, therefore, a prophet and more than a prophet. We should remember that early Islam provided "a porous environment," one that emerged when "the Church of the Great Councils had not yet imposed its dogmas in the Near East . . . Islam was born amid many, often hostile Christian communities and not in the bosom of the universal church."[67] Whatever "christology" the Qur'an ascribes to Jesus, however, is relative to the fact that it is the Book itself that enjoys a functional christology in the foundation of Islam. In the case of Islam, the logic of divine unity rejects *a priori* every incarna-

---

Parrinder, *Avatar and Incarnation* (London: Faber, 1970), 192ff.
  65. Khalidi, *The Muslim Jesus*, 25.
  66. R. Zaehner, *Hindu and Christian Mysticism*, 86ff. Cf. Khalidi: "Jesus was enshrined in Sufi sensibility as the prophet of the heart par excellence," *The Muslim Jesus*, 42.
  67. Khalidi, *The Muslim Jesus*, 6f.

tional concept. Therefore prophets and messengers there may be, but any person or principle even approaching divinity is unthinkable. Let the final word be this: God is always greater, *Allâhu Akbar*!

"Appropriate to God"

This chapter has not tried to include Judaism, and Buddhism only in passing. The former presents the unique challenge of Christianity's origins by denying its identification of the Jewish Messiah. Its own story is a kind of messianic suffering, with the Holocaust the most poignant symbol of the long history of persecution for being the People of God. Buddhism, on the contrary, defies the obvious categories for defining religion itself, and tackles the problem of suffering in a quite different way.

Every religion operates from the touchstone of *theoprêpes*, what is "appropriate to God". The Christian doctrine of the Trinity, developed to conceptualize appropriately the impact of christological confession, operated with the theoretical constructs of its day. Following Plato it knew that "God" is beyond being;[68] following Middle Platonism (e.g. Albinus) it knew that the One is incomprehensible and unutterable (*agnostôs, arretôs*), but apprehensible through the *via triplex* of remotion, causality and eminence. Crowning all is the gradual abstraction (*aphairesis, remotio*) leading to the frontiers of knowing, where the Mystery grants revelation to the initiate (*epoptês*) through participation (*methexis*). Denis' *Divine Names*, for instance, so influential through John of Damascus and the commentary of Aquinas, leads from cataphatic to apophatic, from ascetic to mystical theology, to an ecstatic union with That which is beyond all names, "hyper-essence".[69]

To be without qualities (*apoios*) is to exist *sui generis*. Philo of Alexandria, foundational influence on Jewish, Christian and Muslim theology,

---

68. *epeikeina tes ousias, Rep.* 509B.
69. I have discussed this history in *God the Anonymous* (1971) and *Prometheus Rebound* (1988).

moved the doctrine of God beyond Plato, so that "God" is beyond naming, and clearly beyond qualification.[70] If *That* is not a generic term, how can we qualify Unity? And how can we exist in relation to That which is beyond existence? The Christian answer conflates revelation and reconciliation in the divine Economy. It is in this sense that Raimundo Panikkar notes that strictly speaking, Christianity is not a religion of the Trinity but of the Christ: "The God of theism, thus, is the Son."[71] The dilemma of christology is its attempt to match the traumatic experience of the life and death and reappearance of Jesus of Nazareth with terms appropriate to his finality and absolute status, without qualifying inappropriately the transcendent God. It concludes that there can be no theology except as derived from christology, and no christology without incarnation. (Karl Barth's insistence that the result is a unique "theanthropology" seems to have escaped our dialogue to date).

Hinduism and Islam face the same question: how can the finite relate to the infinite? and operate with a similar problematic, attribution that will qualify positively without conceptual inconsistency. Christian theology has faced the question of a historical faith ever since the Apostolic Fathers struggled to differentiate their faith in an incarnate Logos from the Orphic-Platonic and other Mediterranean religions of their time. Origen in particular was sensitive to the philosophical critique of Celsus, antedating our modern dilemma about "the question of the historical basis of the kerygma."[72] As noted earlier, Lessing phrased the question aptly: "can one base an eternal happiness on a historical accident?" The reply developed by Kierkegaard is still

---

70. Philo Alexandrinus, *Quod Deus Immutabilis Sit*, 1f. See H.A. Wolfson, *Philo: Foundations of religious philosophy in Christianity, Judaism and Islam* (Cambridge: Harvard University Press, 1962), 2 vols.

71. Pannikar, *The Trinity and World Religions* (Madras: Christian Literature Society, 1970).

72. F. Gogarten, *Demythology and History* (London: SCM, 1955), 16ff; McLelland, *God the Anonymous*, 106ff.

to be measured by later philosophy and theology, tending as they both do to dismiss him as irrational or simply "the Father of existentialism." But the two philosophical works that his pseudonym Johannes Climacus composed on the subject provide a unique focus for the current problem of pluralism. In the *Philosophical Fragments* (1844) the thesis of "God in time" as "the Absolute Paradox" was proposed as the limit against which our reason reacts. This resembles Kant's antinomies, but advances beyond to a subjectivity that apprehends the transcendent Truth despite "objective uncertainty." The companion volume, *Concluding Unscientific Postscript to the Philosophical Fragments* (1846), attacks (Hegelian) abstract thought in behalf of the "existing thinker" who stands in need of *becoming*, something accomplished only by a "leap." The dynamism involved requires modal categories, which Kierkegaard explores with the help of Aristotle and Trendelenburg.[73]

The decisive point still remains to be noted, namely that Christian faith is not symbolized simply by a doctrine of Incarnation but by a Cross, the fate of the incarnate Logos. Kenosis denotes the movement of Being into time, denying a docetic christology, positing a break of, and within, human history. This "broken symbol" denies every attempt to achieve logical coherence as a particular instance of a general type: it is not epistemology but soteriology that provides the key. It may be termed a "singularity," analogous to that final limit-concept of historical physics. It anticipates both revelation and reconciliation; it reveals a fault that can be overcome only with an ultimate sacrifice. It is not an answer so much as a question: *Cur deus homo*?

Process thinking offers one way of reducing tension by shifting the question away from physics and metaphysics; Hartshorne puts it best: "What is the *religious* significance of 'absolute'"?[74] The answer recognizes that a bare absolute, particularly in terms of omnipotence, may spell the end of faith rather than its beginning. Moreover, each tradition has

---

73. See chapter 7 above.
74. C. Hartshorne, *The Divine Relativity* (Chicago: University of Chicago Press, 1949).

developed existential ways of relating relative to absolute, and so confirming the spirituality of its theistic devotees. In our postmodern age, it is not becoming for philosophers to insist on conceptual consistency as far as this governs the demands of spiritual coherence. Nor can we mediate among the three sorts of faith at issue here, as if a "transcendental unity of apperception" judges the truth of propositions about Transcendence. Rather, ours is a third-order analysis of (second-order) confessions of (first-order) faith. We can but follow after the traces of those presentations of reality to which the faithful bear witness. Whether or not they will see a need to compare and adjust their statements in light of our unease, whether or not they will acknowledge that some kind of complementarity is possible, is a different kind of issue.

10

SILENCE AND SPEECH

God is honoured by silence—not because we cannot say or understand anything about him, but because we know that we are incapable of comprehending him ... This is the extreme of human knowledge: to know that we do not know God.
— Thomas Aquinas[1]

On the feast of St Thomas in the year 1273 Thomas Aquinas returned to his study after Mass, but was moved to silence by the numinous experience just received. He told his friend Reginald, "All that I have written hitherto seems to me nothing but straw."[2] He stopped writing, never to return to the final section of his great *Summa Theologiae* (it was completed by disciples who missed the point). Thomas did compose one last piece, appropriately a meditation on the *Song of Songs* for the monks of Fossanova. This ultimate motion of grace in the great theologian seems a fitting conclusion to his negative theology. The best example is how he begins his treatise on God: "Now

---

1. *ST,* Ia 3, 1; cf. *SCG* I.14, 2.. See Wm. C. Placher, *The Domestication of Transcendence: How Modern Thinking About God Went Wrong* (Louisville KY: John Knox Press, 1996), "2: Aquinas on the Unknowable God," 21ff.

2. Later he would add: "compared to what I have seen and what has been revealed to me."—Josef Pieper, *The Silence of St Thomas*, trans. Murray & O'Connor (New York: Pantheon, 1957), 39.

we cannot know what God is, but only what he is not; therefore we must consider the ways in which God does not exist rather than the ways in which he does."[3]

In part the negative theology of Aquinas resulted from his commitment to Aristotelian anthropology. If the soul is "the form of the body," its motor, then body is the matter of soul, and limits its intellectual efforts.[4] In noetics this view departed from the Augustinian theory of illumination of the intellect by direct divine light. Thus "it entailed an empirical intellectualism, restricting the data of intellection to sense knowledge only."[5] It must be added, however, that from his different perspective Augustine also recognized the limits of knowledge: "Whatever you understand cannot be God."[6]

Denis the Areopagite was one influence on Aquinas. He was named after Paul's convert at the Areopagus in Athens who responded to the sermon on "the Unknown God."[7] He exhibits the influence of Plotinus, whose famous summary of mysticism runs: "This is the life of gods and of the godlike and blessed among men, liberation from the alien that besets us here, taking no pleasure in the things of the earth, the passing of the solitary to the solitary."[8] While the Areopagite's identity was (fittingly) unknown and remained suspect, confidence in his teaching grew, as

---

3. Aquinas, *ST*, Ia 2,3.

4. J. Pieper, *Scholasticism: Personalities and Problems of Medieval Philosophy* (London: Faber and Faber, 1960), 53f. The quotations are from the commentary on Boethius, *De trinitate*, 2,1 ad 6 and I,2 ad 1, and *Quaest. disp. de Potentia Dei*, 7,5 ad 14.

5. E. Gilson, *Christian Philosophy in the Middle Ages* (New York: Random House, 1954), 382.

6. *Si comprehendis, non est Deus*: *De trinitate* 5,1,1 etc. Cf. D.C. Hall, *The Trinity: An Analysis of St Thomas Aquinas'* Expositio *of the* De Trinitate *of Boethius* (Leiden: E.J. Brill, 1992) on his "profound negativity of *agnosia*," 15.

7. Acts 17:34. Denis was likely a 5thC Syrian cleric. See C.E. Rolt, *Dionysius the Areopagite on the Divine Names and the Mystical Theology* (New York: Macmillan, 1920), Intro.

8. Or, "the flight of the alone to the Alone." Plotinus, *Enneads*, VI.9.11. In fact he developed a noteworthy aesthetics.

shown by the commentaries written by Maximus the Confessor in the East and Albert the Great and Aquinas in the West. The threefold approach to Transcendence that Denis organized so well—purgation, illumination, union—reflects the general mystical tradition but also provides a critique of Western epistemology. For one thing, the latter generally assumes an active intellect (not necessarily identical with the Scholastic *agens intellectus*) which contradicts the insight that human reason is incapable of comprehending the Absolute. It is the latter view that insists that only a "passive intellect" will be able (i.e. receive the grace) to apprehend that which utterly transcends the concepts of human knowing: "Mind beyond mind, word beyond speech." This is especially clear in the teaching of John of the Cross, as shown by the excellent study of Jacques Maritain.[9]

The status of negative theology today is contentious. The traditional comfort with the concept of analogy—from Aristotle through Thomas and Cajetan—has given way to a preference for metaphor, which trades on the difference between sign and things signified. "Enigma lives on in the heart of metaphor. In metaphor, the 'same' operates in spite of 'the different.'"[10] Colin Gunton was one who insisted that the "predominance of the negative" and its worldview should have been "rejected centuries ago on the grounds of a doctrine of creation formed in the light of the Trinity."[11] But now we are familiar with *la différance* (Derrida) and *le différend* (Lyotard). Perhaps Bachelard was right on this point, that modern science demands a non-Aristotelian logic that

---

9. J. Maritain, *Distinguer pour unir, ou Les degrés du savoir* (1932); *Distinguish to Unite, or The Degrees of Knowledge*, trans. G. B. Phelan (New York: Scribner's, 1959).

10. Paul Ricoeur, *The Rule of Metaphor*, quoted by Nicholas Lash, "Ideology, metaphor and analogy" in *The Philosophical Frontiers of Christian Theology: Essays presented to D. M. Mackinnon* (Cambridge University Press, 1982), 78.

11. C. Gunton, *Act and Being: towards a theology of the divine attributes* (Grand Rapids, MI: Eerdmans, 2003), 65.

PLURALISM WITHOUT RELATIVISM

privileges negation.[12] Or more poetically, Amos Wilder said, "The null point breeds new algebras."

UNIO MYSTICA

"Mysticism" is a notoriously difficult term to define.[13] The name derives from the Greek verb *myô*, to close the apertures of eye and mouth, and also from *myeô*, to initiate.[14] Such closure signified a twofold secrecy: some things you *can*not tell, others you *may* not. To stress the point, the Pythagoreans imposed a code of silence on their initiates for some two years or more. The two elements of transcendent ineffability and cultic secret developed into the great Mystery Religions of the classical world. When Dionysos invaded Greece he was a militant deity, destined to inform religious culture with his powerful presence:

> And now I come to Hellas, having taught
> All the world else my dances and my rite
> Of mysteries, to show me in man's sight
> Manifest God.[15]

While the "myth-and-ritual" school of religious interpretation is no longer so influential, its lesson should still be heeded: devotion to the god implies an utter transcendence signified but not captured, apprehended but never comprehended. And if it takes many forms, sometimes complementary and often contradictory, this points not to the inconsistency of the evidence so much as to the richness of the data. This is why mystical theology is inexorably linked with asceticism and its experien-

---

12. G. Bachelard, *La Philosophie du Non: Essai d'une Philosophie du Nouvel Esprit Scientifique* (Paris: Presses Universitaires de France, 1949), esp. 105-34.
13. Dean (W. R.) Inge offered twenty-five definitions in his *Christian Mysticism* (London: Methuen, 1921).
14. See K. Kerenyi, *Eleusis: archetypal image of Mother and Daughter* (New York: Bollingen Series LXV.4) 24ff; McLelland, *God the Anonymous* (Philadelphia Patristic Foundation, 1976), 4ff.
15. Euripides, *Bacch*. 13.

tial knowledge—the *unio mystica* entails a *cognitio dei experimentalis*—and in turn with negative theology. The Beyond (*epekeina*) demands a change in paradigms, "beyond" both positive and negative modes: "C'est pourquoi toute connaissance authentique et sa 'mélioration' s'accompagne d'une augmentation du non-connu: 'docta ignorantia'—ignorance docte, et non pas: sagesse ignorante."[16]

Eastern theology has always looked at doctrine differently from the West. The Alexandrians—Philo, Clement and Origen—had already explored the mystical ladder with telling result; the resulting "Christian Platonism" should not hinder the truth to which they witnessed. Origen once observed: "*Ekstasis*, then, occurs when in knowing things great and wonderful the mind is suspended in astonishment."[17] The very term "orthodox" includes a dimension of "orthopraxy," the liturgical theology that honours the great Mystery of Incarnation and its lesser mysteries the sacraments. Thus whereas in the West orthodox signifies "correctness," in the East it includes (correct) worship. This subtle difference is reflected also by rendering *sacramentum* as *mysterion*, and *Catholic* as *Soborny*, "gathered." In short, the true Sage is the Mystagogue. A striking illustration of this Eastern ethos is the Hesychast controversy of the fourteenth century, the usage of constant prayer linked to a pattern of breathing. This had become associated with the mystical experience of Divine Light. Gregory Palamas defended the monks by referring to the Orthodox tradition of ascetic-liturgical piety. His distinction between divine "essence" and "energies" helped defend the practice by allowing a dynamic presence without sinking into merely rote repetition.[18]

---

16. Maurice Boutin, "Finitude et Transcendance: conditions d'un changement de paradigme," in *Théologie Négative*, ed. M. Olivetti, (Padova: CEDAM, 2002), 346.

17. *Hom. Num.* xxvii.12 (SC 29, 547). See McLelland, *God the Anonymous*, 126ff.

18. See McLelland, "Sailing to Byzantium" in *The New Man: An Orthodox and Reformed Dialogue*, ed. McLelland and Meyendorff (New Brunswick,

PLURALISM WITHOUT RELATIVISM

Now the classic Christian definition of faith, both East and West, is "union with Christ," a *unio mystica* based on Paul's concept of being *en Christô* (e.g. Rom. 6:5, 2 Cor. 5:17). The Cappadocians explore the mystery aptly. Gregory Nazianzen puts the case: "when we have thus become like Himself, God may, to use a bold expression, hold converse with us as Gods, being united to us."[19] Gregory of Nyssa develops the traditional ideas of *apatheia* and *gnosis* as steps towards the true *theôria*, the highest stage of contemplation, in which one achieves perfect union beyond negation and the divine darkness.[20] Later, Gregory Palamas made much of the distinction between the divine "essence" and "energies," teaching that the *energeia* shed an uncreated radiance on human being, leading to *theôsis* or "divinisation."[21] This notion may be compared with the Western idea of sanctification, where the Augustinian tradition of mystical union supplied a similar dynamic to faith.[22] A striking instance of this doctrine is given in Calvin's transition to Book Three of the *Institutes*, when he declares that the previous doctrines are barren unless believers are united with Christ.

> I attribute, therefore, the highest importance to connection between the head and members; to the inhabitation of Christ in our hearts; in a word, to the mystical union by which we enjoy him, so that being made ours, he makes us partakers of the blessings with which he is furnished.[23]

NJ: Agora Books, 1973), esp. 15ff.

19. Gregory Nazianzen, *On the Theophany, or Birthday of Christ* VII (NPNF VII, 347). The context is Gregory's discussion of God's infinity and therefore incomprehensibility: "The Divine Nature then is boundless and hard to understand . . ."

20. Gregory of Nyssa, e.g. *Life of Moses; Homilies on the Canticle of Canticles* (Migne, PG 44).

21. See B. Krivosheine, *The Ascetic and Theological Teaching of Gregory Palamas* (London: Caldwell, 1938), 17ff.

22. See McLelland, *The New Man*, 132ff.

23. Calvin, *Institutes*, III.11.10.

Barth acknowledges the Reformers' definition of faith as *unio Christi*, stating: "In emphasizing this more than mystical and more than speculative statement, that faith means unity with the thing believed in, i.e. with Jesus Christ, Calvin did not in the least lag behind a Luther, or either of them behind an Augustine, an Anselm, a Bernard of Clairvaux. Without this statement the Reformed doctrine of justification and faith is impossible to understand".[24] But Barth offers a strong qualification to the mystical tradition. While he agrees with the Christian doctrine of *unio mystica*, his thesis on "the abolition of religion" noted above, relates mysticism as such to atheism, since both involve the turn to "a relatively new road" of insight. Atheism is "an artless and childish form of that critical turn. Atheism means a blabbing out of the secret that so far as this turn involves anything at all it involves only a negation." Therefore "Mysticism is esoteric atheism."[25] This is surely a strong warning against regarding negation as ultimate, formed in silence.

MODUS LOQUENDI THEOLOGICUS

Augustine had laid the foundation for classical theism's nuanced doctrine of God as ultimately ineffable. Indeed:

> God should not be spoken of even as ineffable, because, when we say this word, we are saying something about Him. There is some contradiction of terms, since, if that is ineffable which cannot be spoken of, a thing is not ineffable which can be called ineffable. We should guard against this contradiction in terms by silence, rather than attempt to reconcile them by discussion.[26]

Yet Augustine will not shirk the responsibility of saying something about the ineffable. In his search for the proper mode of theological speech he can be almost coy in hedging the issue: "we speak because

---

24. Barth, *C.D.* I/1, 274. Barth calls Calvin the theologian of sanctification, as Luther is of justification.
25. Barth, *C.D.* I.2, §17, 318ff.
26. Augustine, *De doctrina Christiana*, I.6.

we must say something." As noted, Gregory Palamas developed his cataphatic theology in sympathy with the Hesychasts for whom silent prayer is the norm, a devotional reflection of the utter simplicity of godhead. If God is ineffable, surpassing all created being (*ousia hyperousios*) then we can and may speak of *That* only in appropriate modes. The ancient question of Greek theology was always: what is *theoprepês*, appropriate to God? This is seen clearly in the Arian controversies, where Athanasius thought that Arians and Tropici were blaspheming against God, arguing from a *deus revelatus* to a *deus absconditus*.[27]

Nicolas of Cusa's famous concept of "learned ignorance" (*docta ignorantia*) notes that "Since the Maximum is the Absolute infinite and therefore all things without distinction, it is clear that it cannot have a proper name." His trinitarian theology proceeds to qualify this by positing a hypostatic union between the Absolute maximum and the limited maximum of the human person; the latter subsists through *enhypostasia*. Moreover, this "maximal humanity" can embrace "the total power of the species and is so much the source of being of each man as to stand far closer to him than ever could brother or most intimate friend."[28]

Such language of losing the self in higher unity was anathema to Emil Brunner. In his study of Schleiermacher he sees only two kinds of relationship with God: mysticism and faith. Schleiermacher's attempt to join them is an impossibility; they form a "glaring contradiction."[29] The famous "feeling of absolute dependence" turns faith into self-consciousness (identical with "God-consciousness") and therefore non-cognitive.

---

27. See G. D. Dragas, "The Eternal Son," in T. F. Torrance, ed. *The Incarnation: Ecumenical Studies in the Nicene-Constantinopolitan Creed AD 381* (Edinburgh: The Handsel Press, 1981), 40ff.

28. Cusanus, *Of Learned Ignorance* (London: Routledge & Kegan Paul, 1954), 53, 139, 146.

29. E. Brunner, *Die Mystik und das Wort: Der Gegensatz zwischen moderner Religionsauffassung und christlichem Glauben dargestellt an der Theologie Schleiermachers* (J. C. B. Mohr, 1924), 312.

When Karl Barth—whose ambivalent attitude to Schleiermacher is well known—reviewed Brunner's book he defended Schleiermacher from what he considered a reduction of his complex thought. One can put too much weight on the Moravianism of the Berlin professor's youth, so missing the strongly apologetic nature of both the *Reden* and the *Glaubenslehre*.[30] That cryptic mystic Angelus Silesius put the case like this:

> God far exceeds all words that we can here express
> In silence He is heard, in silence worshipped best.[31]

The famous aphorisms of Ludwig Wittgenstein are similar:

> There is indeed the inexpressible. This *shows* itself; it is the mystical.
> Whereof one cannot speak, thereof one must be silent.[32]

This insight recalls the saying of Michael Polanyi: "We know more than we can tell. Nothing that we know can be said precisely." His thesis is that all knowledge involves a personal dimension, such that the quest for "total objectivity," even in the natural sciences, is wrong-head-

---

30. K. Barth, "Brunners Schleiermacherbuch," in *Zwischen den Zeiten* 1924, Heft 8, 49–64.

31. Lines 1:240—*Angelus Silesius: The Cherubinic Wanderer*, trans. Maria Schrady (New York: Paulist Press, 1986), xi.

32. Wittgenstein, *Tractatus Logico-Philosophicus*, trans. Pears & McGuiness (London: Routledge & Kegan Paul, 1922), 6.432ff on *das Mystische*. An ambiguity results from his repudiation of the thesis of the *Tractatus* in the *Blue and Brown Books* (New York: Harper, 1958) and the *Philosophical Investigations* (Oxford: Basil Blackwell, 1968). But in view of his own mystical experience on the Eastern Front one might argue that the strict view of scientific language was already bracketed implicitly by a larger notion of language games at play. See W. D. Hudson, *Wittgenstein and Religious Belief* (London: Macmillan, 1975). Cf., Thos McPherson, "Religion as the Inexpressible" in *New Essays in Philosophical Theology*, Flew & MacIntyre, eds. (New York: SCM Press, 1955), 131–43. The latter's conclusion is to deny the possibility of religious utterance: what theologians try to say "belong to the class of things that just cannot be said" (132f).

ed.³³ One thinks of Kierkegaard's idea that "subjectivity is truth," scoring the idealistic fallacy of turning religion into philosophy, as Hegel did so splendidly if mistakenly. (Hegel thought that knowledge should aim at complete speech: "what it is can be said of it!")³⁴ In other words, the nature of faith is to be sought not in reduction or abstraction, but in the living symbols of worship and belief and ethical action. If our intellectual reach after transcendent reality must issue at length in silence, that does not mean the end of faith, only the complementary acknowledgment of its singularity—which is in fact a compliment!

Perhaps "the silence of Plato" also reflects such insight into the claim of transcendence which overcomes speech in order to live. Socrates points at this phenomenon in his myth of the sun, "the child of the Good," when he defines it as being beyond definition—beyond the limit of being: "The Good is not the same thing as being (*Ouk ousias ontos tou agathou*), but far beyond it in dignity and power."³⁵ Thus "The Good must be demonstrated in the quality of one's life and death."³⁶ This sits well with another silence when Socrates is explaining the final stage of education, "at the very end of the world of thought," the study of Dialectics, and a third in the famous Seventh Letter where Plato explains that his higher teaching cannot be expressed in words, but springs out of dialogue, "like light flashing forth when a fire is kindled . . . born in the soul and straightway nourishes itself."³⁷

---

33. Polanyi, *The Tacit Dimension* (New York: Doubleday Anchor Books, 1967)—his thesis is "we can know more than we can tell," (4); *Personal Knowledge: towards a post-critical philosophy* (New York: Harper & Row, 1964).
34. Hegel, *Phenomenology of Spirit* 194.
35. Plato, *Rep.* 509.
36. T. W. Organ, *Third-Eye Philosophy: Essays in East-West Thought* (Ohio University Press, 1987), Ch. 12: "Three Platonic Silences."
37. *Rep.* 532f, *Seventh Letter*, 341. See Organ, *Third-Eye Philosophy*, 154ff.

SILENCE AND SPEECH

THE SILENCE OF THE BUDDHA

Let us consider the Buddhist view of speech and silence. It shares the flavour of Oriental wisdom: "Those who say do not know; those who know do not say."[38] But it has its own peculiar bite; in his Flower Sermon the Buddha's silence before questions of ultimacy has been interpreted variously as cynicism, nihilism, agnosticism, pragmatism, problematicism (every question is a distortion), or dialectics (ultimacy transcends intellection). Most likely is it a case of *apophaticism*: the epistemological form holds that reality is ineffable to us (*quoad nos*) although intelligible in itself (*in se*); but an ontological apophaticism as in Buddhism shifts the ineffability to ultimate reality as such (*quoad se*). We cannot ascribe to It the character of being, of what is manifested. The vexed question as to whether Buddhism is properly termed "religion" turns on this apparent a/theism. In 1966 W.C. Smith lectured on "Religious Atheism? Early Buddhist and Recent American," making his familiar distinction between faith and belief, and arguing that both *Nirvana* and *Dharma* are patient of transcendental meaning, in fact the latter "is also, and indeed more, akin to the notion of God in the West."[39]

This is similar to the Christian view that concepts must be transcended to grasp God. Even the word "God" is not a proper name, but one to be overcome in negation. The famous saying, "When you meet the Buddha, kill the Buddha" is an extreme expression of negative theology, but it has links to the Christian loss of self in mystical union.[40] (T.S. Eliot has a charming account of every cat's third and secret name: "his ineffable effable / Effanineffable / Deep and inscrutable singular Name.")[41] It is also a way of stating the divine "incomprehensibility"

---

38. *Tao Te'Ching*, 56.
39. The Charles Strong Memorial Lecture to Australian Universities (Milla wa-Milla, 1966), 57.
40. See the dialogue on this point involving Thomas Hopko and Eido Roshi among others, in Susan Walker, ed. *Speaking of Silence: Christians and Buddhists on the Contemplative Way* (New York: Paulist Press, 1987), 135ff.
41. T.S. Eliot, "The Naming of Cats," in *Old Possum's Book of Practical*

(*akatalēptos*) so well expressed in Byzantine thought.⁴² The latter yields expressions such as "luminous darkness," "sober inebriation" and "foolish wisdom" to underline the paradox of expressing the inexpressible.⁴³ Thus in turn it resembles the dense meaning of the Buddhist *sunyatta*, since "emptiness" is not itself a concept but signifies the failure of mere conceptualization.

Raimundo Panikkar's reflection on the Buddha's silence is helpful: "When the Buddha refuses to respond . . . it is not for any subjective reason—neither his own, nor that of his hearer, nor that of human nature—but in virtue of an exigency of reality itself. His is not a methodological or a pedagogical silence, but an ontic silence. . . . Not only does the Buddha proscribe every idle word—he proclaims every word idle that purports to bear on the ultimate mystery of reality." Whereas orthodox systems (*astikas*) seek transcendent reality as object of reflection, *nastikas* address immanence, available to the senses, the concrete reality of the subject. Here too the subject is lost, it "is not." "To be" is a verb, not a substantive. "Things *are*, by being, but there is no *esse* (Being) that would sustain them." ⁴⁴

Neither Western nor Eastern scholars identify God with Being in a simplistic manner. Tillich is best known for his explicit rejection, insisting on "Being-itself" or "Ground of Being" as pointers to the ineffable modality of Ultimacy. But this does not entail mysticism, about which he comments: "Mysticism is no real escape from the predominance of space . . . [it] is the spiritual form of the power of space over time, and therefore . . . the most sublime form of polytheism."⁴⁵ Thus the God of ontotheol-

---

Cats, 209.

42. E.g. John Chrysostom, *The Incomprehensibility of God (De Incomprehensibili)* (PG 48.701ff), against the rationalistic theism of the Eunomians..

43. See Thomas Hopko in Walker, *Speaking of Silence*, 138ff.

44. R. Panikkar, *The silence of God: the answer of the Buddha* (Maryknoll NY: Orbis, 1989), 14, 101ff.

45. Paul Tillich, *Systematic Theology*, Vol. 1 (Chicago: Chicago University Press, 1951), 112; *Theology of Culture* (New York: Oxford University Press, 1964), 34; the essay is entitled "The Struggle Between Time and Space."

ogy is "deontologized." If atheism is the negation of Being, apophaticism is the negation of Nonbeing. The truly Transcendent is beyond every determinant, not on the way to abstraction or reduction, but the Sur-real we noted above, apprehended in meditation and silence, where words are denied in behalf of communion. The Kabbalah regards G-d as boundless: *ēn soph*, *ápeiros* and therefore unknowable, described only in negations. Of course, silence may also be an expression of extreme alienation, as in the case of Samuel Beckett, whose novels and plays (written in an alien language) progress in reticence towards "Play without Words." Perhaps such development is a warning: silence cannot be the last "word." It was the Gnostic Basilides who termed God "Nothing" (*ouden*) or "Nonexistent" (*ouk ōn theos*),[46] something akin to the Kyoto School of revisionist Buddhism distinguished by its radical concept of "nothingness."[47] The latter poses its own dilemma, of course, in that by removing all content from consciousness (the opposite of phenomenology's "intentionality") one is left with the simply formless. Western philosophers may conceive of Being as inclusive of non-being, assigning epistemic priority to being. But in the East, one's self, "as pure experience, is an undifferentiated place (Nishida's *basho*)."[48] This represents a considerable step beyond Nāgārjuna's "middle path" of non-attachment. Now William James had detected "pure experience" apart from judgment or reflection, "a *that* which is not yet any definite *what*."[49] But such begs the question of awareness, and presents the same problem as arguing that one can apprehend that God exists apart

---

46. See H. A. Wolfson, *The Philosophy of the Church Fathers*, Vol. 1: *Faith, Trinity, Incarnation* (Harvard University Press, 1956), 522.

47. See J. W. Heisig, *Philosophers of Nothingness* (Honolulu: University of Hawaii Press, 2001).

48. R. E. Baker, *The Nothingness Beyond God: an Introduction to the Philosophy of Nishida Kitarō* (New York: Paragon House, 1989), 84. Cf., xxii: the logic of basho is "nothing ness as field, place, or *topos* borrowed from Plato's *Timaeus*." Cf., F. Franck, ed. *The Buddha Eye: an anthology of the Kyoto School and its contemporaries* (Bloomington, IN: World Wisdom, 2004).

49. James, *Essays*, 46 quoted in Baker, *Nothingness*, 9.

PLURALISM WITHOUT RELATIVISM

from what God may be like. In that case, nothingness is the sign that our silence is a confrontation not with the utterly transcendent so much as with the merely indeterminate, a displacement of theism by a/theism. The posthumous excommunication of Meister Eckhart (for declaring that God is "Nothing, nothing at all") suggests the danger, overshadowing his positive intention. His concept of *Abgescheidenheit*, disinterestedness, denotes more a motion towards the divine purity and simplicity than utter detachment. Thus "Godhead" is "a nothing where there is no path (*apada*) to reach. It is absolute nothingness; therefore it is the ground of being from where all beings come."[50] D.T. Suzuki compares the latter with Zen's *sunyatta*, "a zero full of infinite possibilities."[51]

To return to Smith's happy categories: as distinct from the "cumulative traditions" in which it is structured and nourished (and often distorted), "faith" is that human response to Mystery which itself remains a lesser mystery. To reduce it to formulae is like discussing poetry in prosaic statements. Or like dissecting a frog in the "bios-logos" laboratory. Something is lost in the translation, which in this case is surely a betrayal (*traduttore traditore*). Thus when one has essayed to analyze some dimensions of current philosophy of religion, as this book has attempted, one comes at the end to recognize the need for a new beginning, to try once more but in a higher key. The musical analogy is helpful because we are speaking about transposition (like switching from one tonal modality to another), about moving from theory into practice, from differentiating concepts into unitive relations, and from clarity into mystery. Just as the pause in music or the space in sculpture is part of the whole, so is the silence between words, and especially after words have come to a halt. Therefore might not the last word be a *logos endiathêtos*, inward and potent but unspoken, witness to the meaning and end of human

---

50. R.B. Blakeney, *Meister Eckhart: a modern translation* (New York: Harper, 1941), 82ff.

51. D.T. Suzuki, *Mysticism Christian and Buddhist: Eastern and Western Ways* (New York: Collier, 1957), 28, esp. "Crucifixion and Enlightenment," 98–105.

speech, its fragility in face of the Truth it would fain express, but finds it can but point to, away from itself, beyond even myth and poetry and sighing? These are its signs, and if they constitute the data of religious studies, particularly philosophy of religion, they must never become a substitute for the Reality to which they point. As Origen put it: "I often think of the maxim, 'It is dangerous to talk about God, even if what you say about him is true.' The man who wrote that must, I am sure, have been a shrewd and dependable character. There is danger, you see, not only in saying what is untrue about God but even in telling the truth about him if you do it at the wrong time."[52] If Aristotle is correct that humans are "beings of the word," then this capacity for speech is also the capacity for silence. George Steiner insists that, partly owing to modern physics, "It is no paradox to assert that in cardinal respects reality now begins *outside* verbal language." In particular, "the world of Auschwitz" lies outside both speech and reason.[53]

BEYOND PHILOSOPHY: BARTH AND DERRIDA

We need to heed the warnings of friendly adversaries, of which there are plenty these days. Take Karl Barth, for instance. In his essay "Philosophy and Theology," he notes the reification of two supposed entities that is going on. He prefers to see the two personified as philosophers (such as his brother Heinrich?) and theologians.[54] He bids us confront one another boldly, to determine the differentiations of truth. And in his lifelong affair with Schleiermacher, Barth wrestles with the impact of philosophy of religion, particularly its apologetic form. He rejects both insofar as he "rejects" their author; but admits in his closing years

---

52. *Hom. in Ezek.* I.11; Cf., *Dial. Herac.*, 12ff (149).
53. G. Steiner, *Language and Silence* (New York: Penguin Books, 1958), "The Retreat from the Word," 31–56.
54. See McLelland, "Philosophy and Theology—a Family Affair (Karl and Heinrich Barth)," pp 30-52 in H-M Rumscheidt, ed. *Footnotoes to a Theology: the Karl Barth Colloquium of 1972* (Waterloo: SR Supplements, 1974).

that since he is both a believer and an atheist himself, he sees the confrontation as internal rather than simply outward and historical.[55]

Now Barth has little sympathy for my own vocation (one cannot be a "Barthian" philosopher of religion), nor my department of "Religion and Culture". As we have seen, he offers a spin on Natural Theology that calls in question most of what traditional philosophy of religion thinks it needs to do, and is able to do. Moreover, his claim that Christian theology is the true "science of God" posits as its subject *The-anthropology*, since "only a doctrine of the commerce and communion between God and man" constitutes authentic theology.[56] It is curious that this sort of theological purity has been better heard and more kindly received among cultured despisers of religion than has the sympathetic and overt overtures of a Tillich. Perhaps Barth is correct, that theology is a science and as such is called to determine its own limits and procedures in light of its object (or Subject). In following this strictly rational method it will inevitably engage in dialogue with sister sciences, and will address its cultural context in serious mode. To depart from this singularity is to become irrelevant, even trivial.

Jacques Derrida offers his usual idiosyncratic view of things. (One must always read him with tongue in cheek, of course, appropriate to his manner of writing). The trouble with deconstruction is to build anew once the ontological foundation has been removed—Mark Taylor, for instance, considers Derrida's to be a "linguistic idealism," leaving us with an "empty mirror" demanding subjective constructions of reality.[57] Derrida's recent works include an explicit critique of philoso-

---

55. See McLelland, *Prometheus Rebound*, 288–91, on the Barth-Max Bense dialogue. The latter (in *Zürcher Woche*, 1963) appears in H.M. Rumscheidt, ed. *Karl Barth: Fragments Grave and Gay* (London: Fontana, 1971), 32ff.

56. K. Barth, *Evangelical Theology in the Nineteenth Century* (Richmond VA: John Knox Press, 1960) 11; cf. *The Humanity of God* (Atlanta: John Knox Press, 1960), 55.

57. See Graham Ward, *The Modern Theologians*, ed. D.F. Ford (Oxford: Blackwell, 1997)

phy of religion, *The Gift of Death*.[58] This is more than an advance over Heidegger's being-towards-death. It takes as case study the biblical story (*Genesis* 22) of Abraham's test, the *akedah*. Like Kierkegaard, Derrida is fascinated by the brief encounter among God, Abraham, Isaac, angel and ram. For Derrida this epitomizes the difference between religions of law (debit and credit) and Gospel. The key term is "sacrifice." Since the essence of the encounter is mystery and secrecy, he suggests that God must have told Abraham, "Above all, no journalists!"[59] The singularity of the event, the inwardness of Abraham's call, denies the role of newsgatherer who would turn it into a public event. We tend to miss the bite of the story—Isaac was a special gift of grace, beyond the human nature of Abraham and Sarah to give birth in their old age, a gift to guarantee the fulfilment of covenant (Gen. 17). When the old couple heard the Messenger's news they broke up in laughter. Nine months later they named the child *Isaac*, "he laughs." Thus a double edge is given to Abraham's testing: grace received is to be withdrawn. For Derrida, it is more the sacrifice of Abraham's "patrilocal power," part of the politics (Plato's *polis*) in which religion engages at the cost of the ethical. Like Nietzsche's "Platonism for the people," this critique announces a future epiphany. Derrida refers to the work of Jan Patočka, who declares: "Christianity has not yet come to Christianity . . . the new responsibility announced by the *mysterium tremendum*."[60]

Derrida's meditation on the *akedah* is sparked by Kiekegaard's notorious *Fear and Trembling* (1843), which was written under the sig-

---

58. *Le Don de Mort* (1992), *The Gift of Death*, trans. David Wills (Chicago, IL: University of Chicago Press, 1995).

59. See Derrida, "Above All, No Journalists!" trans. Samuel Weber, *Religion and Media*, H. de Vries & S. Weber, eds (Stanford, CA: Stanford University Press, 2001), 57-93. (I owe this reference to my student Nathan Loewen). Cf., J.D. Caputo, *The Prayers and Tears of Jacques Derrida* (Indianapolis, IN: Indiana University Press, 1997).

60. *Gift of Death* 28; J. Patočka, *Heretical Essays on the Philosophy of History*, trans. C. Kohak (Chicago: Open Court, 1996). He sees the origin of religion's *mysterium* in the inner connection between the sacred and secrecy.

nificant pseudonym of "Johannes *de Silentio.*" Silence befits the secret, and secrecy befits the sacred. This thought-project intends not to stimulate thinking but conversion—after concept, conception! It exemplifies Kierkegaard's fascination with motion, the dynamics of the existing self, which he explored through modal logic.[61] His three "Problemas" offer alternative deconstructions of the text, teasing answers from the hearer. How does one tell such a story? Carefully, without dogmatism or certainty. Perhaps it's a case of simple duty to (heteronomous) authority; or the clash of universal and particular; or a moment of testing where faith and despair come together. The decisive thing is that de Silentio's hesitation unmasks the plot of a religion of duty, the give-and-take of legal and contractual piety. We hear a distinct echo of that much earlier unmasking by Socrates, when the hapless Euthyphro admits that for him religion is a matter of "divine tendance" or fair exchange between the god and his worshippers (a sort of theo-therapy?)[62] For Kierkegaard/de Silentio, "Abraham cannot be mediated; in other words, he cannot speak." His silence on Mount Moriah (the place of "seeing") it not a case of dialogue but of hearing God's Word. The same idea is found in the silence of Job in face of the theophany.[63] Derrida comments: "He must keep his secret. But his silence is not just any silence. Can one witness in silence? By silence?"[64] To which one must recall the saying of Camus that human being is constituted by "the refusal of silence."

TODO Y NADA

Emmanuel Lévinas has stated: "It is so different that in Kierkegaard's eyes it is through suffering truth that one can describe the very manifestation of the divine: simultaneity of All and Nothingness, Relation to

---

61. See above, Ch. 3, "Possible Worlds."
62. Plato, *Euthyphro* 13: "a sort of ministration to the gods."
63. Kierkegaard, *Fear and Trembling* (trans. R. Payne, London: Oxford University Press, 1939); *Repetition* (trans. W. Lowrie, Princeton: Princeton University Press, 1941), 96f.
64. Derrida, *Gift*, 73.

a Person both present and absent—to a humiliated God who suffers, dies and leaves those whom he saves in despair."[65] This is a salutary correction of what we noted above, that Western thought has tended to be driven by a disjunction, "all *or* nothing," on display most clearly in classical theism's questionable concept of divine omnipotence with its fateful consequences for theodicy.[66]

William James and others rightly coined the term "oceanic feeling" for the human experience of the Transcendent. For God has been described as an "infinite and boundless ocean."[67] Kierkegaard's concept of "passional reason" led him to define faith as "objective uncertainty held fast in subjective inwardness." And so to the beautiful gnome: faith is "to be joyful in lying above a depth of seventy thousand fathoms."[68] Such terms imply the tension in philosophy's language game as it stretches words metaphorically as pointers, signs, traces. Here it touches the realm of the mystical, at least in its initial stages of purgation (qualifying terms) and illumination (heuristic thinking). But it cannot take the final step, it cannot reach the mountain-top.

In Carmelite mysticism direct ascent by the most rugged path is the proper way for pilgrims. Once the "dark night" of senses and soul has been lived through, a taste of union with the divine is experienced. This "bridal mysticism" is exuberant in Teresa of Avila and in the poetic "Romances" of her confessor, John of the Cross.[69] Jacques Maritain calls the latter "Doctor of Night," as Thomas Aquinas is "Doctor of

---

65. E. Lévinas, *Proper Names* (Stanford: Stanford University Press, 1996; trans. M. B. Smith) 69. Lévinas is troubled by what he terms Kierkegaard's "violence," (76).

66. See Ch. 1 above.

67. John of Damascus (*De Fide Orth.* I.4), borrowing from Gregory Nazianzus: *immensum et illimitatum essentiae pelagus*. See McLelland, *God the Anonymous*, 155.

68. *Postscript* 126, quoting Frater Taciturnus in *Stagen*; see Stephen Evans, *Passionate Reason: Making Sense of Kierkegaard's Philosophical Fragments* (Bloomington, IN: Indiana University Press, 1992).

69. See Tessa Bielecki, "Bridal Mysticism" in Walker, *op. cit.* 38ff.

Light." His close study of the Carmelite theologian leads Maritain to elaborate an epistemology that moves through three kinds of wisdom, or "supreme knowledge having a universal object and judging things by first principles." They are: metaphysical wisdom, supreme in the natural or rational order ("natural theology"); theology or "the science of revealed mysteries;" and mystical wisdom, seeing God as he is, *deitas ut sic*.[70] The fault of metaphysical wisdom is that it sticks at intellect, without "passing into the heart by love" (Albertus Magnus). For love is the bond of union through which mystical experience achieves its desire and goal.

John of the Cross, author of The *Ascent of Mount Carmel* and *The Dark Night of the Soul*, constantly recognizes the disproportion between intellect and divine Object/Subject. To offer the self to such a One is to experience the void in which selflessness yields to Otherness. This means *suffering* both in the sense of passive reception, "infused grace," and in the higher sense of sharing in the Other's own passion. Teresa termed it "to suffer things divine," *divina pati*, for God is known through his effects, that is changes in our affections. What Pascal called "the motions of grace" create emotions of the heart. Thus love unites by a "connatural knowledge," an identity beyond intellection (hence "a ray of darkness for the intellect") producing a practical way of authentic human existence. For John the reality shifts from disjunction to a radically new conjunction: *Todo y Nada*, All *and* Nothing.[71]

We began with a thesis, that philosophy of religion deals with natural theology, and is false to itself when it strives to go beyond its "religious" data. With such unmasking philosophy of religion reaches its end, for it can deal only with the phenomena, what is objectively given: a religion of legal contract involving Kant's heteronomy/autonomy dilemma, or at best the natural theology of *superbia ratio*, prideful reason. Not a mutual freedom whereby the mystery of self/other is sublated in union. But Franz Rosenzweig issues a warning: the mystic is a "tragic hero,"

---

70. J. Maritain, *Distinguish to Unite or The Degrees of Knowledge*, trans. Gerald B. Phelan (London: Geoffrey Bles, 1959), 247ff.

71. Maritain, *Degrees of Knowledge*, Ch. IX: "Todo Y Nada," 352ff.

locked in his own embrace. He proffered as alternative what he termed "speech-thinking," and observed: "By keeping silent, the hero breaks down the bridges which connect him with God and the world, and elevates himself . . . into the icy solitude of the self."[72] The recovery of authentic selfhood therefore does not come through the isolation, the "alone to the Alone" of Plotinus, but through recognition of that deeper unity of selves with Self. Such covenant dwelling moves from Law to Gospel. When the divine Name was revealed as YHWH (Ex. 3:14)—surely the "I am" is a teaser, it connotes but does not denote[73]—Moses received an alternative route to knowledge of God, the trajectory of the patriarchs: "the God of Abraham, Isaac and Jacob; this is my name" (Ex. 3:15). Such travel and travail had been on view in Abraham's experience, receiving Isaac back from the grave, from the closure of the line of covenant. Surely at that moment he knew why that narrow way of faith was named "Laughter."

SOCRATES' RAFT

At this last stage of life I have learned that facing one's final limit does indeed "wonderfully concentrate the mind," which can then roam freely over a lifetime's essais and their ultimate import. I am clear that the discipline to which I have devoted my academic career suffers from a severe ambiguity, mistaking its subject as the kind of natural theology that is divorced from the claims of revealed theology, and so failing to recognize the possibility of divine existence as a living voice rather than a terminal QED. Long ago, when Socrates was about to die (see Plato's *Phaedo*, a work prone to student misspelling) he told his disciples that we can but "take the best and most unanswerable of human theories" to build a raft to sail through life, unless we can "find some word of

---

72. N. Glatzer, *Franz Rosenzweig, His Life and Thought* (New York: Schocken Books, 1961), 77.

73. Therefore while "He Who Is" is possible, the abstract "One" (as in the LXX) is not.

God which will more surely and safely carry" us.[74] Such uncertainty as knowledge approaches its limits fits well with the Socratic reliance on the "likely story" (*eikôs mythos*) to point beyond limits in the only possible modality. As Kierkegaard put it, to advance one step beyond Socrates requires a dynamic shift, a leap over objective uncertainty to discover subjective certitude. He was thinking of how Aristotle changed gears into modal logic in order to explore the dynamics of that elusive category of motion, *kinêsis*.[75] This entails a need to exchange the modality of physics for a meta-physics that can apprehend (if not comprehend) the kinetics or energetics or pneumatics of properly "spiritual" reality. If philosophy is the practice of dying, preparation for death, as Socrates claimed, is not religion the practice of living, preparation for *hope*? Not tragedy but comedy has the last word, the punch line.

As to the moot question of religious pluralism, our thesis of a "modal theory of religions" offers a way of regarding them as "ways of being in the world" (John Cobb) that resist an essentialist definition. Thus even John Hick's "complementary pluralism" (as Alister McGrath terms it) begs the question, implying merely differing "lenses" through which the Real is apprehended. Rather, we conclude that some kind of disymmetry (Panikkar) or multiple religious ends (Heim) must displace the quest for any universal unitive theory. If this seems but weak gruel after the promise of an academic feast, the current situation of the debate bears witness to the increasingly complex and elusive nature of any solution.

Another conclusion of this rather eclectic foray into modern academia is that the two worlds of university and seminary (or religious studies) may be reconciled without compromising the "objectivity" of the one or the commitment of the other. They need each other—to paraphrase Kant: subjectivity without objectivity is empty, objectivity without subjectivity is blind. If it requires a certain insight to recognize this principle, and

---

74. *Phaedo* 230A—I see Plato as placing *logos* above *mythos*, but positing a series of higher *mythoi* at crucial points in his reasoning: see my *God the Anonymous*, 11f.

75. See ch. 7 above, "Kierkegaard as Aristotelian."

a certain integrity to adopt it personally, then the teacher of religious studies is surely called to do both.

Index of Names

Abe, Masao 137, 145, 151
Abélard 41
Al-Ghazali 190, 192
Anselm 14, 21-22, 36, 65, 95, 163, 166, 190, 203
Apollinaire, Guillaume 127, 132
Aquinas, Thomas 14-15, 17, 24-25, 29, 32, 36, 59, 96, 99, 112, 192, 197-199
Aristotle 16-17, 23, 32, 51, 64, 66, 84, 111, 116, 123, 148-149, 152-153, 159, 171, 194, 199, 211, 218
Armour, L., and Trott, E. 42, 45-46
Athanasius 106, 164, 175, 206
Augustine 15, 46-47, 101, 113, 123, 158-159, 163, 168, 170, 173, 177, 180, 183, 189, 200, 205

Bach, Johann Sebastian 133-134, 155
Bachelard, Gaston 125, 201
Barbour, Ian 82, 86-87
Barr, James 14, 38
Barth, Karl 9, 20, 21, 35, 37, 42-43, 49-50, 56-57, 65, 94-95, 128, 131, 140-141, 151, 161-162, 165-168, 172, 186, 193, 203, 205, 211, 212
Beaven, James 46

Bernard of Clairvaux 120, 205
Black, Max 90
Blake, William 119, 132
Bonhoeffer, Dietrich 49, 141, 160
Boutin, Maurice 66, 148
Breton, André 132
Brunner, Emil 49, 141, 172, 204-205
Buber, Martin 119, 128

Calvin, John 21, 108, 123, 170, 173, 202-203
Cassirer, Ernst 124
Cézanne, Paul 125-127
Cicero 17, 41
Clifford, W.K. 20
Cobb, John 77, 80, 87, 220

Dali, Salvador 133
Denis the Areopagite 188, 200
Derrida, Jacques 50, 53, 56, 58, 103, 128, 201, 214-216
Descartes, René 58, 145, 174
Despland, Michel 42
Dilthey, Wilhelm 91, 117
Duns Scotus, John 149

Einstein, Albert 39-40, 85, 89, 93, 96,

98, 101, 103, 105, 109-110, 146
Escher, M.C. 97, 133-134, 155

Ferré, Fred 54, 91-92, 159, 167, 190
Flew, Antony 68
Frye, Northrop 44, 48, 84, 119

Gellman, Jerome 29
Gilkey, Langdon 101
Gödel, Kurt 65, 97, 106, 133
Goethe, Johann Wolfgang 30
Griffiths, Paul 79, 81

Hamann, J.G. 19
Hamilton, William 46-47
Hanson, Norman 25
Harnack, Adolf von 160, 166
Hartshorne, Charles 21-22, 27, 194
Hawking, Stephen 103, 109-110, 146
Heidegger, Martin 24, 50, 56-58, 110, 116-117, 131, 213
Heim, Mark 80-81, 96, 133, 145, 220
Heisenberg, Werner 65, 67
Hick, John 51, 72, 74, 78, 98, 137, 145, 158, 167, 182, 220
Hume, David 20 85, 96, 145

James, William 211, 217

Kant, Immanuel 18-19, 23, 26-27, 29-30, 42, 47, 57-58, 60, 62, 66, 87, 103, 138, 146, 148-150, 158, 173- 174, 194, 216, 218
Kaufman, Gordon 75
Kaufmann, Walter 29
Kerr, Fergus 16, 28, 35
Kierkegaard, Søren 5, 13, 19, 27, 53, 57, 60, 67-68, 73, 85, 152-154,

162, 166, 174, 194, 206, 213-215, 218
Klostermaier, Klaus 185
Kuhn, Thomas 82-83, 85, 92-93, 98, 127, 142, 149
Küng, Hans 76, 101-102, 122, 139, 142

Lessing, Gotthold Ephraim 67, 73, 152, 189, 195
Lévinas, Emmanuel 216
Lewis, C.S. 66, 97, 108, 115
Lindbeck, George 87 138, 145
Lonergan, Bernard 15, 25-26, 78, 150
Lyotard, Jean-François 50, 55, 58, 201

MacIntyre, Alisdair 15, 54-55, 138
Mackie, J.L. 27
MacKinnon, Donald M. 18, 28, 35
Malcolm, Norman 20
Marion, Jean-Luc 115
Marx, Karl 28, 57, 66
Moore, Henry 115, 125, 127
Mozart, Wolfgang Amadeus 122, 134
Murdoch, Iris 28, 132
Murray, John Clark 46-47

Newton, Isaac 96, 101-103, 119
Nicolas of Cusa 206
Niebuhr, H. Richard 74
Nietzsche, Friedrich 28, 50, 57, 111, 114, 132, 213
Northrop, F.C.S. 136
Novalis 131

Occam, William of 59, 64, 149

INDEX OF NAMES

Palamas, Gregory 203-204, 206
Panikkar, Raimundo 63, 87, 102, 139, 143-144, 185, 195, 210, 220
Pelikan, Jaroslav 121, 136
Picasso, Pablo 126-130, 132-133
Plantinga, Alvin 21-22, 65
Plato 14, 75, 111-112, 118, 123, 145, 194-195, 208, 215, 219-220 (see also Platonism, Neoplatonism, in Index of Subjects)
Plotinus 200, 219
Polanyi, Michael 82, 92, 94, 135, 149, 154, 207
Popper, Karl 92, 147
Prosper of Aquitaine 75, 173
Putnam, Hilary 56, 136

Radhakrishnan, Sarvepalli 181, 183
Rahner, Karl 76, 83, 106, 140, 161, 172, 180
Ramsey, Ian 90-91
Rawls, John 138
Rescher, Nicolas 65, 81
Ricoeur, Paul 28, 57, 99, 113, 115, 131
Rorty, Richard 53, 118
Russell, Bertrand 65, 96, 150

Schelling, Friedrich Wilhelm Joseph 29-30, 152
Schleiermacher, Friedrich Daniel Ernst 23, 29-30, 162, 166, 168, 204-205, 211
Schuon, Frithjof 77
Seerveld, Calvin 123-124
Sharma, Arvind 184
Slater, Peter 145
Smart, Ninian 51, 137, 139, 184-186
Smith, Huston 96
Smith, Wilfred Cantwell 5, 9-10, 19, 32, 51, 67-68, 71-72, 75, 78, 80-81, 136-137, 141-142, 176, 189, 207, 210
Song, C.S. 77, 100, 128, 178, 188
Stout, Jeffrey 54, 56
Surin, Kenneth 80

Taylor, Mark C. 58, 64, 214
Tillich, Paul 20, 30, 49, 56, 76, 117-118, 121, 129, 141, 151, 163, 208, 212
Tolkien, J.R.R. 116
Torrance, Thomas F. 35, 37-40, 93, 95, 97-98, 104, 110, 164-165, 170
Trendelenburg, Friedrich 67
Troeltsch, Ernst 25, 73-74, 76, 105, 181

Van Huyssteen, J. Wentzel 22
Vermigli, Peter Martyr 41, 107, 170-171

Vigneault, Gilles 44

Watson, John 47-48
William of Sherwood 64
Wittgenstein, Ludwig 16, 20, 35, 48, 150, 173, 205
Wolterstorff, Nicolas 21, 36
Wolfson, Harry 9, 159, 167

Young, George Paxton 46-47, 56

Zeno of Elea 130

Index of Subjects

aesthetic 114, 116-118, 123-124, 129-132, 154, 200
agnosticism 32, 36, 99, 139, 207
akedah 215
analogy 31, 58, 61, 82-83, 89, 96, 98-100, 102, 104-105, 110-112, 130, 139-140, 147, 158, 166, 201, 212
analytic philosophy 28, 43
anhypostasia 107, 163-164
anthropic principle 62
apologetics 21, 25, 36, 41, 45, 47, 50
    evidentialist apologetics 21, 36
apophatic 29, 107, 130, 194, 209, 211
aporia 57, 130, 150
apperception 18, 197
archetype 111, 174
argument 13-18, 20-23, 27, 33, 36, 41, 45-46, 49, 58, 62-63, 67, 109-110, 136, 150, 161, 182, 190
    ontological argument 22, 36, 190
asceticism 202
astrophysics 62
atheism 36, 151, 203, 207, 209
Augustinians 161

autonomy 37, 50, 54, 72, 118, 123, 218

beauty 116, 124
Bhagavad-Gītā 180
Bodhisattvas 186-187
Buddhism 63, 105, 128, 139, 186-188, 194, 209, 211

Calvinism 43-44, 62, 108, 169-171
Cappadocians 130, 161, 204
categories 27, 30, 32, 51, 54, 64, 66-67, 77, 89, 100, 115, 122, 135, 142, 148-149, 154, 159-160, 166, 171, 184, 196, 212
chaos theory 147
christology 11, 61, 85, 100, 106-108, 142, 157-158, 161-163, 167, 169-173, 175, 178-180, 184, 186, 190-191, 193, 195-196 (see also Logos Christology)
comedy 50, 112-113, 220
common sense philosophy 44, 47
complementarity 90, 99, 101, 186, 197
contingent 24, 39, 67, 94, 106
Copernican revolution 78, 96,

99-103, 142, 158
culture 23, 25, 42, 53, 59, 74, 77, 101, 118, 132, 136, 139, 202, 214

dance 111-112, 202
demonstration 16-17, 114, 148, 149
dharma 107, 177-180, 185-187, 209
dialectical 16-17, 32, 49, 58, 80, 82, 166
dialogue 9, 10-11, 19, 38, 63, 76-77, 80, 89, 93, 99, 128, 136, 155, 157-158, 170, 185, 190, 195, 208-209, 214, 216
dimensions 68, 84, 88, 96-97, 127, 130, 212
(see also string theory)
Dionysos 202
discovery 21, 39, 66, 90, 93-94, 125, 148, 151
docetism 164
dream 69, 80, 127, 132-133, 146, 183
dualism 39, 54, 90, 93-94, 137, 145

enhypostasia 107, 163-164
Enlightenment 21, 25, 30, 41, 46, 50, 54-55, 57, 72, 101, 111
epistemology 18, 25, 29, 36, 46-47, 58, 80, 83, 86, 109, 114, 118, 128, 146, 149-150, 194, 199, 216
evidentialism 20-21, 35, 57, 68, 85
evidentialist apologetics 21, 36
exclusivism 72, 75, 79, 83, 100, 105, 158
existence 66, 95, 153-154, 168, 170, 172, 193, 216
existence of God 13-14, 16, 18, 22, 33, 45, 148, 217
existentialism 23, 28, 45, 48, 194

extraCalvinisticum 62, 108, 169-170
extra-terrestrial 108-109

fault 18, 57, 113-1145, 152, 196, 218
fideism 20, 22, 41, 49, 60, 86
field theory 98, 110
foundationalism 21, 23, 53, 68, 72, 86

general theory of relativity 84
geometry 40, 60, 96, 124, 154
Gifford Lectures 14, 37, 49, 86, 184

Hinduism 107, 177-179, 185-186, 188, 195

icon 94, 107, 111, 114-115, 120-121, 132, 181
incarnation 61, 63, 83, 87, 93, 97, 100, 104, 158, 160-161, 164-165, 169, 171-172, 177, 183, 185, 190, 192-193, 195-196, 203
inclusivism 72, 75-76, 79, 102, 105, 110, 158
incompatibility 63, 100, 127, 145, 149
ineffability 123, 163, 188, 205-206, 209-210
infinity 19, 97, 130-131, 133, 149
interfaith 63
Islam 104, 107, 141, 179, 181, 188-189, 191, 193, 195, 197
isomorphism 99

Kyoto school 145, 211

Logos christology 61, 107, 169, 171, 186

metamathematics 65, 131
metaphor 58, 63, 89, 99-100, 114,

INDEX OF SUBJECTS

118, 120, 140, 150, 171, 192, 201, 217
metaphysics 23, 32, 46, 48, 50, 56, 63, 65, 90, 92, 116, 143, 146, 196, 220
method 15-16, 24-27, 29, 31-32, 39, 49, 57, 73, 77, 82, 84-85, 95-97, 105, 110, 120, 123, 126-127, 137, 142, 144, 146, 150, 152-153, 166, 212
methodology 24-25, 74, 76, 94-95, 144, 208
modal 9, 14, 16, 21, 51, 60-61, 64-69, 73, 77, 80, 84, 89, 98, 103-104, 111-112, 123-124, 152, 154, 169, 196, 216, 220
modal logic 14, 16, 62, 66, 84, 152, 216, 220
model 14, 24, 31, 76, 78, 82, 83, 85-87, 90-95, 97-99, 101, 103-107, 109-112, 119-120, 123-126, 128-130, 135, 1452, 144, 148, 150, 152, 154, 158, 166, 193
modernism 55, 138
modernity 17-18, 30, 36, 50, 54-55, 59-60, 63, 80, 84, 94, 111, 165, 174
modes of being 61, 80, 162, 165, 167, 178
monarchianism 61, 168
motion 19, 31, 66-67, 96, 103, 113, 139, 151, 153, 194, 199, 212, 216, 218, 220
music 122-123, 132, 212
mysticism 27, 86, 121-122, 127, 143, 164, 187-188, 190, 194, 201-205, 207, 209, 217-218

natural theology 10, 14, 18, 21, 28, 33, 35-37, 39-49, 51, 55, 57, 59, 61, 63, 65, 67, 69, 141, 165-166, 212, 216-217
negative theology 18, 188, 199-201, 203, 209
Neoplatonism 159
Nominalism 59
normal science 93, 142
numinous 86, 187, 199

objectivity 24, 31, 82, 137, 144, 205, 218
omnipotence 27, 51, 64, 132, 195, 215
ontological argument 22, 36, 190
ontology 25, 36, 50, 56, 65, 146, 177
ontotheology 18, 50, 56, 62, 146

paradigm 31, 45, 59-61, 79, 82-89, 92-93, 96, 98-105, 110-112, 126, 128-130, 142-143, 158, 162, 166, 203
paradigm shift 60, 85, 88-89, 98, 101-102, 126, 129-130, 142, 158
paradox 13, 26, 64, 99, 130, 162, 172, 196, 210, 213
perception 46, 113, 118
philosophy of religion 10, 13-14, 23, 26-30, 32-33, 35, 42-43, 45, 49, 210-212, 216
physics 31, 39-40, 51, 61, 67, 84, 87, 90-91, 97-99, 101-103, 109, 142-143, 148, 154, 189, 196, 213, 220
Platonism 16, 27, 41, 138, 142, 145, 154, 158-159, 194-195, 203, 215
play 31, 115-116, 124-126, 211
pluralism 9-11, 13-14, 18, 20-22, 24,

229

26, 28, 30, 32-33, 36, 38, 40,
42, 44, 46, 48, 50-54, 56, 58,
60-62, 64, 66, 68, 71-90, 92,
94, 96, 98, 100, 102, 104-110,
112, 114, 116, 118, 120, 122,
124, 126, 128, 130, 132, 134,
136, 138, 140, 142-146, 148,
150, 152, 154, 157-158, 160,
162, 164, 166, 168, 170-172,
174, 176, 178, 180, 182, 184,
186, 188-190. 192, 194, 198,
200, 202, 204, 206, 208, 210,
212, 214, 216, 218
pneumatology 106-107, 161
positivism 14, 33, 39, 49, 59, 82, 86
postmodernism 9-10, 22, 25, 45, 50,
53-56, 58, 60-63, 68-690, 84,
94, 96, 114, 138, 165, 195
process thinking 29, 196

quantum theory 84, 99, 126

Reformed epistemology 25
relativism 10, 22, 33, 51, 53, 55,
63, 68, 71-76, 79-80, 82,
86, 102-103, 111, 126, 136,
142-143, 154, 158
relativity 39, 51, 61, 68, 71, 73, 84,
87, 89-90, 95-98, 102-103, 105,
107, 110, 143, 158
religious studies 9, 13, 15, 25-26, 71,
76, 82, 103, 110, 135-136, 138,
142,146-147, 154, 176, 211,
218-219
rhetoric 17, 45

salvation 22, 60, 62-63, 75, 79, 81, 85,
100, 102, 104, 108-109, 139,
158, 172-173, 179, 186

sat-cit-ānanda 144
scientific method 32, 57, 82, 110
selfhood 50, 60, 148, 217
sight 118-121, 127-128, 134, 202
sin 63, 100, 104, 113, 139, 186
singularity 10, 82, 99, 173, 192, 196,
208, 214-215
silence 11, 163, 199, 202, 205,
207-213, 216
soteriology 100, 109, 114, 163, 196
space 8, 39-40, 62, 68-69, 93, 96-97,
99, 102, 108, 110, 116, 124-126,
136, 145, 154, 174, 210, 212
special theory of relativity 103
subjectivity 31, 58, 82, 137, 153-154,
194, 206, 218
suffering 63, 104, 139, 179, 189, 191,
194, 216, 218
string theory 147
Surrealism 127, 129, 131-133
syllogism 16, 60, 62, 85, 148

tacit knowledge 94
terminism 47, 59, 64, 66, 93, 147
theodicy 27, 65, 122, 215
theological science 15, 36, 38-39, 93,
104, 123
tragedy 50, 112-113, 122, 132, 184,
220
Trinity 61, 95, 106, 130, 157, 163-164,
167, 169, 172, 179-180, 192,
194-195, 200-201
truth-claims 67, 74-75, 78, 99, 102,
110
twice-born 114, 153
typology 74

ubiquity 108, 169-171
Uncertainty Principle 32

INDEX OF SUBJECTS

unified field theory 84, 88, 102-103, 110

universalizability 63, 87, 102-103, 109, 150

Vaishnavism 180

via moderna 59-60

wisdom 88, 209-210, 218

Yodo-Shin 141

Yodo-Shin-Shu 141

Printed in the United Kingdom by
Lightning Source UK Ltd., Milton Keynes
136598UK00002B/149/P